NELSON'S BATTLES

PEN & SWORD MILITARY CLASSICS

We hope you enjoy your Pen and Sword Military Classic. The series is designed to give readers quality military history at affordable prices. Below is a list of the titles that are planned for 2003. Pen and Sword Classics are available from all good bookshops. If you would like to keep in touch with further developments in the series, including information on the Classics Club, then please contact Pen and Sword at the address below.

2003 List

Series No.

JANUARY

1	The Bowmen of England	*Donald Featherstone*
2	The Life & Death of the Afrika Korps	*Ronald Lewin*
3	The Old Front Line	*John Masefield*
4	Wellington & Napoleon	*Robin Neillands*

FEBRUARY

5	Beggars in Red	*John Strawson*
6	The Luftwaffe: A History	*John Killen*
7	Siege: Malta 1940–1943	*Ernle Bradford*

MARCH

8	Hitler as Military Commander	*John Strawson*
9	Nelson's Battles	*Oliver Warner*
10	The Western Front 1914–1918	*John Terraine*

APRIL

11	The Killing Ground	*Tim Travers*
12	The War Walk	*Nigel Jones*

MAY

13	Dictionary of the First World War	*Pope & Wheal*
14	1918: The Last Act	*Barrie Pitt*

JUNE

15	Hitler's Last Offensive	*Peter Elstob*
16	Naval Battles of World War Two	*Geoffrey Bennett*

JULY

17	Omdurman	*Philip Ziegler*
18	Strike Hard, Strike Sure	*Ralph Barker*

AUGUST

19	The Black Angels	*Rupert Butler*
20	The Black Ship	*Dudley Pope*

SEPTEMBER

21	The Fight for the Malvinas	*Martin Middlebrook*
22	The Narrow Margin	*Wood & Dempster*

OCTOBER

23	Vimy	*Pierre Berton*
24	Warfare in the Age of Bonaparte	*Michael Glover*

NOVEMBER

25	Dictionary of the Second World War	*Pope & Wheal*
26	Not Ordinary Men	*John Colvin*

PEN AND SWORD BOOKS LTD

47 Church Street • Barnsley • South Yorkshire • S70 2AS

Tel: 01226 734555 • 734222

E-mail: enquiries@pen-and-sword.co.uk • Website: www.pen-and-sword.co.uk

1 Nelson

From a bronze-gilt bust by Gahagan (1798)

NELSON'S
BATTLES

Oliver Warner

'As I rise in rank, so do my exertions' – Nelson

PEN & SWORD MILITARY CLASSICS

First published in 1965 by B.T. Batsford Ltd
Published in 2003, in this format, by
PEN & SWORD MILITARY CLASSICS
an imprint of
Pen & Sword Books Limited
47 Church Street
Barnsley
S. Yorkshire
S70 2AS

ISBN 0 85052 941 7

The publishers have made every effort to trace the author, his estate and his agent without success and they would be interested to hear from anyone who is able to provide them with this information.

A CIP record for this book is
available from the British Library

Printed in England by
CPI UK

To
Admiral of the Fleet
SIR PHILIP VIAN

Foreword

Naval or military genius invariably consists of a blend of attributes. The foundation must always be experience, which will result in thought. There is the capacity to learn, from mistakes even more than from successes. With time, comes that serene confidence which is unshaken even by disaster. But the most elusive quality is the particular way in which a commander communicates his personality, as well as his confidence, to those he leads. It may be done in many differing ways, even by fear.

Nelson, so one of his contemporaries was fond of saying, was the man to love. He attracted people by trusting them, so that when it came to a crisis, they always seemed at least to do their best, often excelling themselves on his behalf.

Nelson's capacity was tested in every type of warfare at sea, and his record on land, in Nicaragua and Corsica, was far from negligible. At the battle of St Vincent he showed what was perhaps the highest of all forms of courage in a subordinate officer—a willingness to act on his own initiative, and this in the middle of a formally conducted fleet action directed by a martinet. His triumph at the Nile was the result of impetuous surprise attack on an enemy embayed. Copenhagen, where once again Nelson rightly disobeyed, was a rare instance of success against an opponent with the resources of a dockyard and a city at his back. Trafalgar, like St Vincent, was a purely fleet action, a type of operation for which Nelson had been trained. No amount of sophisticated analysis can rob it of its thrill.

In the narrative which follows, every aspect of Nelson's genius is examined. So many sided was his personality that it is scarcely surprising that the details of his career have continued to enthral posterity. He lived a dedicated life, and to his country this was nothing but an advantage.

O. W.

Contents

Acknowledgment

Figure 2 is reproduced by gracious permission of Her Majesty The Queen.

The Author and Publishers wish to thank the following for permission to reproduce illustrations: the Board of Admiralty for fig. 43; Bibliothèque Nationale, Paris, for fig. 3; the Trustees of the British Museum for figs. 25, 45 and 56; Miss Grethe Buhl for fig. 33; Commander the Hon. John Fremantle for figs. 1 and 36; M. Guilleman for fig. 37; Lloyd's for fig. 47; Musée de la Marine, Paris, for figs. 4, 5, 51 and 52; Musée de Versailles for fig. 6; the National Maritime Museum, Greenwich, for figs. 7–14, 17–21, 28–32, 34, 35, 39, 44, 46, 55 and 58; the Parker Gallery for figs. 26, 27, 49, 50, 53 and 54; Radio Times Hulton Picture Library for figs. 16 and 38; the Royal United Service Institution for fig. 40; J. Russell and Sons for fig. 48; Service Historique de la Marine, Paris, for figs. 41 and 42; Edwin Smith for fig. 57; and the Victory Museum, Portsmouth for figs. 22 and 23 from the Maurice Suckling Ward Collection.

The Illustrations

Maps

PART I

Prelude to Achievement

In the little church at North Stoneham, on the outskirts of Southampton, there is a monument to Admiral Lord Hawke. It is a notable piece of eighteenth-century sculpture, and among the words of eulogy which adorn it there occurs the phrase:

Where'eer he sailed, Victory attended him.

This was a fine thing to say of a sea officer, though it could have been added with truth that Hawke had a long wait between triumphs, and an equally long one before he obtained the peerage which should have been his the moment news was received in London of his annihilation of Conflans at Quibron Bay in November 1759, when Nelson was in the cradle.

Hawke was one of Nelson's heroes, and the veteran survived to see Nelson's name on the list of post-captains, but it could not have been written with any semblance of veracity that victory always attended the younger man. Setback, reverse, disappointment, Nelson knew them quite as often as their opposite. It helped to turn him into the most seasoned commander of his age, perhaps of all time. For better or worse, however, his triumphs have so caught the general imagination that his failures are scarcely remembered. It is partly to make the necessary adjustment in perspective that a summary of all his more important actions is included. The series is one which for variety in scene and circumstance has few equals.

Nelson joined his first ship in 1770 at the age of 12, and his early years at sea included a voyage to the West Indies, another to the Arctic, and a comparatively long spell on the East Indies Station, where he first heard the sound of guns in action. In 1774 the frigate in which he was serving, H.M.S. *Seahorse*, attacked and captured an armed vessel in the navy of Haidar Ali off the coast of Malabar. Haidar Ali, ruling in Mysore, was in arms against the British, who were extending their influence in India.

Invalided home in 1776, Nelson was soon at sea again, first on convoy duty in home waters, and then on the West India Station. At that time Britain was at war with her American Colonies, and Nelson was likely to see action on the far side of the Atlantic. It was there that he was given his first great opportunities. He had been promoted lieutenant in April 1777 at the age of 19, and by the influence of his maternal uncle, Maurice Suckling, who was then Comptroller of the Navy, had been sent to a crack frigate, the *Lowestoffe*, commanded by William Locker, once a favourite with Hawke. When Nelson reached West Indian waters he was taken in hand by Sir Peter Parker, the local Commander-in-Chief, and groomed for further promotion. He was transferred to the *Bristol*, Parker's flagship, and within a few months had risen to be first lieutenant.

Parker's favour did not stop there. In December 1778 Nelson was made commander of the *Badger*, brig, and in the June of the following year he received the most consequential step of a sea officer's life, appointment to a post-captain's command. Parker's promotion was duly confirmed by the Admiralty, and thus at an age which was still a few months short of 21 Nelson had achieved a rank from which nothing but gross misconduct could remove him, and from which, obeying the iron law of seniority, he would in due time rise to flag rank.

It was true indeed that the age of George III was that of youth. Pitt the Younger was Prime Minister at 24, and officers in both armed services with the necessary influence and merit could, if they were lucky in their opportunities, rise high at an early age. If the conditions of the time were exceptional, so, in many cases, were the men.

Nelson's first extended experience of active service was ashore, against Spain in Nicaragua, for when matters began to go badly for the Mother Country, Spain joined France in support of the Americans.

It was thought by the authorities in Jamaica, who exercised general control in the area, that Spain could best be attacked in her possessions in Central America, and a half-baked, ill-equipped amphibious expedition was sent to capture the Fort of San Juan, some distance up the river of that name.

Everything went wrong. The season was ill-chosen, sickness was rampant, and although the fort itself was captured, the affair was of so little importance or effect that it rarely inspires even a footnote in modern history-books. Years later, when Nelson supplied a 'Sketch of my Life' for the editors of the *Naval Chronicle*, he had this to say about the episode:

> In January 1780, an Expedition being resolved on against St Juan's, I was chosen to command the Sea part of it. Major Polson, who commanded, will tell you of my exertions: how I quitted my ship, carried troops in boats one hundred miles up a river, which none but Spaniards since the time of the buccaneers had ever ascended. It will then be told how I boarded, (if I may be allowed the expression), an outpost of the enemy, situated on an Island in the river; that I made batteries, and afterwards fought them, and was a principal cause of our success.

Modesty was not among Nelson's characteristics—until and unless he was assured that his audience knew his stature, when his view of his own achievements took a more proportioned place in the scheme of things. But he had seen hard service, ill-recognised, and it had been followed by another spell as an invalid. Climate and conditions in Nicaragua had got the better of him, and he returned home as a passenger in H.M.S. *Lion*, whose captain, Cornwallis, helped to save his life.

With a good war record, together with an extensive knowledge of the duties of ships of all sizes, Nelson reasoned that once he had recovered, there was the likelihood of a long career before him in command of 'post' ships—that is, of vessels of 20 guns or more. Nor had he long to wait before his next appointment, for the struggle dragged on, and although Nelson was at home convalescing for nearly a year, his new ship, the *Albemarle*, of 28 guns, was ordered first for convoy work in the North Sea and the Baltic, and then across the Atlantic to the main theatre of war.

The *Albemarle*'s commission was arduous though not exciting, and it ended with

2   King George III as a young man

From a pastel on vellum by Jean-Étienne Liotard

(*Reproduced by gracious permission of Her Majesty The Queen*)

3 Napoleon
From a portrait by Dutertre

4 Ganteaume
From a contemporary lithograph

5 Captain Dupetit-Thouars
From a contemporary lithograph

6 M. Poussielgue, financial adviser to the
French Expedition
From a drawing by Dutertre

a sharp disappointment for all on board. In the spring of 1783, when the American war was reaching its final stages, and opportunities for distinction were increasingly hard to come by, Nelson, who was in charge of a detachment of small ships of war, heard that the French had taken possession of Turks Island in the Bahamas. To recapture the place would, he thought, be to end his cruise in a blaze of glory.

Aspiration was one thing, fulfilment another. The plan was hasty, the force insufficient—worst of all, the French were ready, and Nelson met complete frustration. He was repulsed at every move he made, and was forced to withdraw, with casualties, and with no credit whatsoever. Nelson said nothing of the incident in the 'Sketch of his Life', but a few years ago the Navy Records Society published the Memoirs of James Trevenen, an officer who took part. His verdict is unsparing. Writing to his mother to complain of the loss of the value of a prize his ship had taken, he blamed:

> . . . the ridiculous expedition against Turks Island, undertaken by a young man merely from the hope of seeing his name in the papers, ill depicted at first, carried on without a plan afterwards, attempted to be carried into execution rashly, because without intelligence, and hastily abandoned for the same reason that it ought not to have been undertaken at all.

Trevenen was scathing, and no doubt Lord Hood, the Commander-in-Chief, felt much the same when he received Nelson's letter of proceedings, but there is this to be noted. Nelson gave words of praise to all subordinates who took part. It was his way. Seeking fame himself, he never, throughout his life, overlooked merit in others. That is not an attribute of every ambitious man.

From July 1783, when he paid off the *Albemarle*, to January 1793, when he was made captain of the *Agamemnon*, a 64-gun ship-of-the-line, Nelson experienced first the tedium of his one and only peace-time commission, and then a long spell on half pay. His appointment to the frigate *Boreas* took him back to the West Indies, where he made himself unpopular by applying the current Navigation Laws against illicit trading, work in which he found little support from his superiors, and where, in March 1787, he married the widowed niece of the President of Nevis. Her name was Frances Nesbit, and she had a small son, who soon won Nelson's affection.

The years on the beach (1788–93) were mainly spent in Norfolk at Burnham Thorpe, Nelson's birthplace. They were unhappy, for the still youthful captain was longing for another ship, and he believed himself to be out of favour with the authorities for having done his duty. But when fortune changed, it was not half-heartedly. On 7 January 1793 he wrote from London to his wife as follows:

> *Post nubila Phoebus:*—After clouds comes sunshine. The Admiralty so smile upon me, that really I am as much surprised as when they frowned. Lord Chatham yesterday made many apologies for not having given me a Ship before this time, and said, that if I chose to take a Sixty-four to begin with, I should be appointed to one as soon as she was ready; and whenever it was in his power, I should be removed into a Seventy-four. Everything indicates War. One of our ships, looking into Brest, has been fired into: the shot is now at the Admiralty. You will send my Father this news, which I am sure will please him. . . .

The appointment could scarcely have delighted the nervous Fanny, but from the

17

moment he despatched that jubilant missive to the end of his life, some 12 years later, Nelson rarely had a dull moment. From being an enforced spectator, he became once more an active participant in the world's affairs, and it seemed as if the early promise of his life might after all be fulfilled. Final blessing, the *Agamemnon* was ordered to the Mediterranean with a fleet in charge of Lord Hood. This was a sphere Nelson would have chosen, and about the qualities of the admiral he was never in doubt. He considered Hood 'the best officer, take him altogether, England has to boast of; great in all situations which an admiral can be placed in'. This was a slightly exaggerated view, and Nelson in fact had other admirations, including Lord Howe and later Lord St Vincent, but his allegiance to Hood, in the earlier days of the Mediterranean campaign, was a considerable factor in his happiness.

In point of fact the war with Revolutionary France, which was to continue so long, began unpromisingly, and would continue to disappoint belligerent-minded Britons for many years to come. Although the country was strong by sea, her army was inconsiderable, and there was scarcely an area, except the West Indies, where she might hope to take advantage of her opponent. France on the other hand, though suffering from divisions part political, part regional, had found in the principles, practice and sheer ferment of the Revolution a dynamism which was to extend her power beyond the dreams of the greatest of her kings.

Hood began with a swift success. With the help of royalist partisans in the area, he was able to seize and use the port of Toulon, though he was soon threatened by forces intent on its recapture, the artillery commanded by an officer of whom the world would hear more—Napoleon Bonaparte. What Hood most needed was troops, and in September 1793 he sent Nelson and his ship to Naples, to enquire whether Ferdinand III would send a contingent to his aid. At this early stage of the conflict Spain was allied with Britain, and, by reason of dynastic ties, Naples moved with Spain in the matter of her foreign policy. While at Naples, Nelson conducted his business through the medium of the British Minister, Sir William Hamilton, who had been 30 years at Ferdinand's court, and knew Italian politics better than any Englishman living. His wife, formerly Emma Hart, was gracious and attractive, and the visit was successful so far as it went.

Ferdinand indeed sent troops, but their fate was sad, for they had not long reached Toulon before Hood was forced to withdraw from the area, and most of the Neapolitans were driven into the sea. With the port lost, the admiral was forced to look elsewhere for a base for future operations, and it seemed improbable that he would be able to light upon anywhere more favourable than Corsica. There were French garrisons on the island, but the people had asked for British protection, and the likelihood was that the whole area could be reduced without excessive difficulty.

So far as Nelson was concerned, a pattern of service established during the War of American Independence was to repeat itself: then, interception of privateers and contraband, convoy protection, brushes with hostile units had been followed by such activity ashore as had earned him the nickname of 'the brigadier'. Under Hood it was much the same: for instance, he had a protracted engagement with a frigate detachment off Sardinia on 22 October 1793; he was constantly taking or destroying small prizes, and for the remainder of the autumn and in the following year he was at stretch, afloat and ashore, mainly in Corsica or close by.

Nelson lost the sight of his right eye, though not the eye itself, on 12 July 1794, while engaged in reducing the French garrison at Calvi. The incident was so illustrative of his personality, and it so affected his future life, that the details are worth recalling.

The first reference to the incident occurs in a Journal attached to a letter to Hood which was headed: 'Camp, July 11th, 1794, 6 a.m.', the time when the report was begun.

> At daylight on the 12th [wrote Nelson] the Enemy opened a heavy fire from the town . . . which, in an extraordinary manner, seldom missed our battery; and at seven o'clock, I was much bruised in the face and eyes by sand from the works struck by shot.

Nelson was far too busy to refer to the matter again for the next few days, but on 16 July he wrote to an uncle, William Suckling, to tell him something of his Corsican experiences.

> You will be surprised [he said] when I say I was wounded in the head by stones from the merlon of our battery. My right eye is cut entirely down; but the Surgeons flatter me I shall not entirely lose the sight of that eye. At present I can distinguish light and dark, but no object: it confined me one day, when, thank God, I was enabled to attend to my duty. I feel the want of it; but, such is the chance of War, it was within a hair's breadth of taking off my head.

Matters never improved, and to all intents and purposes the eye remained useless, though the fact was so little apparent that when artists got to work on Nelson, they were apt to choose the wrong one when they tried to distinguish which was damaged.

Nelson had a green shade made, soon afterwards, to shield the good eye from the Mediterranean glare. This is the origin of the erroneous belief that he habitually wore a patch. Most considerately, in a letter which he addressed to his wife from Calvi on 14 July, he said nothing about the matter whatsoever, though he was careful to report that her son Josiah 'is very well now sitting by me'.

It was not until March 1795, when Nelson had been a post-captain nearly 17 years, that he had his first opportunity to take part in a fleet action. The occasion was disappointing. By then, Hood had gone home, and had been replaced by Admiral Hotham, a man of less firm stamp: moreover, the relative strength of the maritime forces in the area of the Ligurian Sea had, at least on paper, altered greatly in favour of France. The enemy had had the necessary time to repair the Toulon armament, which had been incompletely destroyed at the time of the withdrawal, while through wear, detachment, sickness and the accidents of war, the British ships were by now seriously under-manned, and every spar and replacement had to reach Hotham by way of the long sea haul from home.

The French Directory, having got together some 17 sail-of-the-line, sent them from Toulon to seek and engage the British. In the event of success, so it was argued, Corsica could be re-taken, and the British would no longer be able to harry traffic along the coast of Italy. Hotham had news of the sortie at Leghorn, where he commanded 15 sail-of-the-line, one of them Neapolitan. He started off at once to face the challenge, and indeed came up with the French, but the result was typical of the many indecisive encounters of the era of sail.

Hotham found that the French, though superior in ships and fully manned, would not stand to meet him. When the conditions of wind at last permitted it, they actually allowed him to give chase, possibly because they were still under the influence of their defeat by Howe in the Atlantic, the result of the battle of the 'Glorious First of June' during the preceding summer. A chase was Nelson's chance for distinction, for the *Agamemnon* was a fast sailer, and he took it. Those were days when the pace of sea warfare was such that it was possible for a captain to compose a letter home when actually within sight of the enemy, and Nelson wrote to his wife on 10 March as follows:

> . . . Whatever may be my fate, I have no doubt in my own mind but that my conduct will be such as will not bring a blush on the face of my friends. The lives of all are in the hands of Him who knows best whether to preserve it or no, and to His will do I resign myself. My character and good name is in my own keeping. Life with disgrace is dreadful. A glorious death is to be envied, and, if anything happens to me, recollect death is a debt we must all pay, and whether now or in a few years hence can be but of little consequence. . . .

In the stately but inconclusive manœuvring which occupied the next few days, a French ship, *Le Ça Ira* of 84 guns—'the largest two decker I ever saw', so Nelson told his brother—carried away her main and fore topmasts. A frigate took her in tow, and two other vessels, *Le Sans Culotte* and *Le Barras* kept within gun-shot for a time, but Nelson in the war-worn *Agamemnon* stood towards the disordered ships, proposing to withhold his fire until he actually touched her stern. This proved impossible, but he battered away at her for over two hours, and further reduced her fighting efficiency. Night then fell, but next day, after further fighting, the prize was his, and *Le Censeur*, 74 guns, fell to other ships of Hotham's fleet.

Nelson was all for pressing the advantage, but he could not move the admiral. 'We must be contented', said Hotham. 'We have done very well.' 'Now', wrote Nelson to Fanny, 'had we taken ten sail, and allowed the eleventh to escape, when it had been possible to have got at her, I could never have called it well done. . . . We should have had such a day as I believe the annals of England never produced. . . .'

Nelson's first fleet action, though it had brought him distinction, and the honorary appointment of Colonel of Marines—which considering his military exploits was singularly appropriate—also brought bitterness, for he had a different conception of war from most of his fellows. He aimed at annihilation as the logical conclusion of bringing an enemy to action. It was a principle endorsed by Napoleon.

> I wish [so Nelson confessed] to be an admiral, and in command of the English fleet; I should very soon either do much, or be ruined: my disposition cannot bear tame and slow measures. Sure I am, had I commanded on the 14th [the final day] that either the whole French fleet would have graced my triumph, or I should have been in a confounded scrape.

Just three months later, there came another opportunity. Nelson had been ordered on detached service, to co-operate with the Austrians in harassing the French then on the

Genoese Riviera. Off Cape del Mele, he fell in with the main fleet of the enemy, who immediately gave chase. He retreated at once upon San Fiorenzo in north Corsica, where Hotham was watering and refitting, and for an hour or two was within possibility of capture while in sight of his friends.

By dint of great exertions, Hotham, though taken by surprise, managed to get under weigh, and for five days gave chase to the enemy. When the main forces came within fighting distance for the second time, the baffling winds and sudden vexatious calms which are a feature of the area of Fréjus made it impossible to shorten the range. Although by the afternoon of 13 July the *Agamemnon* and the *Cumberland* were, in Nelson's words:

> . . . closing with an 80-gun ship with a Flag, the *Berwick*, and the *Heureux* . . . Admiral Hotham thought it right to call us out of Action, the wind being directly into the Gulf of Fréjus, where the Enemy anchored after dark.

Nelson had nearly two years to wait before he once again found himself in a position to affect the fortunes of a fleet engagement. By that time he had left the *Agamemnon*, and he had discovered, in Sir John Jervis, a kind of admiral very different from Hotham. 'Entre nous', wrote Sir William Hamilton from Naples, 'I can perceive that my old friend, Hotham, is not quite awake enough for such a command as that of the British Fleet in the Mediterranean, although he is the best creature imaginable.' Jervis was of another kind.

The war development, in the Mediterranean particularly, increasingly called for the exceptional man, for it was going from bad to worse. By land, France was everywhere successful, and the work which fell to Nelson and his fellow captains was of attempting to contain the uncontainable. Blockading in worn-out ships was gruelling, and in June 1796, when Nelson was acting as a Commodore, it became necessary for him to shift his pendant from the *Agamemnon*, which was almost falling apart, so much was she in need of a home refit, to the *Captain*. This ship, of 74 guns, was commanded by Ralph Miller, an officer who became one of a long series of men of rank who were Nelson partisans. Miller had been born in New York, his parents being fervent Loyalists, and the Navy produced few better officers.

In the later part of the year it became urgent for Jervis to face the fact that it would soon be imperative for the British to withdraw altogether from the Mediterranean, so critical was the supply and health situation, so threatening the enemy dispositions, so uncertain the political climate in the Italian states, and so desperate had the need become to keep the strongest possible force based on Gibraltar and the Tagus. Portugal, which afforded facilities at Lisbon, was at that time Britain's one reliable ally in the west, for active hostility on the part of Spain was a condition which, so it was realised, could not be long delayed. With the resources then at the Admiralty's disposal, it was no longer possible to keep three powerful fleets on active watch, one at the western approaches of the Channel, one further south, and a third based on Corsica.

Nelson's final days on the Mediterranean Station were full of incident. In September and October 1796 he was engaged in the withdrawal from Corsica, which had cost so much to secure. In December he was at Gibraltar, where he shifted his pendant to *La Minerve*, frigate, with orders to help in the withdrawal of troops and stores from Port Ferrajo, in Elba, which had served its turn as a base subsidiary to Corsica. By then, war with Spain was confirmed, and on 19 December, off Cartagena, Nelson had one of the smartest actions of his life. It was against the Spanish frigate *La Sabina*, commanded by Don Jacobo Stuart, an officer descended from James II of England, and renowned in his own navy.

Nelson described the action to his brother William, saying that it opened with his 'hailing the Don' and demanding immediate surrender. 'This is a Spanish frigate', came the dignified reply, 'and you may begin as soon as you please!' Nelson added: 'I have no idea of a closer or sharper battle', for Stuart's reputation was soundly based.

> The force to a gun the same, and clearly the same number of men; we have 250. I asked him several times to surrender during the action, but his answer was: 'No, sir; not whilst I have the means of fighting left!' When only he himself of all the officers was left alive, he hailed and said he could fight no more, and begged I would stop firing.

Hardly had the guns ceased, and a boarding party been sent across, than other Spanish ships were seen approaching. Next day, Nelson was forced to abandon the prize, together with his boarders, in order to protect his own ship. *La Minerve* was able to fight the enemy off, but she could not prevent Spanish colours being rehoisted in *La Sabina*. Stuart, who was enjoying Nelson's hospitality, seemed likely to be the only Spanish prisoner of war.

Soon afterwards, in an exchange of courtesies not uncommon between Spanish and British, Stuart returned home, Hardy and another officer being released, Hardy having commanded the boarding party. It was the beginning of a bond between Nelson and Hardy which was to continue for the rest of Nelson's life, and it was cemented by a startling incident. As *La Minerve* was leaving the Mediterranean on her return to join Jervis in the Atlantic, she was sighted and chased by two Spanish ships-of-the-line. Colonel Drinkwater, a military friend of Nelson's who was taking passage with him, asked if there was likely to be an action. 'Very possibly', said the Commodore, 'but before the Dons get hold of that bit of bunting'—looking up at his pendant—'I will have a struggle with them, and sooner than give up the frigate I'll run her ashore.'

A little later, Nelson and his staff were at dinner, but the meal had hardly begun when it was interrupted by the cry, 'Man overboard!' Hardy went off in the jolly-boat to attempt rescue, but the sailor had been caught in a current which was flowing towards the pursuing Spaniards. He was never seen again. Presently, Hardy and his boat's crew got into difficulty, making no headway towards the ship.

'At this crisis', so Drinkwater related, 'Nelson, casting an anxious look at the hazardous situation of Hardy and his companions, exclaimed: "By G—, I'll not lose Hardy. Back the mizzen topsail."' The order had the intended effect of checking the frigate's speed, and an encounter between unequal forces now seemed certain. But the Spaniards were surprised and confused by Nelson's action. The leading ship suddenly shortened sail, allowing *La Minerve* to drop down to the jolly-boat and pick up Hardy and his men. Once under way again, she was soon safe—at least for the moment.

That same evening, the frigate ran into fog, and when it began to lift, Nelson saw that he was in the middle of an enemy fleet. Spanish look-outs were, so he had long discovered, fallible creatures, and conditions of visibility were such as to make his escape almost a certainty. It was so, and when *La Minerve* reached Jervis's rendezvous off Cape St Vincent on 13 February, Nelson was able to bring him valuable first-hand information. He was ordered to rejoin the *Captain*, and make ready for the battle which obviously could not be long delayed.

Córdoba, the Spanish admiral, had orders to protect a valuable convoy of mercury, and his fleet was also to form part of a larger Franco-Spanish armament whose purpose was invasion of the British Isles. The threat was real. The French had already made a landing at Bantry Bay the previous December, eluding the watch of Howe's successor, Lord Bridport, but bungling their opportunity; and there was another attempt on Wales during this very month of February, which also ended ignominiously. Whatever the result of such sorties, the fact had become evident that they could and might succeed, and as Jervis remarked, a victory was very necessary to the welfare of the country.

When the Commander-in-Chief sighted the Spaniards, on 14 February, Valentine's Day, they were in no regular order. Córdoba himself was to windward of the British, and another group of ships—among which were the mercury-laden *urcas*—were to leeward, making for Cadiz. Jervis had with him 15 ships-of-the-line and four frigates. Córdoba's force was 27, of which one vessel, the *Santissima Trinidad*, was a four-decker, and the largest warship then afloat. Jervis's plan was to lead his well-disciplined line like a wedge between the two Spanish divisions, and then to turn to windward to attack Córdoba. He succeeded, though he may have left his turn somewhat late.

The *Captain*, wearing Nelson's pendant, was the third from the last in Jervis's line. Before the Commander-in-Chief had made his crucial signal to 'tack in succession', that is, to change direction, Nelson realised that the leading ships might well be unable to prevent Córdoba from effecting his junction with the group to leeward. He also realised that if he himself wore out of the line and made at once for the nearest Spaniards, he would disorganise their movements, and allow the head of the British line time to do what Jervis had intended.

Such an act of initiative was unparalleled on the part of a subordinate, and it has never been repeated in a major action. In the Georgian navy, the line of battle was sacred. To leave it, without a direct order, meant court-martial and probably disgrace. Under an extreme disciplinarian like Jervis, disobedience of any kind, however intelligent, demanded supreme courage, and would need to be justified, up to the hilt, by success.

Nelson was not long unsupported. His old friend Troubridge, commanding the *Culloden* and leading the line, was soon in the thick of it, and so was Collingwood in the *Excellent*, another lifelong friend who, incidentally, had brought gunnery drill in his ship to the highest pitch of efficiency then obtainable. The *Captain* was quickly in trouble. Her sails and rigging were shot about, her wheel was smashed, and seeing that she would be able to do no further service in the line that day, or even in a chase,

Nelson ordered Miller to close with the nearest Spaniard. Then he called for boarders. It was no duty of a high-ranking officer to engage in hand-to-hand fighting, his life was far too valuable, but Nelson was no ordinary commodore, and what followed in the Spanish *San Josef* needs to be told in his own words.

> The first man who jumped into the enemy's mizzen-chains was Captain Berry, late my first lieutenant. He was supported from our spritsail yard. . . . A soldier of the 69th Regiment, having broke the upper quarter-gallery window, jumped in, followed by myself and others, as fast as possible. I found the cabin doors fastened, and the Spanish officers fired their pistols at us through the windows, but having broke open the doors, the soldiers fired, and the Spanish brigadier fell as retreating to the quarter-deck.

A detachment of the 69th—later the Welch Regiment—was serving as marines, and did splendidly throughout, and within a few moments the *San Josef* was in British hands. Just beyond her was an even larger ship, the *San Nicolas*, which had been run alongside her compatriot. Nelson ordered Captain Miller to send a party across the *San Josef* to take the *San Nicolas* by the same methods. Nelson followed.

> When I got into the main chains [he reported] a Spanish officer came upon the quarter-deck rail, without arms, and said that the ship surrendered. From this welcome information it was not long before I was on the quarter-deck, when the Spanish captain, with bended knee, presented me his sword and told me the admiral was dying with his wounds below . . . and on the quarter-deck of a Spanish first-rate, extravagant as the story may seem, did I receive the swords of the vanquished Spaniards.

Jervis took four Spanish ships on 14 February, without loss to his own fleet. It was thought at one time that the towering *Santissima Trinidad* had struck her colours, but she got away in the murk and confusion of the winter afternoon, though the admiral had to shift his flag to a less damaged vessel.

Having won his prizes by what he called his 'patent bridge', Nelson had now to face his chief. He need not have worried, for Jervis knew a man when he saw one. Nelson was received with the greatest affection. Jervis, he said 'used every kind expression', which 'could not fail to make me happy'.

Nelson had been bruised in the stomach during the fighting, and although he thought nothing of the matter, pain from this injury was to trouble him on occasion for the rest of his life. The *Captain*'s injuries were still more serious, and Nelson moved to the *Irresistible*, flying his flag as rear-admiral of the Blue, for promotion by seniority came his way almost immediately after the action. He made one more foray into the Mediterranean, withdrawing the last men and supplies from Corsica and Elba, and then settled down to command of the inshore watch on Cadiz. It was an active post for a very active man, about to become Sir Horatio Nelson, Knight of the Bath, with a star and a ribbon for his coat in recognition of his feats on Valentine's Day.

Fanny Nelson, when she hear the news of the battle, begged her husband to 'leave boarding to captains!', but it was as an admiral that Nelson, in company with Captain Fremantle, who had been with him in the frigate *Inconstant* during the attack on the *Ça Ira*, had yet another extraordinary adventure, the details of which would be barely credible did they not appear in Nelson's 'Sketch of my Life'.

It was during this period [he wrote in his uninhibited way] that perhaps my personal courage was more conspicuous than at any other period of my life. In an attack of the Spanish gun-boats [which had made a sortie from their port], I was boarded in my barge with its common crew of ten men, Cockswain, Captain Fremantle and myself, by the Commander of the Gunboats. The Spanish barge rowed twenty-six oars, besides Officers, thirty in the whole; this was a service hand to hand with swords, in which my Cockswain, (now no more), saved my life twice. Eighteen of the Spaniards being killed and several wounded, we succeeded in taking their Commander.

Nelson never questioned the Spaniards' courage, but he had experience of their efficiency, or lack of it, dating back to his service in Nicaragua, and such episodes merely confirmed his view that liberties could be taken with 'the Dons' which would not otherwise be justified. Yet the next fighting in which he was involved showed that military contempt was rash, and could cost him dearly.

While Nelson was off Cadiz, Jervis, now Earl of St Vincent, heard that a Spanish treasure-ship had put into Santa Cruz in the Canaries, and he planned to cut her out. Teneriffe, the island concerned, was well defended, and the operation would require a force of some size. Nelson was the obvious man to lead it.

He was given four ships-of-the-line, with his flag in the *Theseus*, together with three frigates and a cutter. He chose his own officers, who included Troubridge in the *Culloden* and Fremantle, now in the *Seahorse*, successor to Nelson's East Indian vessel. Fremantle actually had his young wife aboard, which was due to the fact that she was a special favourite with Lord St Vincent.

Nothing went right. Owing to unfavourable weather and unsuspected inshore currents, the boats were unable to reach their landing-place during the hours of darkness, and the attack thus lost all element of surprise. The few parties able to get ashore were soon withdrawn, since they found the garrison formidable and ready. Nelson then decided that he would lead a second night attack in person. 'Tomorrow', he wrote to St Vincent on 24 July, 'my head will probably be covered with laurel or cypress.'

Josiah Nisbet pleaded to go with his stepfather. 'No', said Nelson, 'should we both fall, what would become of your poor mother?' 'I will go with you tonight', said the youth, 'if I never go again!' Nelson let him have his way, and it was well that he did so, for his boat was heavily fired upon as she neared the shore, and just as the admiral was about to land, a shot shattered his right arm. Josiah, who was near, saw that Nelson could not stand, and heard him exclaim: 'I am a dead man!' The youngster placed him in the bottom of the boat, took a silk handkerchief from his neck, and with the help of one of the bargemen made a rough tourniquet. The boat then withdrew into the darkness, picking up survivors from the cutter *Fox* as she made her way back to the squadron.

It was the *Seahorse* that Nisbet first sighted, but nothing would induce Nelson to board her, even at risk of his life, for he needed instant attention. 'I would rather suffer death', he said, 'than alarm Mrs Fremantle in this state, and when I can give her no tidings of her husband.'

When the *Theseus* was found at last, Nelson refused help in getting aboard. 'Let me alone', he said. 'I have yet my legs left, and one arm. Tell the surgeon to make haste and get his instruments. I know I must lose my right arm, so the sooner it is off the better.'

The amputation was done in the early hours of the morning of 25 July, and it was successful. Next day, so the surgeon noted, Nelson 'rested pretty well and quite easy. Tea, soup and sago. Lemonade and tamarind drink.' The 'rest' was comparative. The expedition was in ruins, and although the gallant Troubridge got a party ashore he could do little. His ammunition was soaked, his men were outnumbered, and there was nothing for it but retreat. It was Turks Island all over again.

The Spaniards, courteous as ever, were ready to parley. They behaved, said Troubridge, 'in the handsomest manner, sending a large proportion of wine, bread, etc., to refresh the people, and showed every mark of attention.' They even lent boats so that the British could withdraw in comfort! Nelson, not to be outdone in politeness, begged the Spanish governor's acceptance of a cask of English beer and a large cheese.

It was just as well that Nelson had not boarded the *Seahorse*, for when Fremantle did return to his wife, he was also wounded, and his injury, though slighter, was as troublesome as Nelson's, and needed constant dressing. By an odd chance, he too had been hit in the right arm when landing.

On 16 August the force rejoined Lord St Vincent at sea. On the way to the rendezvous Nelson had written, slowly and painfully, to say that 'a left-handed admiral will never again be considered useful. . . . The sooner I get to a very humble cottage the better, and make room for a better man to serve. . . .' Less accurate words were never penned, though Nelson indeed went home in the *Seahorse* with the Fremantles, joining his wife and father after more than four years' arduous service abroad. He seemed to them to possess all the eager, affectionate zest they had loved of old. Convalescence would obviously be protracted, and that he returned a hero, even though a battered one, was a fact which all could rejoice in.

Unbelievably, it was within a year that Nelson was again in action. This time, the story would echo throughout Europe, and the news would come from Egypt.

PART II

The Nile

1 *Eyewitness Ashore*

From Alexandria, the coastline of Egypt runs north-easterly to Aboukir Point—off which is a small island. Between Aboukir Point and Rosetta, where a spit of land conceals one of the two principal mouths of the Nile, there is a curving, shallow bay. It is about 16 miles between the promontories.

On 1 August 1798, or what he himself described, in the style of the French Revolutionaries, as the 14th of the month of Thermidor, Monsieur E. Poussielgue, Controller-General of the Finances of General Bonaparte's Eastern Army, was at Rosetta. At 5.30 in the afternoon, he heard cannon. M. Poussielgue and those who were with him at once went to the highest places they could find—terraces, the tops of houses, natural prominences, from which, away in the distance, they could just see some ten British ships of the line as they swept into Aboukir Bay on a course skirting Aboukir Island ; others followed.

'This', wrote the Controller-General to his wife in France, 'was the beginning of the battle.' He and his party lost sight of the vessels as they headed into shallower water, but gunfire continued, and darkness, when it came, brought no peace to M. Poussielgue and his compatriots.

> The cannonade was very heavy until about a quarter past nine [he continued]. Favoured by the clear night, we saw an immense illumination, which told us that some ship was burning. At this time the thunder of guns was heard with redoubled fury, and at 10 o'clock the ship on fire blew up with the most dreadful explosion.

Other accounts put the time of the event a little earlier or later, but all agree on what happened next. The sound was so shattering that the men of almost every vessel in the Bay thought that they themselves had been hit. Then, in M. Poussielgue's words, 'there was the most profound silence for the space of about ten minutes', lit by the dying blaze of the French flagship *L'Orient*.

> After that significant pause [said the writer] the firing began again, and continued without a break until three o'clock in the morning, when it ceased almost entirely until five. Then it continued with as much fury as ever.

When daylight came, the Frenchman could no longer bear to be without a proper view of what was happening ; so, he said :

> . . . I placed myself on a tower which is about a gun-shot from Rosetta . . . whence I could distinctly see the whole battle. At 8 o'clock I saw a ship on fire, and in about half an hour she blew up, like the other during the night.

Soon, details were discernible, though the general impression was one of the utmost confusion.

> A large ship, entirely dismasted, was on shore on the coast [ran the description]. We saw others of the fleet also dismasted, but the two squadrons were so mingled that it was impossible to distinguish French from English, or to tell on whose side advantage lay.

The battle itself was not quite over, and presently some movement was apparent.

> Firing continued until about 2 o'clock, and then we saw two of the line and two frigates under a press of sail on a wind, standing towards the eastward; we made out that all were under French colours. No other ships made any movement, and firing ceased entirely.

M. Poussielgue had seen the French remnant escaping, led by Rear-Admiral Villeneuve. Then there followed another disconcerting silence.

> Twenty-four hours passed without anyone to give us details [continued the writer]. At last a party from Alexandria told us news, though not tending to our comfort. They said that officers of the French fleet, who had saved themselves in a boat, arrived at Alexandria, and reported that early in the battle Admiral Brueys received three severe wounds, one in the head and two in the body. Notwithstanding, he persisted in keeping his station on the arms-chest, when a fourth shot hit him in the body and cut him in two. They added that our Fleet was totally destroyed, with the exception of the four ships that got away. . . .

The Controller-General had been an eyewitness to the later stages of Nelson's victory over Brueys, at what came to be called, not very accurately, the Battle of the Nile. He termed it, without much exaggeration, 'the most bloody and unfortunate that for many ages has taken place. As yet we know not all the circumstances, but those with which we are already acquainted are frightful in the extreme.'

The missive never reached France. It was intercepted on its way by a British ship of war, and was at once brought to the attention of Nelson, who wrote on the original:

> . . . this Frenchman seems to know so much more of the Battle than I do, that I will not venture to contradict him: I am satisfied with it, if he is. Send it to Lady Nelson when read.

Graphic as it is, M. Poussielgue's account leaves many questions unanswered. For instance, what was this French official doing at Rosetta in August 1798? Where was the General for whose finances he was responsible? What were the circumstances which allowed Sir Horatio Nelson, K.B., Rear-Admiral of the Blue in the Fleet of His Majesty King George the Third, to attack Brueys as he lay at anchor in that shallow bay, and to win the most spectacular of his victories at sea?

The answers make up one of the more dramatic stories in history, its events, by no means confined to the sea, ranging from London to India, and involving the fortunes of two of the greatest men of action their countries ever produced. It was the nearest that Bonaparte and Nelson ever came to personal clash, and the circumstances and results of the battle showed both men, so gifted in imagination and in the art of war, in professional maturity.

2 *French Imagination*

When Nelson sailed into Aboukir Bay, Napoleon Bonaparte was a man of 29, with brilliant grasp of military affairs large and small, with a flair for politics which, had it not been for the French Revolution, might have spent itself in small-scale activities, and with a self-confidence resulting from consciousness of his own capabilities. Even by then, he had afforded proof of them to continental Europe.

He had a less ingrained respect for the British Navy than many of his countrymen. He had already seen it forced from Toulon, largely by his own exertions. Later there had followed an astonishing, swift campaign against Austrian power in Italy, which had ended on 17 October 1797 with the Treaty of Campo Formio. The ancient Republic of Venice had been extinguished in favour of Austria. In her turn, Austria had abandoned her interest in the Low Countries to France, which had secured the left bank of the Rhine, and the islands of the Adriatic. The Treaty meant that the French had only one effective enemy in Europe—Great Britain.

Pitt had actually sent Lord Malmesbury to Lille in the summer of 1797 to open negotiations for peace, and had offered generous terms, but the French government, taking concession as a sign of defeat, insisted on the return of the Cape of Good Hope to the Dutch—it had been captured by an amphibious force as a staging point on the route to India, Holland at that time being allied with France. Compensation had also been demanded for ships destroyed at Toulon. It seemed to Lord Malmesbury that France had no real desire for peace, and he reported in this sense to Pitt. The Prime Minister had already reached the same conclusion.

The breakdown in discussion suited the French Republic. Its rulers believed that England was on the brink of revolution, and made no secret of their hopes. 'It remains, fellow citizens,' ran a manifesto following the announcement of the end of the war with Austria, 'to punish the perfidy of the Cabinet of England, that has corrupted the courts of Europe. It is in London that the misfortunes of Europe are planned: it is in London that we must end them.'

'London' implied large-scale invasion: but the French Fleet was in no state to cover such a venture, and Bonaparte, when he was sent to the northern coasts to report on preparations, soon realised that the idea was impracticable, at least for the time. Instead, he suggested the despatch of an expedition to the Levant, to menace British trade with the East, and to threaten India. Venice, which in Wordsworth's phrase had once 'held the gorgeous East in fee', was no more. It was Britain which had inherited much of her trade with the Orient. She, too, must suffer—she must be attacked in her remoter possessions, and finally at home.

Egypt was not a new idea. Leibniz had suggested the occupation of that country to Louis XIV as long ago as 1672, and the project had been revived in the following reign. Bonaparte found a supporter in Talleyrand.

> To go to Egypt [explained the General to the Directory], to establish myself there and found a French Colony will require some months. But as soon as I have made England tremble for the safety of India, I shall return to Paris, and give the enemy its death-blow. There is

nothing to fear in the interval. Europe is calm. Austria cannot attack. England is occupied with preparing her defences against invasion, and Turkey will welcome the expulsion of the Mameluke.

Nothing was said about command of the sea, but it was Bonaparte's way to devise naval campaigns as if they were to take place ashore, with the French in control of all routes of communication. In the case of the Egyptian project, there was much ground for optimism, since Great Britain had abandoned the Mediterranean. Preparations in Paris went ahead on the assumption that Bonaparte's passage was unlikely to be disputed.

Everything was to be secret, and on a grand scale. The French were to take men of learning, as well as men at arms, to the land of the Pharaohs. Speed was essential, and Bonaparte brought immense energy to the supervision of every detail.

The aims of the expedition were defined by a secret decree of 12 April 1798. They included the occupation of Egypt, and the exclusion of the English 'from all their possessions in the East to which the General can come'. The implication was that the French would revive aspirations in India and Ceylon, which had suffered setbacks in earlier wars of the century. Nothing if not grandiose, Bonaparte's government ordered him to have the isthmus of Suez cut through, 'to assure free and exclusive possession of the Red Sea to the French Republic'. He was to improve the conditions of the inhabitants of Egypt, and to cultivate good relations with the sovereign power of Turkey—with whom, incidentally, France was not at war. The General was also empowered to seize Malta, which was seen as a strategic base of the greatest importance. Bonaparte himself, in one of his more all-embracing day-dreams, added that after conquering the East he would rouse the Greeks and other Christians, smash the Turks, seize Constantinople and 'take Europe in the rear'. There was no limit to his ambitions, no possibility which he overlooked.

His *savants* would give; they would also receive. They would learn the secrets of the mysterious East. In pursuit of learning, Bonaparte himself attended scientific lectures, and was proud to sign himself 'Member of the Institute' in addition to 'General in Chief of the Army of the East'. It was his intention to banish from the life of France that atmosphere of boorish ignorance by which the Terrorists of the Revolution had rendered themselves odious.

Among the *savants* appointed to the expedition were Monge the physicist, Berthollet the chemist, Nouet the astronomer, Geoffroy-Saint-Hilaire the zoologist, Dolomieu the mineralogist, Dupuis the archaeologist, the artist Vivant-Denon, and a number of printers, engineers, surveyors and artificers. Of the soldiers who made names for themselves then or later, Berthier was Chief of Staff; the divisional commanders included Kléber and Reynier; Murat and Marmont were among the brigadiers. The cavalry was commanded by the mulatto Alexandre Dumas, who had with him Davout.

Bonaparte's preparations were made at Marseilles, Toulon, Genoa, Corsica and Civitavecchia. He himself wrote to Brueys that he expected to join him at Toulon on 1 May, and advised the admiral to provide him with a comfortable berth, 'suitable for a commander-in-chief who expects to be seasick the entire voyage'. He was to take passage in *L'Orient*, and the naval staff was approved as follows: Vice-Admiral Blanquet, second in command; Villeneuve, third in command; Ganteaume, Chief of the Naval Staff; Casabianca, Flag Captain. Decrès was in charge of the transports: De Crêpe had command of the frigates. Villeneuve, Ganteaume and Decrès all served in planning or actually took part in the Trafalgar campaign seven years later. Casabianca, like Brueys, died in Aboukir Bay, the subject of heroic verse.

The reason for speed was not fear of the British Navy, it was because, by August, the Nile would be in flood. Its banks would be cut to admit the passage of water over the country. Inundation would hamper the march of any expedition upon Cairo, and would increase opportunities for resistance. Bonaparte estimated his strength at 30,000 infantry, 2,800 cavalry, 60 field- and 40 siege-guns, two companies of sappers and miners, and a bridging train.

There were inevitable delays, in Paris and elsewhere, and Napoleon did not reach Toulon until 9 May. Desertion was already beginning, and there were rumours that an English squadron had been seen off Majorca. His presence restored morale. Two days later a favourable wind allowed convoy and escort to leave harbour, and when the contingents from Marseilles, Genoa and elsewhere met the rest at sea, the armada consisted of 13 ships-of-the-line, 7 frigates, several gunboats, and nearly 300 transports of various sizes. It was an imposing sight, but could have been a rich prey for an experienced opponent lucky enough to have come up, in Nelson's phrase, 'upon a wind'.

Malta was sighted on 9 June, and Bonaparte sent a flag of truce ashore, desiring permission to enter the harbour, and to water the fleet and transports. The request was refused. The island was held by the Knights of St John, the last of those companies of Christian warriors who had once waged war upon the infidels in Palestine. The Grand Master, de Hompesch, as head of a neutral state, regretted that he could not allow more than two ships of a belligerent to shelter in the harbour simultaneously. It was just the excuse that Bonaparte wanted, and he answered that he would take what was needed by force.

De Hompesch's courage failed when he read this uncompromising reply. He retired to his palace, and took no further part in the proceedings. In fact, the Order of which he was head had become degenerate, and was a prey to the intrigue of its French members, who would not fight their countrymen. Brueys had appeared before Valletta in the previous March, hoping to effect a surprise, but he had then judged the enterprise too hazardous, and had sent de Hompesch an explanation so lame that it had served to throw the Knights into the arms of Russia, whose ruler hoped to spread his influence in the Mediterranean by means of a treaty.

Secure within their walls, the Knights might have held the intruders at bay indefinitely, but a revolt of the native Maltese, restless under the yoke of the Order, helped to bring about a quick surrender. After a token defence, the Knights admitted a French garrison. One of Bonaparte's officers, viewing the extent of the fortifications at leisure, remarked: 'Upon my word, General, it is lucky there was someone in the town to open the gates to us!' Once they were admitted, the French showed how long the fortress could have been defended. Four thousand of Bonaparte's men withstood a siege and blockade lasting nearly two years, most of the time on short rations, and some of it near starvation.

Bonaparte stayed a week in the island, showing the organising powers for which he was renowned. He dissolved the Order, pensioning off the French Knights who had been most serviceable to him. He abolished religious houses; established a governmental commission; provided for the imposition of customs dues; suggested improvements for the hospitals and Post Office, paid special attention to the University, directing its studies to the exact sciences and the useful arts, on the model of the more advanced *Écoles Centrales* of France. Having jerked Malta out of its mediaeval calm and launched it into a swirl of progress, having plundered its treasury and churches of gold and silver, he sailed away. He devoted much of the rest of the voyage to browsing in the extensive religious, scientific and geographical library which he had taken in the flagship, which included the Koran, and an account of the voyages of Captain Cook! He had completed his first mission painlessly, and had every reason to be pleased with his success.

One night, on the way between Malta and Egypt, officers in the French Fleet declared that they heard signal guns fired in the distance, and considered giving the alarm. It was that of 22–23 June. Bonaparte did not share their fears. He had no belief that the British could have raised an adequate force in time to intercept him, and preferred intelligent discussion. The weather at first was perfect, and he was finding the voyage more enjoyable than he had anticipated. The talk sometimes turned to religion. Bonaparte's own beliefs were vague. He was ready to acknowledge the existence of a Supreme Being, but subscribed to no creed or dogma. 'In Cairo', he said later in life, 'I was a Moslem. In Paris I was a Catholic.' At bottom, he believed that man's personal destiny was in his own hands. One night, when Monge, eminent among the *savants*, was theorising on the Universe, Bonaparte stared at the heavens. It was a brilliant sight, the whole firmament ablaze with stars. He tapped Monge on the shoulder and said quietly: 'Tell me, O man of Science, who made these planets?' It was a question to which Monge could think of no satisfactory reply.

Off Crete, the wind changed, and the convoy began to face heavy weather, but the end was in sight, and in the early hours of 1 July the ships were opposite Marabut, a little fishing hamlet with a round stone watch-tower, four miles west of Alexandria. There, Bonaparte had news that an English squadron was already in the Levant. Its ships had been seen off the coast of Egypt, two days before.

Bonaparte was faced with the choice of an immediate landing from open boats, or of trying to bring the convoy into Alexandria. The French had few up-to-date local charts, and naval opinion was that the passage would be dangerous in itself, and would be disputed by batteries on shore. Brueys suggested sailing on to Rosetta, so that the transports could shelter in the Nile, and the soldiers disembark at leisure. Bonaparte decided that the risk of undertaking the voyage was now too great, and that he would disembark 5,000 men at once, march upon Alexandria, seize the town and port, and obtain safe mooring for the transports. His decision was justified. Alexandria was in decay. The garrison was small, and the ancient town, with its crumbling forts and the remains of its fabled Pharos, the diminished light perched on the top of a low castle, fell, after desultory fighting, almost as easily as Malta. By 2 July Bonaparte was in possession of Egypt's most celebrated port, and the rest of his army, with its stores and supplies, could be got ashore with ease. Even time seemed on his side. He had a month in which to reach Cairo.

The country which Bonaparte had entered so unceremoniously presented a picture of decay surpassing that of Malta of the Knights. The principal reason for this state of affairs was the same as had caused the decline of Venice. The flow of trade from the Far East had long ceased to pass through Egypt and the Mediterranean to the Adriatic and so into the heart of Europe. Decline, which had begun when the Portuguese discovered the sea route to India and China via the Cape of Good Hope at the end of the fifteenth century, had been gradual. It could perhaps have been arrested but for the greed of those who ruled the country. They inflicted so punishing a tax on the transit of goods (even after an alternative route had been shown to be practical), that no merchant would willingly face it.

Nominally subject to the Sultan of Turkey, Egypt was in fact governed by Mamelukes, a military order who were as picturesque a survival from the time of the Crusades as the Knights of Malta. The word signified in Arabic chattel or male slave, and the Mamelukes were indeed recruited as slaves from their homes in the Caucasus, their future loyalty being to their own Order. They did not mix with or marry Egyptians, and the real slaves of the country were the patient fellahin, the peasants, poor and exploited, on whom the whole economy depended. Oppressive and ignorant, the Mamelukes yet had virtues which the Knights of Malta could no longer claim. They retained their courage, their skill at arms, their scorn of the unbeliever—and of tame surrender.

When news of Bonaparte's landing was brought in alarm to the Mameluke Chief, Murad, who with his fellow Chief or Bey, Ibrahim, governed most of the country, he asked when the last French invasion had taken place, and was told it had been in the thirteenth century, when Louis IX had been defeated and captured at Mansourah. He thereupon told Rossetti, the Tuscan Consul, to give the intruders some coppers and send them away, saying he had no wish to hurt them. It was useless for Rossetti to explain that the invader-in-chief had already defeated the armies of the Austrian Empire on the plains of Lombardy. Murad knew nothing of geography, and cared less. He was confident in the strength of his cavalry and his irregular infantry, his negroes from the Sudan and his Bedouins from the desert. Not many days later, at Shubrakhit, he encountered the French with some of the best of his cavalry, and returned defeated. Bonaparte fought him in square formation, not a favourite tactic with him, but effective in the circumstances.

The skirmish at Shubrakhit was the one formal engagement during the earlier stages of the French advance from Alexandria to Cairo. Otherwise, until they reached the Nile, the principal enemies of the invaders were thirst, the Bedouins who attacked every unwary straggler, and indiscipline. The soldiers had expected a fertile land. They found sand, squalor and a burning sun. They did not hesitate to complain, and it took

Bonaparte's force of personality and a lashing tongue to keep grumbling from becoming mutiny.

The spirits of the French recovered after reaching the Nile at El Rahmaniya, and having news of a contingent which Perrée, a naval officer, was bringing down in gunboats from Rosetta. They were fortified still further by the result of the battle fought on 21 July which secured Cairo, broke, though did not quite destroy, the power of the Mamelukes, and which has gone down to history as the Battle of the Pyramids, since it was fought within sight of them.

The forces on each side were not unequal—about 24,000 men, but the Mamelukes themselves numbered only some 6,000, the rest being made up of irregulars and fellahin. The Mamelukes, formidably armed as they were, had the disadvantage that they could not fight dismounted, owing to their extraordinary dress. This consisted of a cotton shirt next the skin; then followed a light, long-sleeved robe of cloth; a silk under-tunic, girdled, and reaching to the ankles; a heavy cloth pelisse tucked into wide pantaloons; a coat of mail armour; and two or three embroidered shawls. On their heads they wore cylindrical yellow turbans, metal-circled, and wrapped round with many folds of muslin; on their feet they had capacious yellow slippers. They sat their horses on an enormous saddle of iron and wood, across which were stretched three thick blankets; and they slid their feet into copper stirrups weighing 13 pounds apiece. Each soldier had a carbine, a pair of pistols, a lance, a mace and a curved sword. The whole equipment was a fantastic blend of old and new.

Murad, the fighting Mameluke Bey, drew up his line of battle parallel with the Nile, his cavalry occupying the centre. In front stretched the plains of the Pyramids, a level terrain well suited to mounted units. An hour after midnight the French drums beat to arms, and Bonaparte advanced for the last stage of his march. At dawn he presented his army with a noble spectacle. To the left, silhouetted against the Mokattam hills, were the minarets and domes of Cairo, a city surpassing in size and beauty the most hopeful expectations of the soldiers. To the right were the famed Pyramids, gilded by the rising sun. 'Soldiers,' said Bonaparte to his escort: 'from the tops of these monuments, forty centuries look down!'

Murad Bey allowed the French to cross his front unchecked. Then the Mamelukes charged. The French squares, disciplined and patient now that the ordeal of battle was before them, mowed the horsemen down with their steady fire. The Mamelukes charged again. Again they suffered, halted, broke, and fled from the fire of formations which they could not penetrate. The French in their turn advanced, and then, within sight of thousands who had lined the far bank of the Nile to see the infidel perish, they drove the remnants of the cavalry into flight, many being drowned in the river. The irregulars promptly surrendered.

The battle had cost Bonaparte 30 killed, and perhaps ten times as many wounded, some of the victims of the cross-fire of their own squares. He estimated the enemy loss at over 2,000, and he took 400 camels and 50 guns. The soldiers gave over the evening and the night that followed to spoiling the corpses. Many of the striken Mamelukes had been carrying their entire possessions on their person, and the plunder compensated, for the time at least, for the privations of a dusty, arduous march.

7 Lieutenant

8 Carpenter

9 Purser

10 Captain

11 Sailor

12 Admiral

A SHIP'S COMPANY IN 1799
From coloured aquatints by Thomas Rowlandson

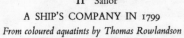

13 Nelson's ships in the Bay of Naples (17 June 1798)

From a watercolour by Giacomo Guardi

14 Capture of the *Guillaume Tell* by the *Foudroyant, Lion* and *Penelope* (1800)

From an aquatint by J. Wells after Nicholas Pocock

15 The Pharos at Alexandria under the French flag

From an engraving by J. C. Stadler after the Rev. Cooper Willyams (chaplain in the 'Swiftsure')

It was a famous though an easy victory, and Cairo was soon in panic. Bonaparte was now faced with the task of crossing the river, which proved a slow process owing to the paucity of boats, and then of reconciling those he had conquered. Afterwards it would be necessary to explore, control and administer Egypt at large, to penetrate to Suez, and to examine the possibility of conveying regiments down the Red Sea.

Near and far, all was promise. Away in southern India another enemy of Great Britain was enjoying local success. Tippoo Sahib, Sultan of Mysore, was engaged in the fourth of those wars by which he and his father, Haidar Ali, against whom Nelson had served as a youth, had hoped to thwart the extension of British influence in the sub-Continent.

Tippoo Sahib was now so hopeful of French help against the British that he had sent envoys to the Île de France, proposing formal alliance with the Republic, and a sub-sidy for French troops. He was thereupon made an honorary 'Citizen', and actually planted a 'Tree of Liberty' at his capital, Seringapatam, though, as those who knew his ways were quick to point out, it was unpromising soil for such a phenomenon.

Tippoo had even been seen to wear a tricolour in his headgear, and his favourite toy was a model of a tiger killing an Englishman. When wound up, the animal emitted realistic noises by means of an ingenious organ, almost certainly devised by a French-man. It is now a popular exhibit in the Victoria and Albert Museum, and in early days as a trophy of war was enjoyed and written about by Keats.

3 Counter-moves

While the Government of France was preparing the Egyptian venture, formulating its plan and assembling its forces, Nelson was trying the amenities of Bath and London, and slowly recovering from his wound. When at last it healed, he pressed the Admiralty for immediate re-employment.

Earl Spencer, the First Lord, was struck by his zeal, and ordered him to hoist his flag in H.M.S. *Vanguard*, lying at Spithead, and to sail for Lisbon. Nelson's flag-captain was to be Edward Berry, his fellow-boarder at St Vincent, a man from his own county who, although recently married, shared all his admiral's ardour for war. Much as he valued the society of his wife, who had nursed him back to health, and of his family, to whom he was devoted, Nelson knew his proper place to be at sea—and if in the force commanded by Lord St Vincent, so much the better.

The *Vanguard*, a fast 74-gun ship then 11 years old, sailed in charge of a convoy on 10 April, arrived off Lisbon on the 23rd, and joined the Commander-in-Chief off Cadiz at the end of the month. St Vincent told Lord Spencer that Nelson's appearance was not merely welcome to him, but that it gave him 'new life'. It was Nelson's way to invigorate, but in this instance his coming led to disturbance on the part of less favoured flag-officers, one of whom, Sir John Orde, quarrelled with the Commander-in-Chief and was sent home.

Nelson confirmed rumours, from what he had heard in London, that the French were preparing a large expedition, from bases in the Mediterranean. Its purpose was undiscovered: even the spies who kept London informed of happenings on the continent of Europe could not pierce the curtain of mystery which surrounded the Egyptian venture. What was evident was that the Royal Navy would need to re-enter the Mediterranean, and that a close watch must once again be kept off Toulon.

> The circumstances in which we now find ourselves oblige us to take a measure of a more decided and hazardous complexion than we should otherwise have thought ourselves justified in taking [wrote Spencer privately to St Vincent], but when you are apprized that the appearance of a British Squadron in the Mediterranean is a condition on which the fate of Europe may at this moment be stated to depend, you will not be surprised that we are disposed to strain every nerve, and incur considerable hazard in effecting it.

What caused the trouble with other flag-officers was Lord Spencer's recommendation (with which St Vincent agreed) that, if St Vincent did not proceed in person with a squadron, he should

> put it under the command of Sir H. Nelson, whose acquaintance with that part of the world, as well as his activity and disposition, seem to qualify him in a peculiar manner for that service.

Even before any formal instructions reached St Vincent, the Commander-in-Chief, with his usual alacrity, had anticipated them, and had sent Nelson into the Gulf of Lion with three 74-gun ships—his own *Vanguard*, the *Orion*, commanded by Sir James Saumarez, and the *Alexander*, under Captain Ball. There were attendant frigates, the *Emerald* and *Terpsichore*, and a sloop. On 19 May St Vincent sent Nelson a message by the brig *Mutine*, a fast-sailing vessel commanded by Thomas Hardy, saying that reinforcements were expected from home, and that the moment their topsails were sighted, Nelson would be given ten additional ships of the line, commanded by 'choice fellows of the inshore Squadron', many of them well known to him already, so that he would have under his hand strength for any contingency. The detachment would be sent to him in charge of his old shipmate, Thomas Troubridge, who in the opinion of St Vincent and other good judges was one of the first officers in the Navy.

Junior as he was on the flag list, Nelson's capabilities were such that it was believed he could fulfil the most difficult and important assignment of the time. If, in the First Lord's view, the 'fate of Europe' might depend on how skilfully he conducted himself, then never was a greater compliment paid to Nelson's character, resolution and understanding. This was all the more remarkable since the only earlier opportunity he had had of conducting an independent operation on a reasonably large scale, the assault on Teneriffe, had met with repulse. Those who were in control of sea affairs were in fact taking a great risk. They knew it; so did Nelson; and in the earlier days of his mission, it must have seemed that they had been misguided, for the admiral met with nothing but setbacks and frustrations, for the first of which he owned himself responsible. A less generous man would have thrown blame on Berry.

On 20 May, when near Sardinia, the *Vanguard* was dismasted, in heavy weather, and was only saved from wreck by the tireless activity of Ball on the *Alexander*, who took the flagship in tow. At one stage, fearing that the ship would be lost, Nelson asked Ball to cast off, but Ball caught up his speaking trumpet and hailed back: 'I feel confident that I can bring her in safe. I therefore must not, and by the help of Almighty God I *will not*, leave you.' Ball was right, but Nelson was never nearer going ashore in his life, and he lost one of his midshipmen in the surf.

Had Nelson been in personal charge of the ship throughout, it is unlikely that, with his long experience of the weather conditions in the area, he would have found himself in so sad a condition. Exact details of the incident are not recorded, but it is possible that Berry, who had never before commanded a ship-of-the-line, was guilty of misjudgment, of which indeed he continued to be capable, though a more intrepid man in action never lived. It is possible that Nelson himself then assumed command, a practice to which he was liable for the rest of his life. It was a useful procedure in the case of Berry, but one which would have been resented by officers who were already masters of their trade.

The episode was described by Nelson in a letter to his wife, which is among the best-known of the many which have been preserved.

> My dearest Fanny [he wrote from the 'Island of St Peter's in Sardinia' on 24 May], I ought not to call what has happened to the *Vanguard* by the cold name of accident, I believe firmly that it was the Almighty's goodness to check my consummate vanity. I hope it has made me a better officer, as I feel confident that it has made me a better man. Figure to yourself a vain man on Sunday evening at sunset walking in his cabin with a squadron about him who looked up to their Chief to lead them to glory and in whom the Chief placed the firmest reliance that the proudest ships in equal numbers belonging to France would have bowed their flags. . . . Figure to yourself this proud conceited man, when the sun rose on Monday morning, his ship dismasted, his fleet dispersed and himself in such peril that the meanest frigate out of France would have been a very unwelcome guest. But it has pleased Almighty God to bring us into a safe port where altho' we are refused the rights of humanity, yet the *Vanguard* will in two days get to sea again as an Englishman of War. The exertions of Sir James Saumarez and Captain Ball have been wonderful and if the ship had been in England, months would have been taken to send her back. Here my operations will not be delayed four days, and I shall join the rest of my fleet on the rendezvous. If this letter gets to you, be so good as to write a line to Lord Spencer telling him that the *Vanguard* is fitted tolerably for sea, and that what has happened will not retard my operations.
>
> We are all health and good humour. . . . Ever your most affectionate husband, Horatio Nelson.

Nelson's allusion to the refusal of 'the rights of humanity' was due to the fact that the Governor of the Island off which he lay, whose Sovereign was an ally of France, had sent a message that the ships could not stay where they were. He added that, as he had no force to compel them, they would doubtless do as Nelson pleased.

The affair had two results. One was good, the other could have been disastrous. On the credit side, it ensured a lasting friendship between Nelson and Alexander Ball, an officer against whom the admiral had conceived a mild prejudice when he met him, years before, while on leave in France in time of peace. Gratitude was always one of Nelson's firmest traits.

The less fortunate turn of affairs was that the frigates and the sloop, believing that Nelson would need to return to Gibraltar to seek help from dockyard resources, parted company, and that on the very day after the French had left Toulon, shaping their course into the Ligurian Sea, and passing between Corsica and the mainland of Italy.

Nelson thought that the captains of his cruisers should have known him better, and said so in round terms. In point of fact, the *Vanguard*, when repaired from the resources of the *Orion* and *Alexander*, could still outsail her consorts.

But the damage and delay had brought one advantage. It allowed time for Troubridge and his ten ships to join Nelson. Had they not done so, and had the French course been discovered, Nelson could have done no more than shadow the armada: he was not in strength enough to cause Bonaparte and Brueys serious loss. Junction was made on 7 June and Troubridge then found himself third in command, since he was a year junior to Saumarez. This was a matter of some concern to Nelson, who confided wholeheartedly in the man he had known since boyhood. Saumarez was a different matter, and it is likely that Nelson felt some degree of jealousy for so senior and so very distinguished an officer.

If so, it was human enough, for Saumarez had already been in four fleet actions, including Rodney's great victory of 1782 against de Grasse in the West Indies. He was of a Channel Island family, a man of 40, with 16 years' service as a captain. He had been knighted in 1793 after a most gallant action, when his frigate, the *Circe*, engaged and took a powerful Frenchman off Cherbourg. He had commanded the *Orion* at the Battle of St Vincent, where he had fought notably against *Santissima Trinidad*, and like other senior officers present, he had not been altogether pleased at the publicity which had accrued to Nelson, whom he referred to as 'our desperate Commodore'. He was, in fact, an officer of quick and imaginative disposition who was as attractive and capable in his own way as Nelson, with an outstanding record. The relationship of the two men, both in England, where their wives were friendly, and on active service, was invariably courteous, but Nelson's fuller trust rested with Troubridge. It was to Saumarez's lasting credit that he gave no open sign of resentment, and that his attitude to Nelson, from the time when he first came under his command to the end of Nelson's life, was one of loyalty and respect. The bearing of Nelson and Saumarez towards one another was an example of the fact that, in the dedicated and the generous-minded, jealousy may be overcome.

In order of the seniority of their captains, the reinforcement was as follows, all but one of the new ships being 74's. Troubridge brought the *Culloden*, in which he had led the line at the Battle of St Vincent. There was Captain Darby in the *Bellerophon*, a ship which was a veteran of Howe's action of 1794, 'The Glorious First of June'. There was Captain Louis in the *Minotaur*; Captain Peyton in the *Defence*, the oldest ship in the fleet, launched in 1763, and present in actions under Rodney, in India, and at the First of June. There was Captain Samuel Hood in the *Zealous*, Hood being a member of the famous naval family, one of whom, Viscount Hood, then Governor of Greenwich Hospital, was a close friend and early patron of Nelson. The *Zealous* had been with Nelson at Teneriffe.

There was Captain Gould in the *Audacious*, another ship which had been at the First of June. There was Captain Foley in the *Goliath*, a ship which had been at St Vincent, her captain at that time being flag-captain to Admiral Sir Charles Thompson, in the *Britannia*. There was Captain Thomas Boulden Thompson in the *Leander*, a 50-gun ship already 18 years old, and scarcely fit to lie in the line of battle, though she did noble duty therein, and had been present at Teneriffe, like the *Zealous*. There was Captain Hallowell in the *Swiftsure*, man and ship soon making names for themselves with Nelson, and there was Captain Miller in the *Theseus*, the Miller of Nelson's earlier days in the Mediterranean, and his captain at the Battle of St Vincent.

It was indeed a magnificent squadron, probably the finest fleet of 74's which was ever assembled, the *Leander* and Hardy's little brig *Mutine* making Nelson's total number up to 15. When it is considered that the Commander-in-Chief, releasing such ships for Nelson's use, only received eight from home as replacements, the measure of his confidence, and his sense of the importance of Nelson's sortie, may be understood. If ever the French could be defeated, it was by such armament, and Lord St Vincent could rest content in the certainty that he had done everything a man in his position could do, even for the most brilliant junior. Such were events, such the uncertainties of communication in the days of sail, that it was months before he heard whether his expectations had been fulfilled. Nelson and his ships disappeared from sight and hearing. They were somewhere in the Mediterranean, and that was all that was known. Gradually anxiety mounted, both off Cadiz and at home in London.

Since at that time Britain possessed not a single base within the Mediterranean, and was without an active ally in Europe, every drop of water, every cask of provisions required by Nelson's fleet during what might prove to be a long chase must come from neutral countries, the authorities in which would be shy of admitting the ships of a belligerent. Nelson was empowered, therefore, to resort to force, if necessary, to secure what he needed. Such was his strength that he knew it to be unlikely that coercion would be called for, even before he had succeeded in his mission. If once he gained a decisive victory, supply would look after itself. He would be welcomed in most ports of Italy as a victorious deliverer. The French might be all-powerful in Europe, but their methods, and the manners of their diplomats, had made them detested.

In the earlier stages of his pursuit, Nelson followed Bonaparte's own course into the Ligurian Sea. On 12 June he was off Elba, and on the 13th and 14th he was at Civita-vecchia, from which place a part of the French expedition had set out. By 17 June he had reached the Bay of Naples, his ships making such a gallant sight, with Vesuvius as a background, that they attracted a sketch by Guardi which is one of the more enduring records of a time of uncommon tension.

Nelson sent Troubridge into the port in the *Mutine*, to get such information as he could of French movements from Sir William Hamilton, the British Minister.

Hamilton was by now nearing 70, married to his famous young beauty, but he had been a Guardsman in his youth, and was acquainted, through personal experience, with the more obvious problems of war. His father had been a sea officer; his mother had helped to persuade Lord St Vincent's parents that the Navy was a fit career for their child, and it was no misguided instinct which led Nelson to look to him in his uncertainty. His confidence was rewarded. Both then and later, Hamilton showed himself active. He could not induce Naples to exceed her duties as a neutral, but as the Court was well disposed—the Queen was sister to the beheaded Marie Antoinette, the King detested the principles of the new France, and the Prime Minister, Sir John Acton, had inherited an English baronetcy—Nelson knew that he could get supplies, in Sicily and elsewhere, without trouble, even if under the rose. There would be a proper show of protest, but he would have what he wanted.

Hamilton's only news was that the armada was likely to be found off Malta, if indeed Bonaparte had not already attacked it. The Neapolitans were fearful for Sicily, despite their neutrality. If the French had passed this island, so Nelson wrote to Lord Spencer, 'I shall believe they are going on their scheme of possessing Alexandria, and getting troops to India—a plan concerted with Tippoo Sahib, by no means so difficult as might at first view be imagined.' He had guessed right, and he added: 'Be they bound for the Antipodes, your Lordship may rely that I will not lose a moment in bringing them to action, and endeavour to destroy their Transports.'

According to Captain Berry, who was in the best position to know the facts, if Nelson had come upon the French expedition at sea, he had arranged that his ships should fight in three squadrons. He himself would take the *Vanguard*, *Minotaur*, *Leander*, *Audacious*, *Defence* and *Zealous*. Saumarez, in the *Orion*, would be given the *Goliath*, *Majestic* and *Bellerophon*. Troubridge, in the *Culloden*, would have the *Theseus*, *Alexander* and *Swiftsure*. 'Two of these squadrons were to attack the ships of war', recorded Berry, 'while the third was to pursue the Transports, and to sink and destroy as many as it could.'

Every contingency was provided for. 'You may be assured I will fight them the moment I can reach,' he wrote to St Vincent, 'be they at anchor or under sail.' His captains were constantly summoned to the flagship, there to discuss every possible type of encounter and manœuvre, until they knew Nelson's mind without possibility of misunderstanding. 'I have passed the day on board the *Vanguard*', wrote Saumarez on one occasion, 'having breakfasted and stayed to dinner with the admiral.' Nelson knew how to blend sociality with serious discussion, and he bound his captains to him by confidence and sympathy. No one who ever served under his command failed to become his partisan, one of a 'Band of Brothers'.

On 22 June, off Cape Passaro, the south-eastern extremity of Sicily, Nelson spoke with a Genoese master who had left Malta the day before. He learnt from him of the surrender of the Knights, but the Genoese thought that the French expedition would by then have sailed elsewhere. Nelson thereupon sent a written questionnaire to representative captains, asking them whether they thought that Sicily could be the real destination, or whether, the French having already gained valuable days, the squadron should push on with all speed for Egypt. Two French frigates were actually in sight, but, having none of his own, Nelson was not to be tempted into scattering his squadron by going in chase of them, for this would have been playing into the enemy's hands. His power lay in concentration.

Ball thought that if Sicily had been the goal, information about French movements would by now have been plentiful, the frigates being simply decoys. 'I am of opinion', he said, 'that they are gone towards Alexandria, and that it is best for His Majesty's Service that we should steer in that direction.' Berry's view was the same. So was Darby's. The matter was clinched by the concurrence of Saumarez and Troubridge. 'Considering all circumstances', wrote Troubridge, 'I am led to think Egypt is their present destination, and that it will be best for His Majesty's Service to endeavour to overtake and destroy them, as their getting possession of Alexandria or any part in Egypt will put our possessions in India in a very perilous situation.'

Fortified by such advice, Nelson could scarcely doubt that his own judgment was right, and that in keeping his ships on an easterly course, he was acting with reason.

Confident though he was that no British admiral could be in close pursuit, Bonaparte, as a precaution, had directed that his armada should steer for the south shore of Crete, instead of straight to Alexandria. If Nelson had had frigates, and thus been able to extend his area of search, even such a course would not have saved the French. As it was, by making direct for Egypt Nelson missed his quarry, actually overtaking the French in the hours of darkness. 'We are crowding sail,' wrote Saumarez, 'but . . . at present it is doubtful whether we shall fall in with them at all, as we are proceeding upon the merest conjecture only, and not on any positive information. Some days must elapse before we can be relieved from our cruel suspense; and if, at the end of our journey, we find we are upon a wrong scent, our embarrassment will be great indeed.'

Saumarez was quick to recognise the stress under which Nelson was suffering. 'Did the chief responsibility rest with me', he added, 'I fear it would be more than my too irritable nerves would bear.'

For some days, not a hundred miles separated the rival forces, making for the same destination. On 26 June, when 250 miles from Alexandria, Nelson sent the *Mutine* ahead, to gain information from Mr Baldwin, the British Consul, whom he begged not to detain the brig. Hardy found that Baldwin was away, but there were no French ships in the port, only some decrepit Turkish men-of-war. Nelson himself sighted the Pharos on 29 June, and sadly confirmed Hardy's report with his own eyes.

Nelson's orders had enjoined that he must not allow the enemy to get to westward of him, but it seemed that, all unknowingly, he had let this happen. He could gain no news from casual vessels encountered, and his only course seemed to be to extend his ships as widely as possible, and to renew search to the north of the way he had already come. '*No frigates*,' he wrote despairingly to Hamilton, 'to which has been, and may be again, attributed the loss of the French fleet.'

Wearily he returned, and by 19 July he had reached Syracuse, having, in his own words, 'gone a round of near six hundred leagues with an expedition incredible'. Yet he was 'as ignorant of the situation of the enemy as I was twenty-seven days ago'. It was true, as he bemoaned, 'the Devil's Children have the Devil's luck'. Even Hamilton's letters, which the Minister had sent to Cape Passaro, had gone back to Naples. Nelson never felt nearer to despair, though at least the Fleet could be replenished. Nelson wrote to the Minister and his wife:

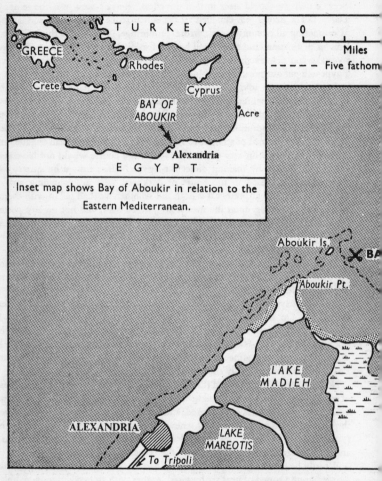

0

Miles

– – – – – Five fathom

TURKEY

GREECE

Rhodes

Crete

Cyprus

BAY OF
ABOUKIR

Acre

Alexandria

EGYPT

Inset map shows Bay of Aboukir in relation to the
Eastern Mediterranean.

Aboukir Is.

✕ BA

Aboukir Pt.

LAKE
MADIEH

ALEXANDRIA

LAKE
MAREOTIS

To Tripoli

Map of the coast of Egypt, with (inset) the Bay o

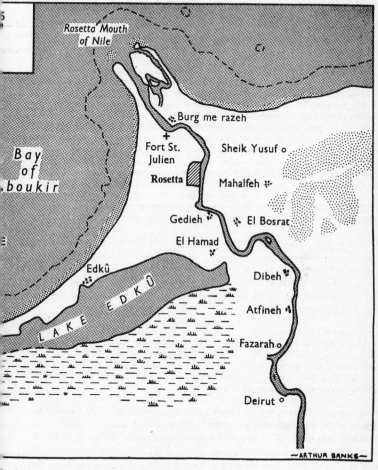

Rosetta Mouth
of Nile

Burg me razeh

Fort St.
Julien

Rosetta

Sheik Yusuf o

Mahalfeh

B a y
o f
boukir

Gedieh

El Bosrat

El Hamad

Edkû

Dibeh

L A K E   E D K Û

Atfineh

Fazarah o

Deirut o

~ARTHUR BANKS~

boukir in relation to the Eastern Mediterranean

Thanks to your exertions, we have victualled and watered; and surely, watering at the Fountain of Arethusa, we must have victory. We shall sail with the first breeze, and be assured I will return either crowned with laurel, or covered with cypress.

It was not the first time he had expressed such sentiments.

Against Ball's advice, Nelson sent a long letter to St Vincent, from sea off Alexandria, giving an account of his proceedings and reasons for his decisions. He concluded:

> I determined, with the opinions of those Captains in whom I place great confidence, to go to Alexandria; and if that place, or any other part of Egypt was their destination, I hoped to arrive time enough to frustrate their plans. The only objections I can fancy to be started is, 'You should not have gone such a long voyage without more certain information of the Enemy's destination.' My answer is ready—who was I to get it from?
>
> The Governments of Naples and Sicily either knew not, or chose to keep me in ignorance. Was I to wait patiently till I heard certain accounts? If Egypt was their object, before I could hear of them they would have been in India. To do nothing, I felt, was disgraceful; therefore I made use of my understanding, and by it I ought to stand or fall. I am before your Lordships judgment (which in the present case I feel is the Tribunal of my Country) and if, under all circumstances, it is decided that I am wrong, I ought, for the sake of our Country, to be superseded; for at this moment, when I know the French are not in Alexandria, I hold the same opinion as off Cape Passaro—viz. that under all circumstances, I was right in steering for Alexandria, and by that opinion I must stand or fall. . . .

It was an able though an anguished letter. Ball's view was that it was unnecessary to justify any course of action before it had been attacked, and St Vincent, so far from blaming Nelson, knew nothing whatever of what he had done. Ball was right. The letter was superfluous, except as an outpouring of Nelson's spirit, and as an example of the forcefulness of his expression, which was never less than clear, and which sometimes rose to eloquence.

> Every moment I have to regret the frigates having left me [he said in a later letter]. Your Lordship deprived yourself of frigates to make mine certainly the first squadron in the world, and I feel that I have zest and activity to do credit to your appointment, and yet to be unsuccessful hurts me most sensibly. But if they are above water I will find them out, and if possible bring them to battle. You have done your part in giving me so fine a squadron, and I hope to do mine in making use of them.

After three days at Syracuse, the fleet once more sailed eastwards. The course first shaped was towards the southern capes of the Greek mainland, and on 28 July Troubridge was sent into the Gulf of Koroni for news. He returned within three hours, with a French brig in tow, loaded with wine, and with information which electrified every man in the squadron. The French had been seen four weeks earlier, from the Cretan coast. They were then sailing south-east. The news was corroborated by a vessel spoken at sea the same day. Suspense was ended. Nelson and his captains had been right in their view, but too swift in their implementation. Within a day or two at most, French dispositions would be discovered, and Nelson, in his own phrase, would have earned a peerage or Westminster Abbey.

16 *Admiral Brueys*
From an early nineteenth-century engraving

Looking into Alexandria, Nelson saw a mass of transports, heavily protected by batteries ashore. There were no ships of war of any size in the harbour. But in the afternoon on 1 August, the masthead look-out in the *Zealous*, then leading the fleet, saw Brueys's ships as they lay at anchor in Aboukir Bay, 15 miles from Alexandria. The long chase was over. 'The utmost joy seemed to animate every breast on board the Squadron, at sight of the Enemy; and the pleasure which the Admiral himself felt was perhaps more heightened than that of any other man, as he had now a certainty by which he could regulate his future operations.'

Nelson had scarcely eaten or slept for days. Now that his strategic problems were resolved, and battle before him, he ordered dinner to be served. Such were the amenities arising from the stately pace of sail.

4 The Battle

Brueys had had the opportunity to make his position at anchor almost impregnable. That he did not do so reflects on his skill, and it arose partly from an over-confidence which may have been caused by an odd fact. When Troubridge had looked into the Gulf of Koroni, he heard that British frigates had been seen off Crete. The report was true. They had gone in search of Nelson, and had actually discovered Brueys, who had recognised them as enemies. They were driven away by superior numbers, but Brueys, far from being warned by the incident, regarded it as a sign that the British were unlikely to attack, and took no additional precautions.

The French admiral had not made use of Alexandria, since he believed the entrance to be difficult for his larger ships. Bonaparte had suggested that he might move to Corfu, which was in French possession, if he did not feel safe at Aboukir; but protected as he was by the lie of the coast, and by batteries both on Aboukir Island and on the castle which stood on the promontory, he saw no reason to suppose that he could not stay where he was in perfect safety, within easy reach of the Army ashore. He had just had news of the Battle of the Pyramids, and intended to celebrate Bonaparte's success in an appropriate way.

Brueys, had he studied his opponent's history, might also have taken comfort from the fact that two admirals, still living, Lord Hood and Samuel Barrington, had repulsed prolonged attacks from much the same position as that which he himself had taken up, Hood at St Kitts in 1782, and Barrington at St Lucia, four years earlier. There were, however, significant differences, and Nelson, as keen a student of history as he was of tactics, was soon to note them. Hood and Barrington had made their anchorages secure—Brueys was less careful. Since time had been on his side, he had no excuse for his oversight. Years later, on his way to St Helena, Bonaparte recalled a conversation he had had with the admiral on the voyage to Egypt. Brueys had explained the very factors which led to the destruction of his own fleet!

The line should have been incapable of being turned, and the ships should have been closed up, with cables between them as necessary, converting them into what was in effect a long, floating battery. It was axiomatic that men-of-war stood little chance against shore batteries, a truth which was often proved. Ships attacking a line in such a condition as Brueys could have established, should also have been repulsed with loss, however often they assaulted, and—within reason—in whatever numbers. Nelson, it is true, encountered a very strong anchored position later at Copenhagen, supported by shore batteries, but, as St Vincent once remarked, there was only one Nelson, and he was the first to realise how near he came to failure at that engagement, and how high was the cost of his success.

Three French flag-officers, Blanquet, Villeneuve and Ganteaume, survived the Nile. It is to Blanquet, who was wounded and made prisoner, that posterity owes the clearest account of the battle from the French side. According to him, the British were sighted by *L'Heureux* about two o'clock in the afternoon. Brueys was at once informed, but there is no record that he or any of his sailors felt elation. Their object had been fulfilled in bringing the army safely to Egypt. They had nothing to gain from a battle, had none of the assurance which came from a succession of sea victories, none of the relief from frustration felt by their opponents.

Brueys at the time had a party ashore, digging wells. So tiresome were what Blanquet called 'the Bedouins and vagabonds of the country' that the diggers had to be reinforced by a sizeable contingent, every ship sending 25 men 'to protect the workmen from attacks'. With the British in sight, everyone ashore was recalled, but only some obeyed the signal. At three o'clock Brueys ordered hammocks to be stowed in the nettings, a measure which helped to protect those on deck from splinters, and he ordered two light vessels into the bay to reconnoitre, and if possible to tempt the British into chasing them into waters where a big ship might run aground.

The eyes of Nelson's Band of Brothers were on more important matters. It was their first glimpse of what they were up against, and they knew soon enough that their task would be formidable. Brueys's 13 ships-of-the-line almost equalled Nelson's in number; but none was as small as the *Leander*. In addition to nine 74's, Brueys had three ships carrying 80 guns, and, in the centre of his line, the huge *L'Orient* with 120 guns and a complement of over a thousand men—larger than any ship in the Royal Navy, a veritable castle.

The Frenchmen were ranged as follows: in the van, anchored towards Aboukir, lay *Le Guerrier*, *Le Conquérant*, *Le Spartiate*, *L'Aquilon*, *Le Peuple Souverain*—all 74's. Then came heavier units, *Le Franklin*, 80 guns, flagship of Admiral Blanquet; *L'Orient* herself, with Brueys and Ganteaume, his Chief of Staff; and *Le Tonnant*, another ship of 90 guns. The rear of the line consisted of *L'Heureux*, *Le Timoléon*, *Le Mercure*, all 74's, *Le Guillaume Tell*, flagship of Villeneuve, carrying 80 guns, and *Le Généreux*, another 74. Brueys was well equipped with frigates. There were four in his fleet, two of them, *La Diane* and *La Justice*, of over 40 guns, not much smaller than the *Leander*, and *L'Artémise* and *La Sérieuse* of 36. Properly handled, the French fleet should have been more than equal to anything they were likely to encounter.

The French commander-in-chief could not at first believe it likely that Nelson would attack the same day. The procedure in his own navy would have been to make a careful reconnaissance, and to test the enemy's reaction to a distant cannonade. When Brueys first saw Nelson's squadron, it was in no set formation, and its scattered appearance must have given the Frenchman some further degree of confidence: there would be night in which to prepare.

At one time he appears to have considered the possibility of engaging under sail, for he ordered his top-sail yards to be got up: then, according to Blanquet, he realised that he had not seamen enough both to man his guns and to manœuvre, and decided to fight it out as he was, anchored. Under the circumstances, however well or ill provided he had been with seamen, the decision must have been right. With the wind blowing into the Bay, as it then was, there was in fact no choice, and in any event his position should have given him strength. Nature had provided for him generously.

From Aboukir Point, shoals stretched north-easterly towards the island, with broken water half covering them. They continued beyond the island, in the same direction, for a further two miles. Within the curve of the bay itself was another irregular shoal. Brueys had only to anchor his van as near as possible to the island, which he had already fortified, and his rear close upon the inner shoal—then, if the ships lay close enough together, his line could neither be turned nor penetrated. Hood and Barrington had had no such ideal conditions in the West Indian actions, yet they had driven off attack after attack by superior numbers. Brueys should have been able to do the same. In fact, he should have awaited with serenity any movement on the part of Nelson, and if the English admiral were rash enough to assault him by night, his discomfiture should have been assured.

At the Nile, every natural advantage was with the French: they were heavier in weight of metal; and to these superiorities, time had been added. A master of war could have smiled grimly, secure in his position, and encouraged by the fact that the remaining hours of daylight were few. Brueys was a brave man, but there is no record that, on 1 August 1798, he was ever seen to smile, even grimly.

Nothing is clearer from Berry's account than that, whatever the circumstances in which the enemy were come upon, Nelson would view them 'with the eye of a sea-man determined on attack'. Although no one could foresee precisely the conditions under which battle would take place, the admiral had planned to cover so many possibilities that, when the moment came, action appropriate to it would have been agreed in principle, if not in detail, in one of the talks with the captains of the squadron. It was so at Aboukir, and an anchored adversary, in a strong natural position, must be given the least possible time in which to prepare himself still further. Nelson would not only attack, he would do so at once, in the full knowledge that darkness would have intervened before all his squadron could expect to be involved.

It is an aim in war, when numbers are fairly equal, to concentrate an overwhelming force on part of the enemy, while containing or immobilising the rest, thus ensuring, at the very least, a limited victory. This was Nelson's idea, expressed in a letter to Lord Howe after the battle: 'By attacking the enemy's van and centre, the wind blowing directly along their line, I was enabled to throw what force I pleased on a few ships. This plan my friends readily conceived by the signals.'

The *Zealous* had originally reported the enemy as 16 ships. Assuming that, although Brueys's flank could not be turned, his vessels were a fair distance apart, Nelson could have achieved his purpose by bringing two to bear upon one of the enemy, attacking bow and quarter, his own ships anchoring by the stern, with a 'spring' or rope attached to the cable, so that their position could be shifted to avoid being raked. He would then gradually proceed down the enemy line, blasting it ship by ship. But had Brueys anchored in closer formation, or had the wind been less favourable, even Nelson might have been frustrated.

When Brueys was sighted, Nelson's ships were not in regular order. The *Alexander* and the *Swiftsure* were away reconnoitring, while Troubridge in the *Culloden*, towing his prize, was some miles to windward. The *Culloden* cast off the French brig in order to rejoin, but later ran aground at the tip of the shoal running out from Aboukir Island, a mishap which caused her commander bitter grief, though he was able to save the ships following him from sharing his own fate. He did not get off until the early hours of the following day, and then at the cost of his rudder and damage below the waterline.

The wind, north-north-west, blew hard enough to ensure ease of manœuvre and a fair speed: it was what the seamen called a top-gallant breeze. After dark, it would drop. The ten 74's nearest to Nelson began to form line of battle, and the admiral then signalled his intention to attack the van and centre of the anchored enemy. 'His idea', said Berry, 'in this disposition of his force was, first to secure the victory, and then to make the most of it according to future circumstances.' Viewed from a distance, Brueys appeared to be in a line 'strong and compact, flanked by numerous Gunboats, four Frigates and a battery of guns and mortars'. Weaknesses were soon observed by the eyes of the leading English captains; yet, said Berry:

> . . . the situation of the enemy seemed to secure them the most decided advantages, as they had nothing to attend to but their artillery, in their superior skill in the use of which the French so much pride themselves, and to which indeed their splendid series of land victories are in a great measure to be imputed.

When the British were off Aboukir Island, Blanquet records that the French brig *Alert* was sent

> . . . to stand towards the enemy until nearly within gunshot, and then to manœuvre and endeavour to draw them toward the outer Shoal lying off that Island. But the English Admiral, without doubt, had experienced pilots on board, as he did not pay any attention to the brig's track, but allowed her to go away: he hauled well round all the dangers.

Nelson, in fact, had no pilots, experienced or otherwise. Captain Hood of the *Zealous* recorded what actually happened in a letter sent to Lord Hood soon after the battle:

> . . . as we got pretty near abreast of the Shoal [he said], being within hail of the Admiral, he asked me if I thought we were far enough to the eastward to bear up clear. . . . I told him I was in eleven fathoms, that I had no chart of the Bay; but if he would allow me, I would bear up and sound with the lead, to which I would be very attentive, and carry him as close as I could with safety: he said he would be obliged to me.

The *Zealous* had the *Goliath* on her lee bow, and presently Hood saw that Nelson was dropping back, so that he could direct the rest of his line to the best advantage. Hood went ahead, continuing to use the lead, and managed to keep clear of reef and shoal. Tension mounted.

If there were the strongest elements of excitement at this meeting off a fabled shore, another factor, not always present in war, is worth emphasis. Personal conviction, as well as physical and moral courage and professional skill, is valuable in leadership. In this respect there was a difference in approach to the French between Nelson and some of his fellows. Nelson held to strong principles: among them was religious belief, partly the result of early upbringing by the clergyman father to whom he was attached, and a devotion, staunch and often expressed, to his King and Country. He sailed as the champion of the Almighty—and of George III—against a foe whose ideas he detested. He was not an egalitarian, and he abhorred atheism. If this was an official creed, as in the case of the French Revolutionaries, so much the worse for them. They were, in his own words, pests of the human race: and there was a marked difference in his hatred for them, and what he felt for the monarchical and Catholic Spaniards, against whom he had also so often fought. He had no exalted idea of the Spaniards as sea-fighters, but as people he could respect them. It was different with the French, however stubbornly they fought, and even in the way of battle, Nelson never cleared for action with them without the most confident assurance, which occasional failures and rebuffs had done nothing to diminish. Right was on his side, or so he believed, and one of his officers recorded that he 'had such a horror of all Frenchmen that I believe he thought them at all times nearly as corrupt in body as in mind'.

In the event, it was not Hood in the *Zealous* but Foley in the *Goliath* who had the distinction of leading Nelson's fleet into battle. The chance could not have fallen more appropriately, since Foley, a big man in every sense of the word, was one of the most experienced captains in the squadron. He had learnt his trade, nearly 20 years earlier, under Rodney, and at St Vincent had been flag-captain in the *Britannia*. Now came one of the great moments of his life. As he rounded the island and ran down the enemy line, he saw two things: the first was that, with any luck, he could take his ship *inside* the French position and fire at his opponent on the side she would not have been prepared for, and on which she might possibly not even have run her guns out. The second was that there was about 500 feet between every Frenchman: room in which to sail through the line, or take up a position from which ships could be raked, that is, fired at along their lengths, either from ahead or astern. Placed as broadsides were, there was no effective retaliation, particularly for an anchored vessel, unless she cut her cable.

It was at once plain that Nelson's decision to attack van and centre was right, if only through the fact that Brueys, anticipating that peril—if it came at all—was likely to affect the rear and centre, had placed his heavier units there to meet it. To reach the van, the British would have to approach through positions where they would be liable to fire from the whole line. That they would make nothing of that particular danger was, in Brueys's view, unlikely. As in other ways, he was mistaken.

There has been argument about the merit and courage of Foley in taking his ship inside the French line without orders to do so. In fact, it was exactly the kind of initiative which would have been most appreciated by Nelson. It has also been said that Foley intended this course all along, but this could not have been so, for its propriety must have depended on circumstances which could only have made themselves clear at the last moment. Foley's seizing of opportunity exactly corresponded to the spirit in which Nelson himself had turned out of the line at St Vincent, knowing that he had a better chance than his Commander-in-Chief of seeing that by so doing he could cut off a group of Spanish ships.

17 Sir James Saumarez
From the portrait after S. Lane

18 Captain Alexander Ball
From the portrait by H. W. Pickersgill, R.A.

19 Captain Thomas Troubridge
From the portrait by Sir William Beechey, R.A.

20 Captain Edward Berry
From the portrait by J. S. Copley, R.A.

21 Nelson wounded at the Nile

From a portrait by an unknown artist which he gave to Lady Parker

22 Sir William Hamilton

From a miniature (1794)

23 Emma, Lady Hamilton

From a contemporary miniature

The log of Foley's sailing-master, George Andrews, records the episode thus: 'At 15 minutes past 6, the *Goliath*, being the leading ship, crossed the van of the enemy's line and commenced the action: having crossed, anchored with the sheet anchor out of the gun-room port, and brought up alongside the 2nd ship.' Hood, amplifying the matter in the letter to his noble relative, said:

> ... the *Goliath* ahead, and the *Zealous* following ... as we approached the enemy, short-ened sail gradually. ... The van ship of the enemy being in five fathoms water I expected the *Goliath* and *Zealous* to stick on the shoal every moment, and did not imagine we should attempt to pass within.

Hood disposes of the notion that Foley's manœuvre was preconcerted, but his letter shows that he himself was as fully equal to the navigational risks as his companion-in-arms. So were the captains of the ships immediately following, the *Audacious*, *Orion* and *Theseus*. The *Vanguard* was the first to attack the outside of the French line, and this not only because Nelson wished to double the enemy, but because, with daylight failing, it would not be possible for later vessels, confused as they would be, at least to some extent, by drifting smoke, to attempt anything so intricate as Foley and others had achieved in the earliest stages of the action.

As the leading ships passed within range of the Island, they came under fire from the battery which the French had placed thereon. The armament consisted of a mere four guns and a mortar, which indicated that Brueys had not taken the fortification of his flank very seriously. The fire was ineffectual.

Foley and Hood not only changed places in the line—they exchanged opponents. Foley should have brought up against *Le Guerrier*, the first French ship, but, Hood wrote:

> ... his sheet anchor (the cable being out of the stern port) not dropping the moment he wished it, he missed, and brought up abreast of the second ship, having given the van ship his fire. I saw immediately he had failed of his intention, cut away the *Zealous*'s sheet anchor and came to in the exact situation Captain Foley intended to have taken.

Captain Gould placed the *Audacious* where she could rake *Le Conquérant*, and it was soon clear that the French van was doomed: even so, they fought stubbornly. Hood made this very plain in his account of *Le Guerrier*:

> I commenced such a well-directed fire into her bow within pistol shot a little after six that her fore-mast went by the board in about seven minutes, just as the sun was closing the horizon; on which the whole squadron gave three cheers, it happening before the next ship astern of me had fired a shot and only the *Goliath* and *Zealous* engaged. And in ten minutes more her main and mizzen masts went; at this time also went the main mast of the second ship, engaged closely by the *Goliath* and *Audacious*, but I could not get *Le Guerrier*'s com-mander to strike for three hours, though I hailed him twenty times, and seeing he was totally cut up and only firing a stern gun now and then at the *Goliath* and *Audacious*.
>
> At last being tired of firing and killing people in that way, I sent my boat on board her, and the lieutenant was allowed ... to hoist a light and haul it down to show his submission.

In *Le Conquérant* the story was much the same. Captain Gould wrote to an uncle afterwards that 'the slaughter became so dreadful in the ship that the French officers declared it was impossible to make their men stand to their guns'. Even had they done so, the *Audacious* and *Goliath* were so placed that they could have done little harm.

Fitting as the tactics were to the occasion, it was not always possible for captains to anchor as they wished. At the best of times anchoring is a test of seamanship. Done under fire, and from the stern, it needed luck as well as skill, and other ships than the *Goliath* fetched up in different places than was planned. Those captains who took an inner station were best off. They included the *Theseus*, Captain Miller, and the *Orion*.

Captain Gould in the *Audacious* had placed himself somewhat redundantly, for Hood and Foley were capable by themselves of crushing the leading French ships, particularly as the *Theseus* soon reinforced them. The *Orion*, ably handled by Saumarez, ran farther down the line, and concentrated her fire on the fifth opponent, *Le Peuple Souverain*.

Nelson, when he brought the *Vanguard* into action, opened up on the third ship, *Le Spartiate*. At half past six, according to the log, he himself came under very heavy fire, and suffered severely until Captain Louis in the *Minotaur*, sailing past him to engage *L'Aquilon*, afforded some relief. Then followed Captain Peyton in the *Defence*, which attacked *Le Peuple Souverain* from the outside, while the sixth French ship, *Le Franklin*, escaped attention until the *Orion* shifted her target away from *Le Peuple Souverain*, which did not stand up well against good gunnery.

The mighty *L'Orient*, seventh in the line, had been awaiting her moment, her men ready, her guns double-shotted. Her wrath fell upon the *Bellerophon*, Captain Darby, a ship of half her weight and size, whose proper target should have been *Le Franklin*. Darby missed his mark in the smoke and confusion of what had by then become a general action, and fetched up against the towering flagship. Many captains claimed a hand in the fight with the French giant, but to the *Bellerophon* belongs the honour of engaging her alone for not less than an hour, with such courage that, although she was herself dismasted and reduced to a wreck, she left *L'Orient* comparatively easy prey for others.

Darby, who was wounded, was a notable fighter who had sustained a battering not many months before, when his ship had been becalmed off Cadiz, and had come under the combined fire of a score of Spanish gunboats. He had the heaviest casualties in the squadron, nearly 200 of his officers and men being killed or wounded, and when at last he was forced to cut his cable and drift away to leeward, it must have seemed doubtful whether he could survive the night. Had the French van been ably led, he would not have done so.

The *Majestic*, Captain Westcott, was almost as pressed as the *Bellerophon*. Groping her way down the blazing line, she ran into *L'Heureux*, where she remained for some time in a position of disadvantage, and where her captain was killed. Swinging clear, she then anchored off the bow of the next astern, and there she continued in a deadly duel.

The fight had begun a little after six. *Le Guerrier*'s masts fell at sundown, which was shortly before seven, and ships retained their relative positions until past eight o'clock, when the second phase began. This was brought about by the arrival of the *Alexander*, Captain Bell, and the *Swiftsure*, Captain Hallowell. Their distance from the rest of the fleet had originally been such that they were able to act as a mobile reserve, and to throw their strength upon the French line where it would be most effective. The *Leander*, Captain Thompson, which, with the *Mutine*, had been trying to help the stranded *Culloden*, now joined the battle with them, and these three fresh ships were able to turn success into a victory which was very nearly annihilating. Nelson thought it would have been completely so, had he not been wounded and for a time—as he explained to Lord Howe—'stone blind'.

At this point, drama piled on drama. The *Bellerophon*, leaving the line crippled and in darkness, with some rags of sail on her one remaining mast, was nearly fired upon in error by the *Alexander* and *Swiftsure*, for she could hoist no distinguishing lanterns like the rest of the British ships. The admiral was wounded; the *Goliath*—always a focus of interest—was shifting her berth, and the French flagship was about to provide the climax of that dreadful night. Now that the French van was crushed, the British began to gather round the French commander-in-chief's ship, and to batter away at her until she was rendered helpless.

The *Swiftsure* anchored outside the enemy line, the *Alexander* inside. Then a shot from the *Orion* cut the cable of *Le Peuple Souverain*, which drifted out of her place, leaving a gap of a thousand feet, into which the *Leander* glided. Without risk to himself, Captain Thompson was able to rake both *Le Franklin* and *L'Orient*. It was an ideal situation for a 50-gun ship, and the *Leander* made the most of it.

Many eyes took in details of the last hours of *L'Orient*. She was at the core of the defence, and her capture or surrender would be momentous. One of those who had a ringside view was John Theophilus Lee. He was a midshipman serving in the *Swiftsure*, which was the only ship anchored closely on the Frenchman's weather side. Captain Hallowell's position was good. He was fine on *L'Orient*'s bow, and could hit without serious danger of retaliation from the three-decker, though some of his guns had to be kept trained on *Le Franklin*, which was active on his starboard quarter.

Lee was acting as Captain Hallowell's aide-de-camp, and must have been among the youngest people present. He was not yet eleven, but he could already consider himself a veteran, for he had been present in the *Barfleur* at the Battle of St Vincent.

When the *Swiftsure* first anchored, *L'Orient* still flew an immense tricolour at her main-mast, and was at a point in the French line where it bent at a slight angle. Writing his reminiscences nearly 40 years later, Lee recalled that at that stage in the battle

> . . . the incessant flashes of the numerous guns, discharged at nearly the same instant [were] so vivid at times as to enable each party to distinguish clearly not only the colours of the respective contestants, but the disastrous results of battle upon them.

Lee had been sent by his captain, during the hottest part of the fight, 'to bring a few bottles of ginger beer from the cabin locker round the mizzen mast for the refreshment of himself and other officers actively engaged on the quarter-deck'. Needless to say, the young midshipman was invited to share in the amenities of the moment, and Captain Hallowell, enjoying his drink, remarked that *Le Franklin* was shooting well. Then he turned away from a gangway near which he and Lee had been standing. They had not long left it when it was shivered by a heavy shot.

The captain soon noticed that a fire was growing near the mizzen chains of *L'Orient*. He ordered every available gun to bear on the spot, as well as the fire from marines stationed on the poop.

> But the French [said Lee], nothing daunted, still gloriously maintained the honour of their flag. . . . The brave Brueys having lost both his legs, was seated with tourniquets on the stumps in an armchair facing his enemies, and giving directions for extinguishing the fire, when a cannon-ball from the *Swiftsure* put a period to his gallant life by nearly cutting him in two.

The fire grew, and those who could do so began to jump from the doomed ship. Lee's version of the incident of Commodore Casabianca and his son, the subject of Mrs Hemans's popular though much parodied poem, *The Boy Stood on the Burning Deck*, is probably nearer the truth than most.

> The son of Casabianca [he wrote] had lost a leg, and was below with the surgeon, but the father could not be prevailed upon to quit the ship even to save his own life, preferring to die beside his son rather than leave him wounded, and a prey to the flames, thus placing parental affection in a most trying and awful situation, as if to show the extremities to which it may be carried.

Other narratives say that, as the flames spread, Casabianca and his son did in fact leave the ship together, only to be drowned before they could be picked up.

As the heat increased, helped by jars of oil which the French had left about on the middle deck, where they had been painting before the action, the pitch began to run out of the *Swiftsure*'s seams in streamlets down the side. It was clear that, sooner or later, flames would reach *L'Orient*'s magazine, and she would explode. Nothing could save her.

Nearby ships tried to move away: not so Hallowell. He considered that he was so close that the explosion would arch over him. He refused to change his position: in fact, wrote Lee:

> . . . two sentinels were placed by the cable round the mizzen mast, with directions to shoot anyone who might attempt to cut it, while the ports were ordered to be lowered, the magazines and hatchways closed, and every man to go under cover, provided with wet swabs and buckets of water, in order to extinguish any burning fragments which might come on board during the explosion.

By that time, the 'cold, placid light of the moon', as Lee described it, added an unforgettable touch to the scene, and officers and men from *L'Orient* began to swim clear of her. The *Swiftsure* rescued 14, including the first lieutenant and the commissary, and most ships in the neighbourhood picked up their quota, including the *Goliath*, showing how far a determined captain could move even a much damaged ship, her keel by that time scraping the bottom.

No two accounts agree exactly when *L'Orient* went up, but there is little doubt that it was at or soon after ten o'clock, as M. Poussielgue, from his vantage point ashore, duly noted. Every witness accounted it the most awe-inspiring incident in their lifetime. The noise was shattering, and was heard away in Alexandria. Light and flames lit the whole expanse of the Bay, and in a second the few Frenchmen aboard her who had until then survived, and some who were already in the water, perished by blast or drowning. Not only did the ship herself disappear, she took with her, in her

24 '*L'Orient*' *blows up*
Woodcut from a Banbury Chap Book, c. 1800

hold, over half a million pounds in bullion, three tons of plate, life-sized silver statues of the Apostles, the principal treasures of the Knights of Malta. Bonaparte's financial sinew and much of his loot were lost in the conflagration.

When the glow at last faded, every ship ceased fire, as if by consent. It was a pause of wonder and exhaustion. Men slept where they stood.

Battle was resumed within a few minutes, but it was on a different scale. Decision had been attained, and it only remained to make victory absolute. As Nelson's friend Collingwood said of him, out of the fullness of experience: 'An enemy that commits a false step is ruined, and it comes on him with an impetuosity that allows him no time to recover.' Brueys and Casabianca had gone. Blanquet remained—and Villeneuve. The final challenge came from Blanquet. Villeneuve, with more sense than valour,

59

shifted anchorage farther eastward. There would be time for further encounter, or for escape, when morning light showed him a fuller picture. The wind had fallen, and Villeneuve would not attempt to make sail until he knew where he was going.

Nelson had been wounded in the head by a fragment of iron shot, which had cut the skin rectangularly above his sightless eye. The flap fell down over his good one, and the flow of blood blinded him. The shot came from *Le Spartiate*. He exclaimed: 'I am killed. Remember me to my wife . . .' and was about to fall when Captain Berry, who stood near, caught him in his arms, and led him below, to the cockpit. There, the surgeon went to him immediately, but the place was full of dead, dying and wounded, and Nelson said that he would 'take his turn with his brave fellows'. It was the sort of consideration which is never forgotten.

Presently the surgeon was able to assure the patient that, though messy and painful, the injury was not grave. Nelson was unconvinced. He renewed his messages to Lady Nelson, and then directed that Captain Louis of the *Minotaur* should be hailed to come aboard, so that he could thank him in person for the help he had given to the *Vanguard*. 'Your support', he said, 'prevented me from being obliged to haul out of the line.' The inference was that, until the coming of Louis, *L'Aquilon* had joined her guns with those of *Le Spartiate* upon the *Vanguard*, with the result that her casualties were next in severity to those of the *Bellerophon* and *Majestic*.

After his head had been tied up, and his good eye cleared of debris, Nelson was enjoined to lie quiet, but his responsibility was still so great that he could not possibly stay long inactive. He ordered his secretary, Mr Campbell, to attend him, as he wished to begin a dispatch. Campbell, who had suffered a slight wound himself, was too agitated to write, and the chaplain was no better, so Nelson tried to draft a few lines himself, and it was typical both of his confidence in a victory not yet quite achieved, and of his belief in Providence, that he began, in words which later rang round Europe: 'Almighty God has blessed His Majesty's arms in the late Battle. . . .' Then *L'Orient* was seen to be on fire, and Berry went below to report the fact to the admiral. Nelson demanded to be led on deck, where he gave orders that the one boat still fit to use should be sent, with the *Vanguard*'s first lieutenant, to help save the crew. He stayed on deck, watching the spread of the fire, but felt increasingly sick. He went below once more, but only to issue a stream of orders designed to follow up success.

Capel, the signal lieutenant, was sent in a borrowed boat to the *Goliath* and other ships, urging them to join in the fighting towards the French rear, if their condition allowed them to move.

George Elliott, who was signal midshipman to Captain Foley, recorded that Capel

> . . . came on board and said, with a considerable smile on his face, that the captain of the *Audacious* could not move his ship down to the assistance of other ships, as we were in the way.

Capel saw at once that the *Goliath* was disabled, but, said Elliott:

> . . . Captain Foley, in his quiet way, said 'Not so much disabled that we cannot go down with the wind' and immediately ordered the Master to go down and cut the cable. We had

not a sail to set, but the fore top-sail was let fall, and hung down on each side of the stay which, directly before the wind, kept her steering, and in half an hour we came into action.

The incident accounted for the *Goliath* being present at the climax of the battle. Foley, like his admiral, could not be kept away from the point of danger.

Nelson's immediate wish to record what had already been done was in keeping with his character, in which the man of action and the artist were blended. He had always said that, next to doing great things, it was fine to record them. He liked others to do so too, and not the least curious relic of the Nile is a picture which Nelson commissioned for his friend Lady Parker. This shows him in his shirt, with his head freshly bandaged by the surgeon. In spite of the distractions of that crowded hour, Nelson apparently continued to wear, over his shirt, the gold medal which he had won for his part in the Battle of St Vincent, correctly suspended from its white and blue riband. No doubt, had it been the custom to have worn the insignia of the the Order of the Bath in such circumstances, they also would have been included. Posterity may smile at such instances of vanity in a great man, but it was his weakness as much as his brilliance which helped to endear him to those who knew him best.

Admiral Blanquet, like Nelson, was wounded in the head, and was carried below soon after the arrival of the *Alexander*, *Swiftsure*, and *Leander*. 'The severe wounds of Admiral Blanquet', so ran his own account, 'must have deeply affected the people who fought under him, but it added to their ardour for revenge, and the action continued on both sides with great obstinacy.' The admiral was able to give details of what happened in *Le Franklin* which are lacking in so many other instances.

> At half past 9 [he said], Citizen Gillet, Capitaine de Pavillon of *Le Franklin*, was very severely wounded, and carried off the deck. At three quarters past 9, the arms-chest, filled with musket-cartridges, blew up, and set fire to several places on the quarter-deck, but was fortunately extinguished.
>
> The situation, however, was still very desperate; surrounded by enemies, and only eighty fathoms to windward of *L'Orient* (entirely on fire), there could not be any other expectation than falling a prey either to the enemy or the flames. At 10 o'clock, the main and mizzen masts fell, and all the guns on the main deck were dismounted.

When *L'Orient* blew up, *Le Franklin*'s decks, like those of other ships, became littered with flaming debris. This, said Blanquet, was extinguished, and she was the first ship to renew the action. The sky was by then full of black smoke, and the issue not in doubt, but:

> . . . *Le Franklin*, anxious to preserve the trust confided to her, recommenced action with a few of her lower-deck guns. All the rest were dismounted, two-thirds of her ship's company being killed or wounded, and those who remained much fatigued. She was surrounded by enemy ships, some of which were within pistol-shot, and who mowed down the men with every broadside. At half past 11 o'clock, having only three lower-deck guns that could defend the honour of the Flag, it became necessary to put an end to so disproportionate a struggle, and Citizen Martinet . . . ordered the colours to be struck.

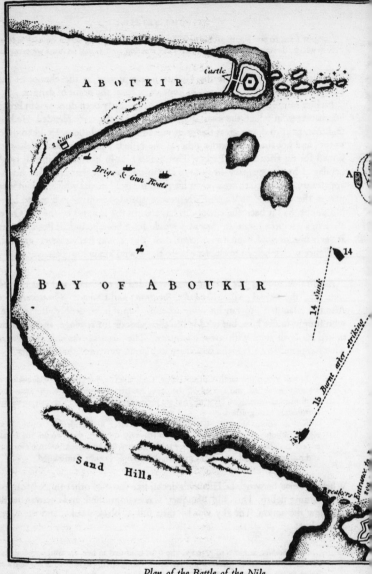

Plan of the Battle of the Nile

From Clarke and M'Arthur, Life of Admiral Lord Nelson, K.B., *1809. Ba*
on a plan by Captain Miller of H.M.S. Theseus, *this differs from others in resp*
of H.M.S. Audacious, *which anchored so as to rake the* Conquérant, *not as show*

BRITISH SHIPS	D	*Audacious*	H	*Bellerophon*	M	*Swiftsure*
A	*Goliath*	E	*Theseus*	I	*Defence*	N	*Leander*
B	*Zealous*	F	*Vanguard*	K	*Majestic*	O	*Culloden*
C	*Orio*	G	*Minotaur*	L	*Alexander*	P	*Mutine*

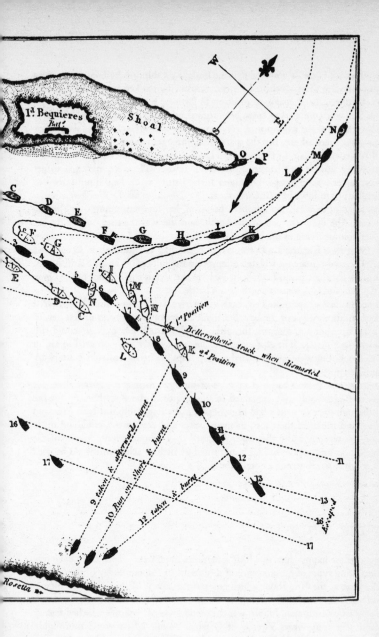

When dawn at last came, it was seen that the leading six ships of the French line were in British possession. The seventh, L'Orient, was on the sea-bed, and there were six survivors. Of them, Le Tonnant, next astern to Brueys, was still dangerous, though grounded. She was a mile away from her original position, having slipped her cable to avoid the effects of the explosion. L'Heureux and Le Mercure, which had slipped her cable for the same reason, were ashore. But the spars of the three remaining ships, Le Guillaume Tell, with Villeneuve's flag, Le Généreux and Le Timoléon, were still standing, and they had all received little if any battering. At about noon, Villeneuve managed to get under way, but it was to escape. Damaged as the British were, he did not intend to fight them. He was followed by Le Généreux and Le Timoléon: but Le Timoléon, after an ineffectual attempt to wear, ran aground, bows on, her foremast going over the side as she struck. The crew escaped to the beach, and she was then set on fire by her captain, her colours flying as she burnt. Le Guillaume Tell and Le Généreux got away together, with two frigates, La Diane, wearing the flag of Admiral de Crêpe, and La Justice. The two remaining frigates, attempting the impossible against British 74's, had been sunk for their pains, La Sérieuse early in the action by the guns of the Orion and the Goliath, and L'Artémise after the main battle.

Hood in the Zealous attempted to chase Villeneuve, who passed near the shattered Bellerophon on his way out of the bay, but made no serious attempt to molest her. In this he may have shown wisdom, for, although dismasted, her gunners could still have shown their mettle. The Audacious, Goliath and Leander were ordered to sail in support of Hood, but were soon recalled to help ships in distress or liable to attack by the escaping enemy.

On 31 July 1798 Brueys had had 13 ships-of-the-line, their companies trained for battle. By 2 August only two remained in the service of the Republic. As for the British, although their casualties had been heavy, not a single ship had been damaged irreparably, and much of their loss, in masts, spars and equipment, could be made good from the wreckage and the prizes scattered over Aboukir Bay. A less volatile man than Nelson might have had his head turned by such an achievement. As he said: 'Victory is not a name strong enough for such a scene.'

5 In the Ships

By one of those happy chances which sometimes illuminate events, there have survived contrasting types of reminiscence of service under Captain Foley of the Goliath, one of the ships at the Nile about which any information is likely to be both picturesque and valuable.

Foley's signal midshipman, Elliott, was the second son of Nelson's attached friend, Lord Minto, for some years Viceroy of Corsica. Young Elliott was a thoroughly happy character, who would have been completely at home in a novel by Marryat. In the fullness of time, he became a distinguished flag-officer, and it is not to be wondered at that he wrote his memoirs for his children. These afford glimpses of events at the Nile.

At the other end of the scale there appeared a little book from Edinburgh, 24 years after the battle, presenting the recollections of 'John Nicol, Mariner', a much-travelled man who had volunteered for the Navy at the age of 21, and who, in the course of a packed life, had thrice been round the world, been twice to China, knew the American littoral from Alaska to Cape Horn, and been present at St Vincent, like so many fellow seamen of Nelson's squadron.

Unlike Elliott, poor Nicol fell on hard times. When one of Messrs Blackwood's editors persuaded him to relate some episodes from his life, he was so poor that he was keeping himself warm in his humble lodging on pieces of coal picked up in the streets and alleys of Edinburgh—anything rather than beg.

The contrast between Mr Midshipman Elliott and plain John Nicol lies in the fact that they saw the Nile not merely from different places, one from the upper deck and the other from below, but that Nicol records incidents such as were rarely noted anywhere. The seamen lived, fought, and died or survived: it was mainly the officers who had education and opportunity for print.

Elliott's version of the battle opens in high style. That morning, he said:

> I, as signal midshipman, was sweeping round the horizon ahead with my glass, from the royal yard, when I discovered the French at anchor in Aboukir Bay. The *Zealous* was so close to us that had I hailed the deck they must have heard me; I therefore slid down by the backstay and reported what I had seen.

Enterprise and activity were, alas, ill-rewarded, for in running the signal up, the flags fouled, and the keen-eyed *Zealous* had meanwhile sent her own message to the *Vanguard*. But Foley, though robbed of the pleasure of being first with good news, was not discomfited. Guessing that Nelson would signal his ships to form line as most convenient (not in any specific order), and knowing that Captain Hood, who was senior, would be certain to push for the honour of the lead, Foley gave orders:

> ... to have our stay-sail and studding sails ready to run up, to keep our place, and I [said Elliott] fortunately saw the flags under the flagship's foresail as they left the deck, so that by the time they reached the royal yard, to show over it, our sails were going up and we got a little start and took the lead. Captain Hood was annoyed, but could not help it.

Hood and Foley, said an admiring junior of 14, were 'fine competitors for such an honour'.

Elliott next recorded an incident unmentioned in the logs of the ships concerned, though these were by custom sparse. He said that after the squadron had begun to form line, Hardy sent a boat from the *Mutine* to a small coasting vessel and 'took out the crew to act as pilots'. This, he said, was the cause of the *Vanguard*'s slowing up, and of the *Audacious* following her example. But Elliott was never fond of the *Audacious*, and memory may have played him false.

He was emphatic as to the value of cheering, a respect in which he and Nicol were at one. Those in the *Theseus* cheered the *Goliath* as she went into action:

The French [he remarks] were ordered by their officers to cheer in return, but they made such a lamentable mess of it that the laughter in our ship was distinctly heard in theirs.

Some officers held that cheering should not be allowed. 'I say decidedly yes', said Elliot with the experience of a lifetime. 'No other nation can cheer. It encourages us and disheartens the enemy.'

Both Elliott and Nicol record the fate of the French frigate *La Sérieuse* which, had her captain obeyed the conventions of the time, would have kept well clear of the ships-of-the-line, and brought no discredit on himself by so doing. 'Sink that brute, what does he here!' exclaimed Foley; while an observer in the *Orion* says that Saumarez manned the guns for a single broadside on the opposite side to that on which he was regularly firing, in order to rid himself of the nuisance. Elliott goes into more detail. *La Sérieuse*, he records, was actually driven ashore because her rudder jammed, and it jammed, as he found with his own eyes after the battle, with a large fragment of shot, fired from a Spanish 68-pounder howitzer from the poop of the *Goliath*. Foley's ship had four of these heavy weapons. They had been taken out of a gunboat off Cadiz, on a night when Nelson had made an attack on that port. Unfortunately, the *Goliath* had only Spanish ammunition, and very little of that, and she was too short of men to use all four guns. In fact, the decisive shot was fired by two midshipmen and two signalmen, in an interlude from their more ordinary duties.

One of the reasons for Foley's reasonable hope that he would be able to outflank the French was that he had with him a French atlas, only 20 years old, which showed the depths of water in the Bay. Hood, who depended on a London publication, found it 'very incorrect'. Elliott was sure that 'had we been running by it, we should have gone ashore by the spit'.

No one but Elliott mentions that the *Goliath*, and perhaps one or two other ships, had half a company of Austrian grenadiers—about 50 men—and others of various nations serving their guns.

The Austrians had been taken near Genoa by Bonaparte's army, and retaken by us going from Genoa by sea; they offered to serve and behaved very well at their guns, and so did all the foreigners.

John Nicol's details are of interest as being by a man of over 40, a cooper by trade and rating, who, though a veteran at war, was regarded as too old, even had his occupation allowed it, for an active part in the fighting of the ship. This was, he said, 'wounding to my feelings, and trying to my patience'.

His first revelation is that there were women aboard, and that they did excellent service in supplying ammunition. One of them died of her wounds, and was afterwards buried on Aboukir Island; another gave birth to a son in the course of the action. Nicol's own station was at the powder magazine, with the gunner.

I was much indebted to the gunner's wife [he said], who gave her husband and me a drink of wine every now and then which lessened our fatigue much.

Nicol added other touches:

As we entered the Bay [he wrote] we stripped to our trousers, opened our ports, cleared, and every ship we passed gave them a broadside and three cheers.

For cheering he had the utmost respect. Recollecting St Vincent, he said that:

> ... when everything was cleared, the ports open, the matches lighted, and the guns run out, then we gave them three such cheers as are only to be heard in a British Man of War. This intimidates the enemy more than a broadside, as they have often declared to me. It shows them all is right, and the men, in the true spirit, baying to be at them.

Two incidents at the Nile would be forgotten but for Nicol. One was of a boy on a cartridge chest, sitting bolt upright with his eyes open. Asked for more ammunition, he did not jump to the order, as he would normally have done. The gunner gave him a push, upon which he fell stiffly on the deck. He had been killed by blast, with not a mark upon him. His body was at once thrown overboard.

Then there was the case of

> ... a lad who had the match in his hand to fire his gun. In the act of applying it, a shot took off his arm. It hung by a small piece of skin, and the match fell to the deck. He looked to his arm, and seeing what had happened, seized the match in his left hand, and fired the gun before he went to the cockpit to have it dressed.

Such was 'British phlegm'.

Two men were killed in Nicol's own mess, but in the press of events of 'the busiest night of my life' Nicol did not hear of it for two days. He himself had one near shave.

> In the heat of the action a shot came right into the magazine, but did no harm, as the carpenters plugged it up, and stopped the water that was rushing in.

After the battle ended, Nicol

> ... went on deck to view the state of the fleets, and an awful sight it was. The whole Bay was covered with dead bodies, mangled, wounded and scorched, not a bit of clothes on them except their trousers.

One last impression, from a man who had served in King's ships in earlier wars, is worthy of record.

> One thing I observed [said Nicol] in these Frenchmen quite different from anything I had ever before observed.
>
> In the American war, when we took a French ship ... the prisoners were as merry as if they had taken us, only saying '*Fortune de guerre*'—'you take me today, I take you tomorrow'. Those we had on board were thankful for our kindness, but were sullen, and as downcast as if each had lost a ship of his own.

Captain Samuel Hood in the *Zealous* provides the only confirmation of George Elliott's statement that Nelson, when bringing the *Vanguard* into action, hailed and spoke a boat, which may have been the coastal craft intercepted by Hardy in the *Mutine*. His account of the battle supplements those written from the viewpoint of the *Goliath*, and his description of what a Frenchman looked like after attention from his broadsides is as graphic as it is concise. Her men, he said:

> ... had been driven from the upper decks by our canister and musketry, and ... from her bow to her larboard gangway the ports on the main deck were entirely in one, and her

> gunwale in that part entirely cut away, two of the main deck beams fallen on the guns in consequence.
>
> She is so much cut up that we cannot move her without detention and expense, so I fancy the Admiral will destroy her. And in doing all this I have pleasure to say the *Zealous* had only seven men materially wounded.

Hood remarked that it was almost inevitable that, in the process of doubling the French line, with the light failing, some of Nelson's ships should at times fire on one another. By and large, this was avoided with great skill, and, viewing its risks dispassionately, Hood remarked of Nelson's plan of battle: 'Had I been in his situation, and so late in the evening, I should have acted the same way.'

Speaking of the trials of the *Majestic*, Hood referred in generous terms to her first lieutenant, who was promoted immediately after the battle. 'Captain Westcott', he said, 'was killed by a musket ball early in the action, but the loss was not felt; his first lieutenant, Cuthbert, who was in the *Montagu* in the West Indies, fought the *Majestic* most gallantly during the remainder of the action.'

Of Nelson's wound he said he thought that the admiral was 'now doing well, as it is dangerous but not troublesome'. The *Vanguard*'s surgeon wrote an entry in his journal on the same subject that: 'The cranium was bare for more than one inch; the wound three inches long.' It was, in fact, to be more tiresome than anyone could have realised at the time, and left an ugly scar which Nelson later hid under a lock of hair. There is not much doubt that he suffered from concussion. A fortnight after the battle he was writing to St Vincent: 'My head is so upsett that really I know not what to do . . .', and he was not a man who made much of his wounds without good reason. No man had suffered from them more, generally without complaint.

Lieutenant Webley, in a memorandum now in the Hood Papers, contributed a note about his captain which adds a touch of the picturesque to a brave scene. When Hood obtained leave from Nelson to sound ahead of the Fleet, Nelson, answering his request, raised his hat, as was the custom of the time.

> Captain Hood [said Webley], in endeavouring to do the same, let his fall overboard; and immediately said: 'Never mind, Webley! There it goes for luck! Put the helm up and make sail.'

Of the *Audacious*, not many details are known. Her Captain, in later years Sir Davidge Gould, rose by seniority to the head of the list of admirals, and survived longest of the Band of Brothers, but he left no account of his impressions.

It is clear, both from indications from other ships, and from his letters, that Gould was a cheerful, kindly man, brave as a lion but without any strong sense of what was happening in the action as a whole. His brief note of congratulation was the first received by Nelson, before the battle was half over, but having done his duty as he conceived it (and at light cost) Gould was content to stay near the van of the French line.

Gould could perhaps have done more—given drive and initiative, but as it was Nelson himself who wrote: 'On my honour, I am satisfied that each did his very best', it is possible that conditions in the *Audacious*, in spite of her few casualties, were less easy than they seemed to be to those in other ships, and Gould certainly gave such aid to others as he could after the battle, standing by the *Bellerophon* for several days.

The log of the *Orion*, next astern, records an incident not observed elsewhere. Soon after Saumarez came into action, his sailing-master, Mr Bruff, saw 'a fire-raft coming down on us from one of the enemy's headmost ships'. The boat towing from the *Orion*'s stern had been shot through, and could not be used defensively, so a party of seamen 'prepared to boom the raft off: a little time after, she drifted clear of our larboard bow about 25 yards, and passed on our lee quarter'. The danger was then over, and no other such raft was seen by the *Orion* or any succeeding ship.

When the fighting was done, Bruff relates that the Captain 'gave the ship's company 36 gallons of wine as an extra allowance'. They had assuredly earned it, and no one had done more than Saumarez, who had been wounded in the side early in the action. He made light of the matter, and does not even appear to have gone below for more than a few moments. Certainly he was well enough to visit Nelson next day, and to enquire after an injury which seemed to be more troublesome than his own.

It was on this occasion that Nelson and his second-in-command came nearest to a difference. Saumarez was known in the squadron as one who did not favour the tactic of 'doubling'—for two reasons. The first was that he believed that one British ship would always be more than a match for one Frenchman. The second was that he viewed with more concern than Nelson the inevitable risk of British ships firing into one another.

Saumarez, after greeting and congratulating his chief, was beginning to form the sentence: 'It was a pity that . . .', when Nelson cut him short with the words: 'Thank God there was no order.' He had read Saumarez's thoughts, and refused to go over the details of a fight which had so clearly been a triumph. Both men had reason and experience behind their opinions, and it was good that Nelson did not allow a professional disagreement to mar their mutual pleasure.

Captain Miller, always a favourite with Nelson and with his fellow captains, was yet another pupil of Rodney. Alas, he did not long survive the Nile, dying off the coast of Palestine when serving with Sir Sidney Smith. He wrote a long letter to his wife, after the action in Aboukir Bay, from which may be learnt many details which would otherwise have been forgotten. Indeed, so meticulous was Miller in what he put down that if his letter home was the only surviving account of the battle its main events could be accurately known.

Miller said that the *Theseus* was 'in the most perfect order'. Like most of the ships present, French and English, she had yellow sides with black streaks. Where the *Theseus* differed from others was in the fact that Miller, with much ingenuity, had had ports painted on the outside of the hammock-cloths which were placed in nettings on the upper deck, to give the impression that she was a three-decker. Miller noted, as did others, that Brueys's line was 'in the form of a bow, with the convex part to us, *L'Orient* making the centre of it'. He observed that the French frigates, all four of them, were anchored behind the ships-of-the-line, a certain indication that Brueys had not been expecting attack, or they would have been under sail, out in the Bay or beyond it.

Miller thought that Saumarez in the *Orion* actually took the ground as he swept down inside the French line, for his ship suddenly seemed to slow up, though she got free. It was one more sign of the risk Foley had taken in his first approach.

> In running along the enemy's line in the wake of the *Zealous* and *Goliath* [said a captain experienced in war], I observed their shot sweep just over us, and knowing well that at such a moment Frenchmen would not have coolness enough to change their direction, I closed them suddenly, and, running under the arch of their shot, reserved my fire, every gun being loaded with two and some with three round-shot, until I had *Le Guerrier*'s masts in a line, and her jib-boom about six feet clear of the rigging; we then opened with such effect, that a second breath could not be drawn before her main and mizzen masts were gone.

Miller next turned his fire upon *Le Spartiate*, until Nelson in the *Vanguard* fetched up on the other side of her, when he directed some of his guns to *L'Aquilon* and some to *Le Conquérant*, 'giving up my proper bird (*Le Spartiate*) to the Admiral'.

Miller had much of the same hatred towards the French felt by Nelson, for when he saw *L'Orient* ablaze:

> . . . displaying a most grand and awful spectacle, such as formerly would have drawn tears down the victor's cheeks, pity was stifled as it rose, by the remembrance of the numerous and horrid atrocities their unprincipled and bloodthirsty nation had and were committing; and when she blew up, though I endeavoured to stop the momentary cheer of the ship's company, my heart scarce felt a single pang for their fate.

His sympathy was concentrated on the trials of his friend Ball, in the *Alexander*. Although he did not know it, Ball had been wounded: what he could see was that his ship was on fire from *L'Orient*'s debris, and he at once organised a boat's crew to go to her help. 'I had the unspeakable happiness of seeing her go before the wind, and extinguish the flames', he said.

Miller's account of the later stages of the battle shows how certain captains, notably Hood, Foley and himself, were at all times eager, with or without instructions, to pursue every advantage.

Soon after *L'Orient* went up, Miller saw a dismasted frigate in the moonlight, and sent a lieutenant to demand surrender. She was *La Sérieuse*, which had been wrecked by Foley and Saumarez, and she was by then aground on her side, with about 30 men clustered on the poop. Miller's lieutenant brought four of her officers aboard, and next day Midshipman Elliott, in charge of one of the *Goliath*'s boats, went over to salvage useful material.

Elliott's head and neck were by that time bandaged from a slight wound, but this did not deter him from diving inside the wreck. To accomplish this, he had to manœuvre the bloated corpse of a marine through a hatch, in order to get it out of the way. By that time Hardy was in the neighbourhood in the *Mutine*, and he was thunderstruck at the apparition he saw popping in and out of the water like a white-headed porpoise.

After the surrender of the frigate's officers, Miller snatched half an hour's sleep, 'from which I was roused by Captain Hood', he said, 'who had come to propose that our ship and the *Goliath* should go down' towards the French rear.

Meanwhile a message had come from the *Vanguard* asking ships to help the *Alexander* and *Majestic*. This they did by slipping their cables. At one stage Miller was amazed to find that, before the *Zealous* and *Goliath* could join him, the broadsides of three Frenchmen bore directly upon his own ship. 'Happily', he said, 'the enemy made no use of the opportunity.' 'Finding myself thus situated', he added, 'a principal object to the French ships . . . I was resolved to remain quiet as long as they.'

By that time the ship's company were 'so extremely jaded, that as soon as they had hove our sheet-anchor up they dropped under the capstan bars, and were asleep in a moment in every sort of posture, having been then working at their fullest exertion, or fighting, for near twelve hours'.

At daylight Miller saw *Le Guillaume Tell* and *Le Généreux* on the move.

> I could no longer wait [he said], particularly as none of the other English ships were yet in motion, but precisely at sunrise, opened my fire on these two ships, as the *Alexander* and *Majestic* did immediately after; this was directly returned, principally by *Le Guillaume Tell*.

There followed some mopping-up operations, after the undamaged Frenchmen had moved out of range. *L'Heureux* struck, and was boarded: so was *Le Mercure* and *L'Artémise*, frigate, which surrendered to Nelson's pupil, William Hoste. But *L'Artémise*, having fired a random broadside, had been set on fire, and later blew up, by design. 'This dishonourable action', said Miller, 'was not out of character for a modern Frenchman: the devil is beyond blackening.'

Then there was *Le Tonnant*, a ship which had been stubbornly fought, in the earlier stages of the action, by her captain, Dupetit-Thouars. After this gallant officer's death she had been boarded by many survivors from other French ships, so that on the morning of 2 August she had no fewer than 1,600 men crowding her decks.

Miller recorded seeing the *Swiftsure* sending a boat with a flag of truce to summon *Le Tonnant* to surrender. The lieutenant came back with the answer, from the senior Frenchman, that unless Nelson would give him a ship to convey them all back to Toulon, he would fight to the last man. Miller diagnosed this as 'a true French gasconade'. He prepared for immediate action by running down under topsails for *Le Tonnant*, the master sounding ahead in a boat. But in the meantime the ship had hoisted truce colours, and surrendered tamely enough to a party sent over from the *Leander*.

Miller now had time to examine his own ship, and was amazed to find that although she had been struck by 80 large shot, some of which had gone through both sides, he had only five killed and 30 wounded. He himself had a slight graze, but it was not serious enough to include in the casualty list. He watched the *Zealous* chase the escaping ships out of the Bay before she had to be recalled, and then went to pay his respects to Nelson, who he heard had been wounded.

> I found him in his cot [he said], weak but in good spirits, and, as I believe every captain did, received his warmest thanks, which I could return from my heart, for the promptness and gallantry of the attack.

Few details have survived of the actions of Captain Louis in the *Minotaur* and Captain Peyton in the *Defence*. Both did well, and Nelson was sure that the *Vanguard* owed her survival to Louis's gunnery. Louis was a descendant of the Kings of France, and a man of charm. He afterwards flew his flag, as a rear-admiral, in *Le Franklin*, a fine new ship which was renamed *Canopus* after her capture by the Royal Navy. She was afloat for nearly a century. Calling her after the ancient Egyptian city formerly at one of the silted mouths of the Nile had been an idea of Nelson's own.

Captain Peyton's account of his duel with *Le Peuple Souverain* is typically laconic in its record of one of the slow and terrible duels between the iron cannon in the wooden ships. 'At 7', he wrote in his journal, 'came to an anchor with the sheet cable out of the gunroom port, and engaged our opponent until 10 o'clock, when she ceased firing, being totally dismasted. At the same time, our fore-topmast went over the side.'

Peyton was representative of the more active captains, for without a pause his journal continued: 'At 5 minutes past 10, veered away on the sheet cable, in order to get alongside the next ship of 80 guns.' This was *Le Franklin*. Not a moment was lost: not a break for recovery. It was no wonder that the Band of Brothers were invincible.

The *Bellerophon*, before she sheered away from the flaming *L'Orient*, picked up two Frenchmen who had swum away to escape. She was herself on fire in several places, but the flames were soon put out. On examination, Captain Darby, wounded but active, saw that 14 of his guns had been rendered useless, and one of the carronades on the poop 'broke to pieces'. When he mustered his people next day he

> ... found we had lost 3 lieutenants, 1 master's mate, 32 seamen and 13 marines. The captain, master, captain of marines, boatswain, 1 midshipman, 126 seamen and 17 marines wounded.

This was four more than the next most injured ship, the *Majestic*.

The ship had been saved largely through the exertions of John Hindmarsh, who lost an eye in the battle, fought later at Trafalgar, and waited nearly 60 years for his admiral's flag, so congested did the Navy List become when the war was over.

For an unusual glimpse of Ball of the *Alexander*, it is necessary to go to no less exalted a source than the works of Samuel Taylor Coleridge, to whom Ball was, without qualification, 'a truly great man, the best and greatest public character that I ever had the opportunity of making myself acquainted with'.

Coleridge had an extended chance to know what he was talking about, for in 1804, six years after the Nile, Ball, by then a baronet, was governing Malta, with a skill and devotion which the Islanders never forgot. He appointed Coleridge his secretary and the arrangement, though brief, was happy. Ball admired Coleridge's learning and range of thought, while in his turn Coleridge recorded episodes from Ball's career in the pages of *The Friend*, which form a sympathetic interpretation of a man of action who was also a man of wisdom.

'Courage', Ball used to say, 'was the natural product of familiarity with danger, which thoughtlessness would oftentimes turn into foolhardiness.' He told Coleridge that 'he had always found the most usefully brave sailors the gravest and most rational of his crew'.

At the Nile, said Coleridge, Captain Ball: 'with his characteristic forecast and activity of practical imagination, had made arrangements to meet every probable contingency'; and when his sails caught fire from L'Orient's blazing debris, Ball soon had the danger mastered, with help from a party from other ships.

In the later stages of the action, so Coleridge related:

> . . . the first lieutenant came to Captain Ball and informed him that the hearts of his men were as good as ever, but that they were so completely exhausted, that they were scarcely capable of lifting an arm. He asked therefore, as the enemy had now ceased firing, that the men might be permitted to lie down by their guns for a short time. After some reflection, Sir Alexander acceded to the proposal, taking of course the proper precautions to rouse them again at the moment he thought requisite. Accordingly, with the exception of himself, his officers and the appointed watch, the ship's crew lay down, each in the place to which he was stationed, and slept for twenty minutes. They were then roused, and started up, as Sir Alexander expressed it, more like men out of an ambush than from sleep, so co-instantane-ously did they all obey the summons! They recommenced their fire . . . and it was soon discovered that during that interval . . . the French . . . had sunk down by their guns, and there slept, almost by the side, as it were, of their sleeping enemy.

There is not much doubt that Ball edited his reminiscences to suit the taste of his learned but unpractical secretary, yet they are worth quoting, if only as an illustration of how some of the greatest seamen the nation ever produced were regarded by some of its most famous men of letters. Coleridge served, and was valued by, one of Nelson's favourite officers; Southey wrote the admiral's life; and Wordsworth, in the year of Trafalgar, made heroic virtues the theme of *The Character of the Happy Warrior*.

The final items of information for which an historian of the Navy may be grateful are that Coleridge puts it on record that it was reading *Robinson Crusoe*, in his home in Gloucester, which first roused in Ball a desire to make the sea his profession, and that he shared with Nelson a fondness for the writings of William Dampier, that colourful buccaneer-explorer so popular in the eighteenth century.

Of the *Swiftsure*, which had such keen observers in young John Theophilus Lee and the Chaplain, Cooper Willyams, one odd incident is related. Just before L'Orient blew up, one of her lieutenants, Berthelot, appeared on the *Swiftsure*'s deck, stark naked but for his hat! Hallowell asked who the devil he was, and the Frenchman gave his name, adding that he had gone back to L'Orient for his headgear, to prove that he was an officer! Hallowell's journal merely says: 'Picked up 9 men, 1 lieutenant and commissary which escaped', but the master of the *Alexander* noted: 'Served to the French prisoners saved from L'Orient when blown up, and came on board naked, shirts 28, trousers 28 pair'—so M. Berthelot's tale is not wholly improbable.

The *Swiftsure* was one of the four British ships badly damaged below the waterline. 'Made at the rate of 8 inches of water an hour', noted Captain Hallowell. 'Carpenters employed stopping the shot-holes. Found one of the cutters cut away and the other stove in such a manner as rendered her quite irreparable; cut her adrift; the oars, masts, sails and everything washed out and lost. Received several shot in the hull, masts, yards &c and a good part of the rigging cut in pieces.'

As for the *Culloden*, Berry's narrative gives a good account of her trials:

> From the over-anxiety and zeal of Captain Troubridge to get into action [he wrote], the *Culloden*, in standing in for the Van of the enemy's line, unfortunately grounded upon the tail of a shoal running off from the Island, on which were mortar and gun batteries . . . and notwithstanding all the exertions of that able officer and his ship's company, she could not be got off.
>
> This unfortunate circumstance was severely felt at the moment by the Admiral and all the officers of the Squadron, but their feelings were nothing compared to the anxiety and even anguish of mind which the Captain of the *Culloden* himself experienced, for so many eventful hours.
>
> There was but one consolation that could offer itself to him in the midst of the distresses of his situation, a feeble one it is true—that his ship served as a beacon for other ships . . . which were advancing with all possible speed close in his rear, and which otherwise might have experienced a similar misfortune, and thus in a greater proportion still have weakened our force.
>
> It was not till the morning of the 2nd that the *Culloden* could be got off, and it was found she had suffered very considerable damage in her bottom, that her rudder was beat off, and the crew could hardly keep her going with all pumps going. The resources of Captain Troubridge's mind availed him much, and were admirably exerted upon this trying occasion. In four days he had a new rudder made upon his own deck which was immediately stripped, and the *Culloden* was again in a state for active service, though still very leaky.

This description, which is paralleled by others, indicates the respect in which Troubridge was held throughout the Navy, though his luck was never of the best. He had been present at the Glorious First of June—but as a prisoner in a French ship, which Howe took. He had led the line at St Vincent, to the Commander-in-Chief's admiration, but although, by Nelson's pressing desire, he was included in the Nile honours, he did not live long to enjoy them, and had no further chance of distinguishing himself in a Fleet action.

Nelson's dispatch, the draft begun so oddly in the heat of battle, was soon complete. The final version, headed: '*Vanguard*, off the mouth of the Nile, 3rd August, 1798', took the form of a letter to the Earl of St Vincent:

> My Lord [it ran], Almighty God has blessed His Majesty's Arms in the late Battle, by a great victory over the Fleet of the enemy, who I attacked at sunset on the 1st of August, off the mouth of the Nile. The enemy were moored in a strong line of Battle for defending the entrance of the Bay (of Shoals) flanked by numerous gunboats, four frigates, and a battery of guns and mortars on an Island in their van; but nothing could withstand the Squadron your Lordship did me the honour to place under my command. Their high state of discipline is well known to you, and with the judgment of the captains, together with their valour, and that of the officers and men of every description, it was absolutely irresistible. Could anything from my pen add to the character of the Captains, I would write it with pleasure, but that is impossible.
>
> I have to regret the loss of Captain Westcott, of the *Majestic*, who was killed early in the action: but the ship was continued to be so well fought by her first lieutenant, Mr Cuthbert, that I have given him an order to command her till your Lordship's pleasure is known.

The ships of the enemy, all but their two rear ships, are nearly dismasted: and those two, with two frigates, I am sorry to say, made their escape; nor was it, I assure you, in my power to prevent them. Captain Hood most handsomely endeavoured to do it, but I had no ship in a condition to support the *Zealous*, and I was obliged to call her in.

The support and assistance I have received from Captain Berry cannot be sufficiently expressed. I was wounded in the head, and obliged to be carried off the deck: but the service suffered no loss by that count: Captain Berry was fully equal to the important service then going on, and to him I must beg leave to refer you for any information relative to this victory. He will present you with the Flag of the Second in Command, that of the Commander-in-Chief being burnt in *L'Orient*. . . .

I have the honour to be, my Lord, your Lordship's most obedient servant,

HORATIO NELSON.

So ran Nelson's report. Brief as it was, and famous as it became, it is notable for the omission of names except in the cases of poor Westcott, his subordinate Cuthbert (who was duly confirmed in his promotion), the ever-active Hood, and Berry, who did duty as Nelson's Chief of Staff in the absence of a properly appointed Captain of the Fleet. There was nothing said about the second-in-command, Sir James Saumarez.

This was unlike Nelson. His 'Letters of Proceedings' while he was a captain and a commodore had never been less than generous to those who served under him, and his private expressions, to Saumarez as to the rest, lacked nothing in appreciation and warmth. But he was in something of a quandary. He wished to mention Troubridge, but could not. He should have mentioned Saumarez, but did not.

In spite of his enthusiastic, almost lyrical tone, Nelson was perhaps treading delicately. He would have been aware of the heart-burnings caused by the dispatches of other commanders, notably those of Earl Howe after the Glorious First of June, 1794, a matter which had been aggravated by the eccentric way in which the coveted gold medals were withheld from some captains—Westcott included—and bestowed on others. Nelson did better, though he must have caused Saumarez some sad moments, so deeply did that officer feel slights, real or imaginary, and he possibly deferred the baronetcy which should have been due to Saumarez, for which his later actions caused him to be recommended, until two years after Troubridge got his. However, as was the case after the Battle of St Vincent, every captain received the King's Gold Medal except Hardy, and Hardy would not have looked for one, since his brig did not rate as a major war vessel, and in any case he received special promotion. Every officer and man also had a medal from Alexander Davison, the Prize Agent: the captains' were gold, other officers' in silver, and the men's in bronze. The men valued theirs so little that specimens are now uncommon.

With his dispatch, Nelson forwarded lists of ships and casualties, of which there is a more detailed balance sheet in the Nelson Papers. Perhaps it is too neat, since the complements of both British and French ships are given at their Authorised Figures (e.g. 800 men for a French 80-gun ship: 700 for a 74, etc.), whereas in fact they were short in numbers, like the victors.

Nelson noted that he had taken seven ships-of-the-line, that three had been burnt, and that *L'Orient* was 'destroyed'. Two frigates and a bomb vessel had also been destroyed, and a number of small vessels had either escaped, like *Le Salamine*, in which Ganteaume had got away, or had beached themselves in the shallows under the guns of Aboukir Fort. He reckoned that the numbers in ships taken or destroyed amounted to 8,930. He had sent 3,105 men ashore, including wounded, while some 400 had escaped before their ships were burnt or given up. He had 200 prisoners, including captains, officers, carpenters and caulkers (the principal technicians), and he reckoned that some 5,235 of the enemy were killed or missing. Seven French captains had been wounded, and three killed.

British casualties were 218 killed and 677 wounded, a total of 895, roughly one for every ten Frenchmen put out of action.

Bonaparte formed the remnant from his Fleet into a Nautic Legion, which served with the Army of Egypt. Their services were of no special distinction, and it is improbable that, in their role as soldiers, the men were assigned to the more considerable tasks. The General seldom had much tenderness for the unlucky, or indeed for the Navy.

It was otherwise in Britain, and a popular discovery on the part of a gentleman clever at puzzles and oddities was that the anagram HONOR EST A NILO could be made from Nelson's two names.

Midshipman (1799)

PART III

Aftermath

1 Follow-up

It is one thing to win a victory—another to follow it up. Nelson was now one of the only two living men to have achieved success in a major fleet action against the French. Lord St Vincent's had been a triumph over Spain, and Duncan at Camperdown had defeated the Dutch. Howe alone, then in the last year of his life, could claim the Glorious First of June as a tactical masterpiece against the most competent enemy.

Yet it was held against Howe (even by Nelson, who revered him) that he had not pursued his success as a younger and more vigorous man might have done. The criticism is implicit in some remarks which Collingwood addressed to a correspondent during the winter after Aboukir:

> I know, my dear Sir [he wrote], what joy you would feel at the unparalleled victory of . . . Nelson. It was indeed a charming thing. It was the promptitude as much as the vigour of the attack, which gave him the superiority so very soon: the Frenchman found himself assailed before he had determined how best he should repel the assault, and when victory had been decided on our side, the fruits of it were carefully gathered in. . . .

It was the professional who was 'charmed', the experienced sea officer who knew how often success was not fully exploited. And certainly, whatever the ultimate disappointments, no one could fairly have charged Nelson—wounded as he was, and without an experienced secretary—with leaving any matter of importance unattended to immediately after the battle. As the staff work was done in his own head, and most of the orders drafted by his one remaining hand, his powers of endurance, together with the range of his understanding, were never shown more clearly.

First came Thanksgiving. 'The Admiral intends returning Public Thanksgiving . . . at two o'clock this day', wrote Nelson in a memorandum to his captains the day after the battle, 'and he recommends every ship doing the same as soon as convenient.' He then sent a letter of congratulations addressed to all his 'Captains, Officers, Seamen and Marines', which was courteously reciprocated from the *Orion*, with captains' signatures appended. They wished him to accept a sword and to have his picture painted. The sword became a treasured possession, and, in the next few years, Nelson sat to many artists.

The Revd Mr Comyn held divine service in the *Vanguard*, 'the other ships following the example of the Admiral, though perhaps not all at the same time', said Berry. He added:

> . . . this solemn act of gratitude to Heaven seemed to make a very deep impression upon several of the prisoners, both officers and men, some of the former of whom remarked

The Captains of the Squadron under the Orders of Rear admiral Sir Horatio Nelson K B, desirous of testifying the high Sense they entertain of his Prompt decision, and intrepid conduct in the attack of the French Fleet in Bequier Road, off the Nile the 1st of August 1798, request his acceptance of a Sword, and as a further proof of their esteem and regard, hope that he will permit his Portrait to be taken, and Hung up in the Room belonging to the Egyptian Club now established in Commemoration of that glorious day

　　　　　Dated on Board of His Majesty's Ship
　　　　　Orion this 3rd of August 1798

25　Letter to Nelson from his captains after the battle, lacking the signatures of Captain Thompson of the Leander, and Captain Westcott of the Majestic, who was killed. Reproduced from B.M. Add. MSS. 34,907 f. 142

'that it was no wonder we could preserve such order and discipline, when we could impress the minds of the men with such sentiments after a victory so great, and at a moment of such seeming confusion'.

The 'confusion' was more apparent than real. Gradually, the floating devastation cleared; corpses were disposed of, wounded cared for, and the sandy Island, which was later known as Nelson's, became a scene of burial. Soon there began the cheerful work of repairing damage, and making prizes seaworthy. Troubridge was much to the fore in this, and so was Miller. The French ships which were thought worth taking into British service were Le Franklin, Le Peuple Souverain, L'Aquilon, Le Conquérant, Le Tonnant and Le Spartiate. The rest were stripped of such material as was useful, and were sunk or destroyed, being too much knocked about to reward attention. Miller observed to his people 'that our business was not finished till the prizes were fit for sea, exhorting them to obtain by their work as much credit as by their courage'. He was soon as proud of their exertions as he was astonished at how quickly work was finished.

Young Theophilus Lee of the Swiftsure remembered one vivid incident of salvage, worth recording both as illustrating the responsible work which could fall to a boy of ten, and as a glimpse of the easy-going attitude assumed by Captain Gould of the Audacious. Lee was sent with four boats to Le Mercure:

> ... then on shore to leeward, near the mouth of the Nile, with orders to bring her mainyard on board the Swiftsure, to replace the same spar, which was much crippled.
>
> The Mercure lay very far to leeward, and it was slack water when the boats left the Swiftsure, but while launching the main-yard, and getting it in tow, the tide began to make towards the Nile; and although for some time after this the boats gained ground with this heavy yard, and succeeded in towing it past some of the English ships most to leeward, yet this success was but of short duration; as in consequence of the tide increasing in strength, and the wind beginning to blow fresh from the northward, the boats were gradually drifted to leeward, in spite of every exertion that could be made. But our young Mid. being well aware that the yard was much wanted, he still persevered with the towing of it, until at length the coxswain of his boat, a valuable old sailor named Johnson, who was a quarter-master ... said to him that it was useless to strive any longer to save the yard, as the result would only be the loss of all the boats and crews, and spar also.

Reluctantly Lee agreed, and decided that the boats must make for the nearest English ship. The yard was cut adrift, and after an hour's exhausting pull, they reached the Audacious.

> Our young Mid. [continued Lee], on getting on board, said to Captain Gould that he hoped he would tell Captain Hallowell that he had done all in his power to save the yard; and the reply from this worthy man was: 'Do not fear, my fine little fellow, I watched you till dark, with a spy-glass, and since that, I entertained serious fears that you had all gone together; however, I am delighted to see you safe. Come into my cabin, and get refreshment, and lay down on my sofa for the night, and I will send a letter by you in the morning to your excellent captain, telling him how hard you struggled to save the spar, and that you did not abandon it till it was absolutely necessary to do so, to save the lives of your boats' crews.'

Gould and his first lieutenant added to their kindness by housing the Swiftsure seamen snugly for the night.

Meanwhile, communication with the shore opened. 'The Admiral', said Berry:

> . . . knowing that the wounded of his own ships had been well taken care of, bent his first attentions to those of the enemy. He established a truce with the Commandant of Aboukir, and through him made a communication to the Commandant of Alexandria, that it was his intention to allow all the wounded Frenchmen to be taken ashore to proper hospitals, with their own Surgeons to attend them.

As for the Bedouins and Mamelukes, they had lined the shore of the Bay during the whole of the action. Berry said that they

> . . . saw with transport that the victory was decisively ours, an event in which they participated with an exultation almost equal to our own; and on that and the two following nights, the whole coast and country were illuminated as far as we could see, in celebration of our victory.

There was no lack of firewood for a blaze, and the onlookers reaped the harvest of loot from an affray which had cost them nothing. The bonfires, said Berry:

> . . . had a great effect upon the minds of our prisoners, as they conceived that the illumination was the consequence, not entirely of our success, but of some signal advantage obtained by the Arabs and Mamelukes over Bonaparte.

The sailors were depressed enough already, and the thought of the French army suffering reverses made them utterly dejected. In fact, there was no ground for their surmise.

After courtesies were over, Nelson ordered Berry to take passage with Captain Thompson in the *Leander*, bearing his dispatch to the Commander-in-Chief. He arranged for a duplicate to go to Naples in the *Mutine*, giving command of her to Capel, and taking Hardy into the *Vanguard* as his captain. It was one of the wisest appointments he ever made. Hardy, though a year younger than Berry, was much better at running a ship, and never gave Nelson a moment's disquiet.

It was as well that Nelson made plans to use the *Mutine*, for the *Leander*, sailing on 6 August, was captured on 18 August not far from Crete, being delayed by light airs. She had the ill luck to run into the escaping *Généreux* whose 74 guns far outnumbered her own, while the Frenchman's complement had been made up to some 900 men, largely from other ships, against whom Thompson could oppose only 343. Thompson himself was hit four times, and Berry more than once, and in a calm sea the gallant *Leander* fought till her men could fight their guns no more, having Mr Midshipman Downes and 34 others killed, and over 50 wounded. She was afterwards plundered, the captors taking every stitch of clothing from Berry. They even robbed the British surgeon of his instruments. Chivalry vanished from the French Navy at the time of the Revolution, as the officers admitted. 'Our men', they said wryly, 'are good at plunder', and M. Lejoille, *chef de division* and captain of the ship, seemed unable or unwilling to stop them.

Dispatches to St Vincent for British consumption were only part of the story, for Nelson, remembering his own service of years before on the East Indies Station, was aware of the alarm which would have been caused to the Indian settlements by news of a French landing in Egypt. He therefore wrote to the Governor of Bombay, telling him what he knew of Bonaparte's movements, and the probable result of his victory. This, he felt certain, would relieve India from immediate anxiety, and save great expense in defensive preparations. Tippoo in Mysore could be dealt with in isolation. The Honorary Citizen would get no support from his friends.

Hood had a lieutenant in the *Zealous*, Duval by name, whom he recommended to Nelson as a very fit person, by reason of languages, and diplomatic connections, to 'go to India by way of Alexandretta, Aleppo, Basra and the Persian Gulf'. Duval had an interesting journey, which he completed successfully, and the relief resulting from his tidings was such that the Company voted Nelson a present of £10,000.

The squadron was then divided. Hood was left in charge of the blockade of the Egyptian coast. The *Vanguard*, so Nelson judged, must go to Naples for repairs, and to enlist the activity of the Bourbon Court. To Saumarez fell the honour of escorting the six prizes down the Mediterranean to Gibraltar. He had with him, besides the *Orion*, the *Bellerophon*, *Defence*, *Minotaur*, *Audacious*, *Theseus* and *Majestic*, the *Audacious* and *Minotaur* being detached later to rejoin Nelson. It was a goodly company, though Saumarez's progress, undermanned as he was owing to the prize crews, was slow. But if slow, it was triumphant. He even summoned the garrison of Malta to surrender, sending boats ashore from some of the very ships which had taken part in the humiliation of the Knights. The French Commander returned an insolent reply.

As a last immediate act, Nelson wrote direct to Earl Spencer at the Admiralty, his letter being dated 9 August.

> My Lord [he said], was I to die at this moment, want of frigates would be found stamped on my heart. No words of mine can express what I have, and am suffering for want of them. Having only the *Mutine* brig, I cannot yet send off Captain Capel, which I am very anxious to do: for as an accident may happen to Captain Berry, it is of some importance, I think, for your Lordship to be informed of the success as soon as possible.
>
> If the King of Naples had joined us, nothing at this moment could prevent the destruction of the Store Ships and all the Transports in the Port of Alexandria . . . but, as I have not means, I can only regret the circumstances.

On 12 August Nelson was overjoyed to find the *Emerald*, *Alcmene* and a sloop saluting his flag. The sloop was in charge of his stepson, Josiah Nisbet. Next day, off went Capel, to spread joy throughout those regions of Europe not yet under French control or influence.

2 *Repercussions*

'The glorious victory of the first of August is like the Church of St Peter's at Rome', wrote Sir William Hamilton to Lord St Vincent. 'It strikes you at first sight from its magnitude, but the more you examine into its dimensions and details the more wonderful it appears.'

Battles as shattering as that of the Nile, rare in history, cannot be looked at in isolation, or as events in themselves, since their effects will be widespread and may be unexpected. Nelson's feat had repercussions which demand consideration, while its effects upon the career and character of the victor were so considerable and lasting that they too require attention. Echoes reverberated long after the final shot.

For his own part, M. Poussielgue of the Army of Egypt was in no doubt as to its effects on the French Expedition. Some months after his graphic account of the action itself, he committed his thoughts to paper in a letter, which, like its predecessor, was intercepted by a British cruiser on its way to France.

> The fatal engagement [he said] ruined all our hopes; it prevented us from receiving the remainder of the forces which were destined for us; it left the field free for the English to persuade the Porte to declare war against us; it rekindled that which was barely extinguished in the heart of the Austrian Emperor; it opened the Mediterranean to the Russians, and planted them on our frontiers; it occasioned the loss of Italy and the invaluable possessions in the Adriatic which we owed to the successful campaigns of Bonaparte, and finally it at once rendered abortive all our projects, since it was no longer possible for us to dream of giving the English any uneasiness in India. Added to this was the effect on the people of Egypt, whom we wished to consider as friends and allies. They became our enemies, and, entirely surrounded as we were by the Turks, we found ourselves engaged in a most difficult defensive war, without a glimpse of the slightest advantage to be obtained from it.

On any reckoning, the French official's summing up was too pessimistic. Bonaparte, had he read the letter, would not only have disagreed with it, but would have reproved a responsible civilian for giving expression to such views, particularly in a form which might be used as evidence in a country where the Expedition already had critics in high places, all too eager to denigrate and intrigue. And in fact, although there is both substance and shrewdness in some of M. Poussielgue's remarks, there was another side to the story, one of the more remarkable aspects being Nelson's own mistakes, once he had withdrawn from the coast of Egypt.

The nearest and by far the most important diplomatic representative of Great Britain, so far as the Fleet was concerned, was of course Hamilton at Naples. Nelson did not know the Ambassador at Constantinople personally, while Greece was at that time still under Turkey. To Hamilton, therefore, he wrote on 8 August, though with less than his usual care, knowing as he did that the news he sent could be supplemented by word of mouth.

> My dear Sir,
>
> Almighty God has made me the happy instrument in destroying the Enemy's Fleet, which I hope will be a blessing to Europe. You will have the goodness to communicate this happy event to all the Courts in Italy, for my head is so indifferent that I can scarcely scrawl this letter. Captain Capel, who is charged with my Dispatches for England, will give you every information. Pray put him in the quickest mode of getting home. You will not send by post any particulars of the Action, as I should be sorry to have any accounts get home before my Dispatches. I hope there will be no difficulty in our getting refitted at Naples.
>
> As this Army will never return, I hope to hear the Emperor has regained the whole of Italy. With every good wish, believe me, my dear Sir,
>
> Your most obliged and affectionate,
>
> HORATIO NELSON.

> 9 August: I have intercepted all Bonaparte's dispatches, going to France. This Army is in a scrape, and will not get out of it.

It was as rash for Nelson to pronounce upon soldierly affairs as it was for his adversary to plan campaigns by sea; unhappily, Nelson was soon in a position where he could directly influence military events, and where there would be no restraining hand. For Hamilton himself, despite age and experience, was affected by enthusiasm, and even before the battle, when Nelson had been chasing Brueys the length of the Mediterranean, he had written: 'You know how much I am the enemy of half measures.' He had been trying to infuse warlike energy into the Neapolitans ever since. Now he had the best of instruments—news of wonderful success.

He and his wife were looking forward to receiving the victor in person, having already written to him ecstatically. Nelson himself wrote an impression of his feelings on the way to Naples in a letter to his wife which was one of the last of those full, personal outpourings that he afforded her. Soon after he had sent the letter home he grew so engrossed in the management of his ships and in the affairs of Naples that she receded into the background of his mind, never to regain her place.

The letter was begun on 16 September, from sea:

> My dearest Fanny [Nelson wrote]. It is hardly possible to know where to begin. My head is almost turned by letters already, and what am I not to expect when I get on shore? My head is healed and I am better . . .

It had always been one of Nelson's characteristics to conceal his sufferings, so far as possible, from a woman who felt them as if they had been her own. It had been so with his eye, and it was so now. In fact, his head continued to give him pain, and made him liable to fits of acute irritation.

> The Kingdom of the Two Sicilies [he continued] are mad with joy: from the throne to the peasant all are alike. From Lady Hamilton's letter the situation of the Queen was truly pitiable. I only hope I shall not have to be a witness to a renewal of it. I give you Lady Hamilton's words: 'How shall I describe the transports of the Queen? 'Tis not possible. She fainted, cried, kissed her husband, her children, walked frantic about the room, cried, kissed and embraced any person near her exclaiming: "Oh, brave Nelson: Oh God bless and protect our brave deliverer! Oh Nelson, Nelson, what do we not owe you. Oh victor, saviour of Italy . . ." You may judge of the rest, but my head will not allow to tell you half . . .

The 'transports' were explained by the fact that this was the first news the Queen of Naples had had which led her to suppose that the destroyers of her sister were not invincible in battle.

The *Vanguard* anchored off Naples on 22 September. Three days later Nelson concluded his letter with a graphic description.

> Sir William and Lady Hamilton came out to sea, attended with numerous boats with emblems, etc. [he wrote]. My most respectable friends had really been laid up and seriously ill, first from anxiety and then from joy. It was imprudently told Lady Hamilton in a moment.
> The effect was a shot. She fell apparently dead and is not yet properly recovered from severe bruises.

That this was no exaggeration (so violent were feelings in that less inhibited day) is shown by the fact that exactly the same thing happened to Lord Spencer, when he first heard news of the Nile at the Admiralty. He fell senseless outside his room.

> Alongside my honoured friend came [continued Nelson]. The scene in the boat appeared terribly affecting. Up flew her Ladyship and exclaiming: 'OH GOD IS IT POSSIBLE!' fell into my arm more dead than alive. Tears, however, soon set matters to rights, when alongside came the King. The scene was in its way affecting. He took me by the hand, calling me his deliverer and preserver, with every other expression of kindness. In short all Naples calls me *Nostra Liberatore* for the scene with the lower classes was truly affecting. I hope one day to have the pleasure of introducing you to Lady Hamilton. She is one of the very best women in this world. How few could have made the turn she has. She is an honour to her sex, and a proof that even reputations may be regained, but I own it requires a good soul. Her kindness with Sir William to me is more than I can express. I am in their house, and I may now tell you it required all the kindness of my friends to set me up.

Nelson meant that he had at first suggested going to an hotel, seeing that he would be constantly receiving sea officers and conducting a press of business, but had been persuaded to make the Hamiltons' palace his home, when ashore. He concluded:

> May God Almighty bless you, my dearest Fanny, and give us in due time a happy meeting. Should the King give me a peerage I scarcely need state the propriety of your going to Court. Don't mind the expense. Money is trash. Again God Almighty bless you.
> Ever your most affectionate husband,
>
> HORATIO NELSON.

Fanny Nelson cherished this letter, and was right to do so, for it was long before she received her next news, and then it was less exultant. Malta was holding out; while, however fervid his welcome and grateful the praise, Nelson soon found that he received little but lip service in a place he described, in a disillusioned note to St Vincent, as 'a country of fiddlers and poets, whores and scoundrels'.

If Hamilton had allowed his excitement, his patriotism, his pride in the Navy, and his wife's sense of the dramatic to unbalance his political judgment, the same was not true of his superiors at home.

At the time when the French armada had first sailed, there had been general fears for Naples or Sicily. Even while threats hung over the country, the Neapolitan Court had been in treaty with Austria for a new alliance. Negotiations were concluded on 16 July, after which Hamilton had notice that Neapolitan ports would be fully open for the use of British ships of war. The Viennese Court, where the Queen of Naples's daughter reigned as Empress, was thereupon asked to send an experienced general to help the Neapolitans with preparations.

At home, Pitt, Grenville and Spencer, Ministers in Office, had no belief that it was possible to catch armed Frenchmen napping, and they were inclined to discourage belligerence from Naples, at any rate until larger plans had been concerted. Nelson thought otherwise, and he carried Hamilton entirely with him. It was his view that there was no time like the present, and that if Ferdinand did not act on his own initiative, and at once, the French, in their own good time, would 'kick him out of his dominions'.

With the arrival of General Mack from Vienna, Nelson urged Ferdinand to act, promising the use of his ships to ensure supplies and support by sea.

The advice was as strange as it was unfortunate, for Nelson, serving on the western coast of Italy in the earlier years of the war, had had long, close and disastrous experience of Austrian generals ashore. He had no adequate reasons to suppose that Mack would prove to be different. As for the Neapolitans, he had seen their troops training in 1793, and knew their record at Toulon. Nothing in history could have afforded either Nelson or Hamilton any grounds for hope that the Neapolitans had skill or eagerness in fighting. Nevertheless, so infected were Ferdinand and his Queen by Nelson's fire and enthusiasm that they agreed upon a campaign which was to free Rome from French occupation, and to transform Ferdinand from a monarch who cared only for hunting, eating and making love into Ferdinand Victorious; a hero after the Nelson pattern.

Having been ashore at Naples from 22 September to 15 October, Nelson sailed with four of the line to observe the blockade of Malta, complaining that the Neapolitans would take no active part in the affairs of the island, though Ferdinand had claims to sovereignty therein. He was back at Naples by 5 November, and on the 22nd sailed with a small squadron and troops for Leghorn. His idea was that Ferdinand's army under Mack should attack Rome, while his own squadron made a surprise landing in the rear of the French. Meanwhile, the cautious Austrians would promise no help unless the French attacked first, which they had the wisdom not to do.

Leghorn surrendered unconditionally, on Nelson's summons, and Ferdinand entered Rome in triumph. Captain Louis of the *Minotaur* was rowed up the Tiber in his barge, and saw the British flag flying below that of the Papal States on the Castle of St Angelo. Leaving some infantry at Leghorn under General Naselli, Nelson himself returned to Naples, to learn that everything had suddenly gone wrong.

Mack's advance on Rome had, it is true, taken the French by surprise, since their country was not officially at war with Naples. Their troops obligingly withdrew, and were promptly reorganised outside the city. Ferdinand had entered on 29 November, but he left hurriedly just over a week later, to avoid capture. The French were on the move, and two days later, they were back in Rome. The Neapolitan army proved as useless as its Austrian general, and fled at the first sign of the enemy.

Ferdinand's sudden return to his capital spread general alarm. The local Jacobins took courage; the Queen panicked, and by the last weeks in December it had become inevitable that Nelson would have to convey the entire Court, the royal treasure, friendly diplomatic representatives and the principal English merchants to exile in Sicily. A hasty, ill-conceived campaign had ended in the way it deserved.

Hamilton was politically disgraced; Nelson henceforward considered his first duty lay in expiating his bad advice by guarding the Neapolitan territory in Sicily, and the first fruit of the Battle of the Nile was the gratuitous loss of Naples. It was a result which the wildest partisan of Bonaparte would not have dared to prophesy a few months earlier, with the smoke of battle still ascending from the ships in Aboukir Bay.

As if to cap the misfortunes of the time, one of the little Bourbon princes died in Lady Hamilton's arms, in the course of a stormy passage. Christmas Day, 1798, was spent at sea, and it was certainly the least festive in Nelson's life.

During the passage to Palermo, the one and only serene passenger was the King of Naples. Now that he was out of immediate danger, his thoughts at once returned to hunting. He asked that one of Nelson's overloaded transports should send ashore for additional dogs and guns. In his view, there were more rewarding things than making war on Frenchmen.

3 The Wider Scene

'If I was King of England,' wrote Emma Hamilton to Nelson while he was at sea, 'I would make you the most noble, puissant Duke Nelson, Marquis Nile, Earl Alexandria, Viscount Pyramid, Baron Crocodile and Prince Victory, that posterity might have you in all forms.'

On 6 October, when he was preparing to sail for Malta, Nelson became Lord Nelson of the Nile and Burnham Thorpe, as was officially notified in the *London Gazette*. 'Sir William is in a rage with the Ministry', wrote Emma to Lady Nelson when she heard the news, which took some weeks to reach Naples, 'for not having made Lord Nelson a viscount, for sure this great and glorious action, greater than any other, ought to have been recompensed more. Hang them I say!'

Emma Hamilton was not the only surprised person. Even the eminent Lord Hood had murmured to Fanny Nelson that he thought she would find herself a viscountess, while Maurice, the modest Nelson brother who served in the Navy Office, was astonished at the award, even though a pension of £2,000 a year for life, and for the admiral's two next heirs, was added to it, together with many tributes from abroad such as the Chelengk, or Plume of Triumph, which had been sent by the Sultan of Turkey. This was a garish ornament in diamonds, the centre revolving by clockwork, which Nelson wore in his hat.

The fact was that the authorities were in a dilemma. Nelson was a junior flag-officer, on detached service, without the status of a commander-in-chief. Lord Spencer wrote that he had 'particular pleasure in remarking, that it is the highest honour that has ever been conferred on an officer of your standing in the Service'. He might well have thought that if Nelson continued to win victories on this scale, no adequate rewards could be in prospect.

There were two recent instances of peerages being given for naval victories which were in the minds of partisans when they said that Nelson had not been recognised on the scale that his merit claimed. St Vincent had been made an earl after the battle of February 1797, and Duncan had been made a viscount after Camperdown, fought

26 On board *Le Tonnant*: the death of Captain Dupetit-Thouars

From a lithograph by A. Mayer and Bayot

27 'Victors of the Nile'

Nelson

| Saumarez | Troubridge | Hardy | Louis | Peyton | Ball | Hood |
| Gould | Foley | Westcott | Thompson | Hallowell | Miller | Berry |

Engraved from designs by R. Smirke (1803)

eight months later. But there was good reason for both these awards. Both flag-officers concerned were very senior at the time their peerages were granted, and in one case at least, that of St Vincent, a barony was about to be conferred, battle or no battle. St Vincent fought against great odds: and at Camperdown Duncan took 11 ships: even so, neither victory was as remarkable as Nelson's.

Where Nelson also suffered was that whereas both St Vincent and Duncan had had their pensions swollen by £1,000 a year from the Irish Parliament, before Nelson's reward could be augmented in this way, a Union of the Parliaments at Westminster and Dublin had been arranged, and the matter was overlooked.

Capel had arrived in London on 2 October 1798, and the following day news-papers came out with what might fairly be described as Nelson numbers. The re-cognition by way of honours was swift, partly the result of popular clamour, and the general rejoicing, at a time when the nation was only beginning to recover from news of a serious rebellion in Ireland, was of a kind which those who experienced it re-membered all their lives.

Typical of other news-sheets was *The Times*, dated 3 October, in which the very first item was an advertisement headed 'Ranelagh'. It offered the following attraction:

> Grand Gala in honour of Lord Nelson's Glorious Victory over the French at the Mouth of the Nile. The proceeds to be devoted to the relief of the Widows and Orphans of the brave men who fell on the occasion.

Not only was this an instance of immediate exploitation of a great event under the guise of beneficence, but it showed most intelligent anticipation, since, at the time they drafted the notice, the proprietors of Ranelagh could not possibly have known that Nelson would be made a peer.

The leading item on the news pages naturally concerned Capel's advent. He was said to have reached the Admiralty at a quarter past eleven on the morning of 2 October, when: 'the Park and Tower guns, and the merry peals of the bells from the steeples of several churches soon announced this happy news to the Public. Lord Spencer wrote official information of it to the Lord Mayor: and Mr Winchester, the Messenger, was sent off express to the King at Weymouth, in order that His Majesty might learn the glad tidings before he went to rest.'

Then there followed Nelson's official letter of 3 August, with a covering note to the Secretary of the Admiralty, written four days later, just before Capel sailed for Naples, saying that already 'eight of our ships have got topgallant yards across, ready for any service; the others, with the prizes, will soon be ready for sea'. Lists of ships on both sides were appended, as were the British casualties, including names of officers killed and wounded.

The Times' own comment on the news as first received was that:

> The narrative of this glorious action is much too concise to satisfy the curious eye of the public; it is written in the true style of a seaman who understands how to lead his fleet to victory better than to write a long letter.

It was Capel himself who supplied details which helped to fill out the picture: Nelson's wound; Brueys's death; Troubridge's grounding; the rejoicings of the

Bedouins ashore. The paper enumerated the many strategical advantages which could be looked for from the battle, ending on a closer note:

> The Illuminations at night were general throughout the metropolis and its neighbourhood. The Admiralty, the Navy and Victualling Offices of course took the lead in point of splendour, and such was the zeal shown by the Public at large that to particularise any house would only appear invidious.

Just as the Nile had spread into the advertisement columns, so were other manifestations of joy reported: for instance, after a performance of *Leonora*:

> . . . the news of Admiral Nelson's glorious victory produced a burst of patriotic exultation that has rarely been witnessed in a theatre. *Rule, Britannia* was lustily called for from every part of the house. The acclamations were the loudest and most fervent we have ever witnessed.

Lloyd's opened a subscription for the widows and orphans. A man at Drury Lane, who called boisterously for the singing of 'Britons Strike Home!', was silenced by a shout from someone nearby: 'Why, dammit, they *have*!'; and an affray was reported, opposite the Admiralty, when some officers refused to pull off their hats at the orders of what the paper called 'the mobility', and drew swords. They were no denigrators of Nelson, but they would not be dictated to!

Other items of news—and there was a great deal from Ireland—were pushed to the back of the paper. This was Nile day, and certainly attention was paid on no mean scale.

Such were the principal newspaper accounts. Letters followed, wild with joy, making lavish use of the word 'immortal', as was the custom of the day. One of the most uninhibited was from the patrician Lady Spencer, usually restrained and dignified in her expression. She had entertained Nelson and his wife earlier in the year, and had been as startled by his appearance as she had been impressed when 'his wonderful mind broke forth'.

Admiralty, 2 October 1798

> Captain Capel just arrived! [she wrote]. Joy, joy, joy to you, brave, gallant, immortalised Nelson! May that great God, whose cause you so valiantly support, protect and bless you to the end of your brilliant career! Such a race surely never was run. My heart is absolutely bursting with different sensations of joy, of gratitude, of pride, of every emotion that ever warmed the bosom of a British woman, on hearing of her Country's glory—and all produced by you, my dear, my good friend. All, all I *Can* say must fall short of my wishes, of my sentiments about you. This moment the guns are firing, illuminations are preparing, your gallant name is echoed from street to street, and every Briton feels his obligations to you weighing him down. But if these strangers feel in this manner about you, who can express what *We* of this House feel about you? What incalculable service have you been of to my dear Lord Spencer! How gratefully, as First Lord of the Admiralty, does he place on *Your* brow these laurels so gloriously won. In a public, in a private view, what does he not feel at this illustrious achievement of yours, my dear Sir Horatio, and your gallant Squadron's! What a fair and splendid page have you and your heroic companions added to the records of his administration of the Navy! But I am come to the end of my paper, luckily for you, or I should gallop on for ever at this rate. I am half mad, and I fear I have written a

strange letter, but you'll excuse it. Almighty God protect you! Adieu! How anxious we shall be to hear of your health! Lady Nelson has had an Express sent to her.

It was, indeed, an exuberant age. It compensated for the lack of quick and widespread means of communication, such as we take for granted today, by giving news of great events (when it did at last arrive) every particle of value. Nelson, at one bound, became a national hero, the darling of drawing-room and tap-room alike, and he would never be supplanted from his place in the popular imagination. 'He has turned all our heads', said the Duchess of Devonshire. She spoke for her race.

Honours and awards dispensed, the problem for the home authorities, who knew nothing of the Neapolitan land campaign until it was under way, and, therefore, until it was too late either to approve it or to countermand Nelson's part in it, was how best to support the newly won entry into the Mediterranean for the furtherance of the war in general.

Decisions were reached to seize Minorca as a base—the island had been in British hands more than once during past campaigns—and to strengthen the blockade of Egypt, off the coast of which Nelson had had to leave what was little more than a token force. The most effective way of bringing pressure on the French expedition, blockade apart, was to invoke Turkey and Russia in belligerent movement.

Both countries were ripe for action. Turkey regarded the French invasion as a gross affront to her suzerainty, however loosely this had been exercised, hence the Sultan's lavish gift to Nelson; but she had not formerly declared war on the Republic. Russia, with ambitions in the Aegean as well as at Malta, was preparing to act.

Spencer Smith, a diplomatist of great ability, was already at work in Constantinople, urging a Government in whom sloth was habitual to move against the aggressors. Smith had an elder brother in the Navy, a flamboyant personality who soon talked himself into being made joint British representative to the Sultan. The fraternal partnership was to have large consequences, some fortunate, others less so.

Captain Sir Sidney Smith's instructions were imprecisely worded, and this caused much disturbance. He was six years junior to Nelson, and was sent from England in the 80-gun *Tigre*. He soon began to issue directions, in his joint role as sea officer and man of state affairs, calculated to rile both Lord St Vincent and Nelson, into whose sphere he entered with all the assurance of a character in which the histrionic made up a large element. Nothing could have been more likely to enrage an admiral smarting from the failure of a land campaign, and Nelson soon made his displeasure apparent.

The letters exchanged between Nelson and St Vincent leave no doubt as to their mutual irritation with Smith's pretensions, and this was not soothed by Smith hoisting a broad pendant as commodore, a purely self-ordained appointment which the Commander-in-Chief refused to recognise. Nevertheless, Lord Spencer was right when he wrote to St Vincent, on Smith's first coming out:

> I am well aware that there may perhaps be some prejudice . . . but from a long acquaintance with him personally, I think I can venture to assure your Lordship that, added to his unquestioned character for courage and enterprise, he has a great many very good points about him, which those who are less acquainted with him are not sufficiently apprised of . . .

It was not long before Nelson received a directive telling him the Government's policy in the area of his command. With the objectives he could have found no fault. They were the protection of the territories of the Kingdom of Naples; the severing of all communication between Egypt and France; the blockade of Malta; and co-operation with Turkish, Russian and Portuguese squadrons. Implementation was another matter. Naples itself was already lost. Communication between Egypt and France was by now hazardous in the extreme, though it never ceased entirely. The blockade of Malta was a principal charge on Nelson's energies; while for reasons of language, outlook, and standard of efficiency, liaison between his own ships and those of the friendly Powers enumerated could, he found, be only on a limited scale. If Nelson wanted anything done by sea, he knew it would need to be done from within his own resources.

Minorca fell, without serious resistance, on 19 November, and St Vincent, cheered by this further evidence of re-establishment in the Mediterranean, began to hope that, if supplies could be got from Leghorn, it might once more be possible, as in the earlier days of the war, to maintain a regular watch on Toulon.

It was thus that, while the opening of the year 1799 saw Nelson sadly established at Palermo, protecting the Bourbon Court in Sicily, triumphs attended others: Duck-worth and Stuart at Minorca, and the brothers Smith at Constantinople. With the *Tigre* riding at anchor in the Bosphorus, and with Spencer Smith skilful ashore, the Sultan's grand vizier, impressed by floating strength and cogent argument, signed an offensive and defensive alliance with Great Britain. Russia had come to a similar understanding a few days before, and thus three great Powers bound themselves to expel France from the Levant.

An island base in the western Mediterranean, and a promising alliance in the east, were a fair counter-balance to the loss of Naples. All three events were directly due to the Battle of the Nile.

As the year proceeded, so did complexities grow. Soon after news of the defeat of his admiral became known, Bonaparte faced trouble in Cairo, and had to suppress insurrection, though he was careful to antagonise as few Moslems as possible. He then made the journey to Suez which had long been planned, taking Ganteaume with him. He found little but decay, and half-obliterated traces of ancient waterways. Though he ordered Ganteaume to prepare a flotilla for use in the Red Sea, it was soon clear that adventures in that direction were not practical.

Syria was another matter, and it was to this country that his energies were next directed. It was there that he could attack the Turk, at once expanding his own conquests, and preventing the recapture of territory already won. He had heard that the Sultan planned to send an army overland for the recovery of Cairo, and that a force was being assembled at Rhodes to be used in support of the British fleet, and for coastal landings. It was never Bonaparte's way to wait on the defensive, and by early in February he was on the move.

His first success was against Jaffa, which was stormed on 7 March. The victory was marred by a massacre of prisoners, after their lives had been promised, owing to shortage of food. He then decided to push on to Acre, threatened as he was by cases of plague, an enemy liable to be deadlier than the Turk.

Acre, like so many other places in the Levant which had been fortified of old, was crumbling, and Bonaparte expected a victory as easy as that which he had enjoyed at Jaffa. He had reason on his side, for Captain Miller of the *Theseus*, sent by Sir Sidney Smith to survey the defences, wrote:

> I found almost every embrasure empty except those towards the sea. Many years' collection of the dirt of the town had been thrown in such a situation as to cover completely the approach to the gate from the only guns that could flank it, and from the sea. . . . None of the batteries had casements, traverses or splinter-proofs. They had many guns, but generally small and defective . . .

Miller himself was soon at work, and when Smith arrived in person, on 15 March, the defences had been put in better shape. The decisive event, in the earlier stages of the siege, was the capture of Bonaparte's siege-train, which had been sent—at great hazard—by sea, and of seven small vessels in which it had been conveyed. Mounted on the walls they were intended to breach, the guns played a great part in the defence. So did a French royalist officer, Phélippeaux, who had helped Smith earlier in his career to escape from Paris.

Nine confident attacks were repulsed by the Turks, stiffened by British seamen. Bonaparte was then forced to detach a number of his troops to meet a threat in his rear. A decisive battle was fought near Mount Tabor, which resulted in a victory of Bonaparte and Kléber over greatly superior forces of Turks and Mamelukes. Bonaparte and his staff spent the ensuing night at the Convent of Nazareth, Bonaparte checking the ribald laughter of his men when the Prior told the story of the breaking of a pillar by the Archangel Gabriel at the time of the Annunciation of the forthcoming birth of Christ.

On returning to Acre, Bonaparte learnt of the death of Phélippeaux from sunstroke, but his place as an engineer had been filled by an English volunteer, Colonel Douglas, who foiled the efforts of the French sappers, and enabled the fortress to hold out until it was known that Turks from Rhodes were approaching.

By 4 May a practicable breach in the walls had been made by French heavy guns which had been brought overland. Two days later an assault was ordered. The besiegers hoped that this would take place under cover of the explosion of a mine; but Douglas destroyed it. By 7 May, the Rhodes contingent were on the horizon, and Bonaparte knew it was then or never. Led with reckless gallantry by Lannes, the French gained part of the wall, and planted the tricolour on the north-east tower. But all further progress was checked by the British bluejackets, whom Smith at once threw into the town. The Turks from Rhodes, wafted landwards by a sudden favourable breeze after being becalmed, were landed in time to dislodge the French, and a renewed assault next day met with bloody repulse.

Both sides were now worn out with the extraordinary siege. 'This town is not, nor ever has been, defensible according to the rules of art: but according to every other rule it must and shall be defended.' So wrote Smith to Nelson, on 9 May, and he was as good as his word.

He soon had a new ally—disease. As the summer advanced, the sickening heat increased, and so did the plague. After the failure of an assault on 10 May, certain French battalions refused to advance over the putrid remains of their comrades. Finally, having clung to his enterprise with desperate tenacity, the general gave orders to retreat.

In later years Bonaparte spoke of Smith as the man who spoilt his destiny. It is unlikely that, in any event, the French leader's fate would have held him long in the East, but Smith had certainly shown him, and those under his orders, that he was not invincible, even on land.

Smith won much honour from his defence of Acre, all of it deserved. Acre was prophetic of later triumphs by British arms, the last of them on the plain of Waterloo.

At sea, had the skill and co-ordination of French and Spanish admirals equalled their ability to plan and to time, they should have regained the Mediterranean. For in March 1799 the French Directory, determined upon at least one great effort for the relief of Egypt, ordered Admiral Bruix, then Minister of Marine, to hoist his flag at Brest, and to bring out the Atlantic Fleet.

Bruix evaded the blockaders under Lord Bridport, who should have been relieved, or such was the view of good judges, when the French expedition to Ireland eluded him in the previous year, and from April to October a powerful force was constantly in motion, though never seeking battle. It set the British a series of problems which were never satisfactorily resolved.

Bruix's first intention was to join a Spanish squadron at Cadiz, but he was foiled by Lord Keith, and his later movements kept both friend and foe guessing. St Vincent, who was in failing health and about to relinquish his command to Keith, was determined to prevent Bruix from joining forces with any other large squadron, and to defend Minorca, but there was nothing strong or fast enough to stop Bruix from suddenly entering the Mediterranean from the wastes of the Atlantic, and this is what he did. At first he made for Toulon. Then, since the news from Italy was bad, he was diverted to Genoa; thence back to Toulon, and at last to Cartagena.

At Cartagena, the Frenchman found the Spanish admiral Mazareddo, with 19 sail-of-the-line. If combined, the two squadrons could, so far as numbers were concerned, not merely have secured ascendancy in the Middle Sea, but brought relief to Bonaparte. In the upshot, they never sailed together, for divided policy ruined an incomparable chance. The interest of the Court of Madrid was westwards, and it was not prepared to risk ships to bring home a republican general from an expedition which appeared to have failed, and which was no business of Spain. Mazareddo was ordered to make for Ferrol, and Bruix returned to Brest, chased for weeks on end by the luckless Keith.

It had been a useless cruise, but it had caused acute anxiety to many, Nelson included, for in May, when the danger became serious, his force was so scattered, and employed so variously, that he could have offered no effective resistance had Bruix appeared in strength. Smith and Miller were at Acre; Ball, with three ships, was watching Malta; Duckworth, with four ships, was prepared to defend Minorca. They were penny packets, and needed combining if they were to offer a bold front.

On 12 May, Nelson, still at Palermo, learnt for certain that the French had appeared in strength in the Mediterranean. He at once concentrated his squadron, stationing it off the north-west of Sicily, where he cruised between the 21st and 28th. He then returned to Palermo, and on 8 June transferred his flag to the *Foudroyant*. On 13 June he embarked Neapolitan troops, nominally under the Hereditary Prince, to go to Naples, which was on the point of being recovered by royalists from Calabria led by a remarkable character, Cardinal Ruffo, who combined ability as a leader of guerrillas with high office in the Church.

Hardly were the troops embarked when Nelson had news from Keith of the presence of Bruix's large fleet off the Italian Riviera. In view of Keith's orders, Nelson again took up a position where he could protect Sicily, and where he could dispute the passage of any hostile force making for the Levant. Then he returned to Palermo, and deciding that the chance to recover Naples was worth a grave risk, though inwardly doubting the wisdom of his own decision, he sailed with his whole squadron to the capital, taking the Hamiltons with him.

It was a bold and successful step, though it brought odium upon the admiral and his friends, since they made themselves the instruments of a restoration of Bourbon rule which was accompanied by unwise excesses, shockingly protracted.

Nelson was off Naples between 25 June and 4 August, for most of which time Ferdinand was a guest in his flagship, exercising his authority therefrom. When he returned with the King to Palermo, Nelson was given the Sicilian Dukedom of Brontë, together with an estate commensurate with the title. He accepted it with some reluctance, though he was soon proud to sign himself (without the leave of his own Sovereign) 'Brontë Nelson of the Nile', a usage which was later modified to the simpler 'Nelson and Brontë'. He had now expiated the misfortunes of the land campaign of the previous winter, but at much risk to his reputation.

The crisis had come on 13 July, when Nelson received orders from Keith, who was his senior, to take all the ships he could spare to the defence of Minorca. Keith himself had with him 31 sail-of-the-line, and was faced with the possibility of opposing 43. Nelson's squadron would ensure equality in numbers, and the probability of success if the forces once made contact.

Nelson considered that he was bound by his word to stand by the King of Naples, and that the defence of Naples and Sicily was of overriding strategic importance. 'It is better', he said, 'to save the Kingdom of Naples and risk Minorca, than to risk the Kingdom of Naples to save Minorca.' If the truth of the proposition was itself open to argument, Nelson himself had no business to weigh such high matters, and to decide in a manner contrary to his superiors. He defied Keith's orders, and stayed at Naples. For his disobedience he was rightly censured by St Vincent, by Keith, Spencer and the Board of Admiralty. He had jeopardised his professional character, and although no harm resulted (such was Bruix's mismanagement) it was the gravest risk of the kind that even Nelson ever ran, and it was a good thing for the country that his luck held. Even though it did so, he could easily have been disgraced, had not his seniors shown him quite astonishing forbearance.

If Nelson's luck held, so did that of Bonaparte, who had need of it even more. There were further risings in Egypt, though not of a grave nature, and a brief reappearance of scattered forces of Mamelukes—nuisances which he was able to counter. But early in July, just about the time that Keith's message was on its way to Nelson at Naples, Marmont, who commanded at Alexandria, sent a note to his chief with the news that 60 transports, crowded with troops, and escorted by Russian, Turkish and British ships of war, had come to anchor in Aboukir Bay, among the wreckage of the ships destroyed by Nelson just a year before.

It was Smith's doing, as Bonaparte soon guessed: he had found a new use for the amphibious force from Rhodes. The Turks landed on 14 July and entrenched themselves on the narrow spit of land which formed the western arm of the bay. There had been a sharp struggle for possession of the tip of the peninsula, on which stood the fort of Aboukir, but the issue had not long been in doubt, since the French numbered less than 300 men. Mustapha Bey, the Turkish general, was left in possession, and Marmont did not dare attempt relief from Alexandria.

When Bonaparte arrived, he was agreeably surprised to find that Mustapha, content with the early success, had made no move. Next day, with 6,000 men to oppose double that number, Bonaparte achieved yet another of his astonishing victories. One of the comparatively few important survivors among officers serving with the Turkish forces, pulled from the sea into Sir Sidney Smith's own gig, was Mehomet Ali, later to be the founder of a royal dynasty of Egypt.

> The name Aboukir [wrote Bonaparte] has had a melancholy meaning for all Frenchmen; but the triumph of the seventh day of Thermidor has effaced the memory. It is a victory that will hasten the return of the army to France.

Bonaparte was wrong in respect of the army, yet it hastened his own. Soon after his success, he opened a correspondence with Smith about an exchange of prisoners, and Smith allowed a young officer aboard the *Tigre*, who was hospitably entertained, and given a bundle of English newspapers. As he stepped into the boat to return, Smith remarked, in his impeccable French: 'Lord Nelson understands that the Directory desires your Commander-in-Chief to return at once to France.'

The young Frenchman could hardly believe his ears, but the news was true. The Directory had written to that effect, and had entrusted the letter to Bruix, who had been unable to deliver it. Smith had been looking for a chance to deliver the message: but it was craft, not generosity, which prompted the action. He hoped to prevail on Bonaparte to sail, and to capture him at sea.

Bonaparte was glad enough of the papers, though their news was gloomy. In Italy, the situation was growing critical. France, too, was in confusion, and Jacobins were hinting at the need for a new purge. La Vendée, royalist in sympathy, was in revolt, and conspiracy was active elsewhere. On top of all this was Smith's message, which Bonaparte was glad to believe. He sent for Ganteaume, and asked him to make the two remaining frigates then serviceable ready for sea. They were *Le Muiron* and *Le Carrère*. Bonaparte thereupon returned to Cairo, with Mustapha Bey a prisoner at his side. He would leave the city as he had entered it, on a triumphal note, however secret he kept his actual departure.

It was not long before Ganteaume reported that the *Tigre* and the *Theseus* were out of sight of the Egyptian coast, and that the frigates were waiting. In order to lure Bonaparte to sail, Smith had himself to vanish. No responsible officer, least of all Ganteaume, would put to sea with his commander-in-chief on board and an efficient enemy ship-of-the-line within sight. Smith had to risk that Ganteaume would sail, and gain sufficient sea room before one of the lighter British ships could catch him and by a bold attack delay him until the *Tigre* came up to decide the issue.

On 18 August, with the Nile in flood, Bonaparte embarked at Bulac, leaving Kléber as his successor in Egypt. All was mystery, and with a party which included Berthier, Beauharnais, Monge and Berthollet, Bonaparte transferred on 22 August to *Le Muiron*, wearing Ganteaume's flag. He sailed from Marabut, where the expedition had landed the year before. In *Le Carrère* was another party, which included Lannes and Marmont.

The voyage was long and risky, with winds light and uncertain. But the ships themselves were well found, particularly *Le Muiron*, newly built at Venice, and they could probably have outsailed anything hoping to intercept them. At the end of September Bonaparte put in at his native Corsica, his escape almost accomplished. There the mistral blew for more than a week, and *Le Muiron* could not get to sea again until 6 October. That evening, as twilight was fading, look-outs sighted an English fleet. It was Keith's, cruising off the coast of Provence. Keith knew nothing of Bonaparte's departure from his army, and his ships held on. Presently their topsails merged into the darkness.

Ganteaume, had he had his way, would have returned to Ajaccio, but Bonaparte ordered him to hold his course. His instinct was right. Early on 9 October, while Nelson was on passage between Palermo and Minorca on a visit of duty to Port Mahon, Ganteaume anchored in the bay of St Raphael. The news spread like wildfire, and the inhabitants of Fréjus hurried to the coast. News of the second Battle of Abou-kir had just reached France, and Bonaparte was once again the hero of the hour. 'Go, General, go', said the townsmen, urging their guest towards Paris, 'and if you wish, we will crown you King!' Bonaparte was, in fact, soon master of France, and when at length he chose a title, his ambitions soared beyond mere kingship. A quicker transition, from fugitive at sea to mastery of a great country, has seldom been recorded.

4 *The Last of the French Ships*

There was an artistic unity about Nelson's victory of the Nile which extended to the submission of the two remaining French ships of the line, *Le Généreux* and *Le Guillaume Tell*, though they continued to fly the flag of their country for nearly two years after the battle.

The encounter with *Le Généreux*, against which Nelson had a particular grudge since she had taken the *Leander*, came about in an unexpected way, by a stroke of luck which led Alexander Ball to call his chief a 'heaven-born admiral'.

All the winter of 1799 Nelson had been at Palermo, his flag sometimes in the *Foudroyant* but more often in a transport. He grew increasingly under the influence of Lady Hamilton, increasingly tied to the Court, and as his friend Lord Minto wrote:

> ... he does not seem at all conscious of the sort of discredit he has fallen into, or the cause of it, for he writes still not wisely about Lady Hamilton and all that. But it is hard to condemn and use ill a hero for being foolish about a woman who has art enough to make fools of many a wiser man than an admiral.

At last, towards the end of the year, the patient Keith grew peremptory, and Nelson was summoned to join him at Leghorn, which he reached in the *Foudroyant* on 20 January 1800. It was Nelson's first seamanlike activity in the new century.

Three days later Keith and Nelson sailed together for Palermo, which they reached on 3 February, Nelson reluctant to introduce his chief to the Court of Palermo, where he himself had been principal adviser for so long, and Keith sharply aware of the figure which Nelson was cutting there, since even devoted naval friends like Troubridge were growing shocked at his deterioration, and had the temerity to say so.

On 12 February Keith and Nelson sailed for Malta, but were separated by a fog. Nearly a week later the *Foudroyant*, *Northumberland*, *Audacious* and the frigate *Success* came upon a French squadron under Rear-Admiral Perrée, who had taken advantage of the thick weather to try to bring relief and supplies to Valetta, Perrée flying his flag in *Le Généreux*. There could be only one end to such a meeting, and by good fortune one of the *Foudroyant*'s midshipmen, G. S. Parsons, recorded a glimpse of Nelson as he appeared in action.

After some days of groping about in a heavy sea, interspersed with fog, Nelson heard the sound of firing, and ordered Sir Edward Berry, who had by now resumed his old place as flag-captain, to steer towards it. Soon the admiral grew impatient, and took personal charge of affairs.

'Make the *Foudroyant* fly!' he said to Berry. 'This will not do, Sir Ed'ard, it is certainly *Le Généreux*, and to my flagship she can alone surrender! Sir Ed'ard, we must and shall beat the *Northumberland*!'

'I will do my utmost, my lord', said Berry. '. . . hand butts of water to the stays— pipe the hammocks down, and each man place shot in them—slack the stays, knock up the wedges, and give the masts play. Start off the water, and pump the ship.'

The *Foudroyant* began to draw ahead, and slowly took the lead. 'The admiral is working his fin' (the stump of his arm), noted Parsons. 'Do not cross hawse, I advise you.' He was right, for Nelson suddenly burst out to the petty officer who was conning the ship:

'I'll knock you off your perch, you rascal, if you are so inattentive! Sir Ed'ard, send your best quartermaster to the weather-wheel.'

'A strange sail ahead of the chase', called the look-out man.

'Youngster,' said Nelson to Parsons, 'to the mast-head! What—going without your glass and be damned to you! Let me know what she is immediately.'

'A sloop of war or frigate, my lord.'

'Demand her number.'

'The *Success*.'

'Signal her to cut off the flying enemy. Great odds though. Thirty-two small guns to eighty large ones.'

'The *Success*, my lord, has hove-to athwart-hawse of *Le Généreux* and is firing her larboard broadside. The Frenchman has hoisted the tricolour with a Rear-Admiral's flag.'

'Bravo, *Success*, at her again.'

'She has wore, my lord, and is firing her starboard broadside. It has winged the chase, my lord.'

Le Généreux then opened fire on the frigate, and 'everyone stood aghast', said Parsons, 'fearing the consequences. But when the smoke cleared, there was the *Success*, crippled it is true, but bulldog-like, bearing up for the enemy.'

'Signal the *Success* to discontinue the action and come under my stern', said Nelson. 'She has done well for her size. Try a shot from the lower deck at her, Sir Ed'ard.'

'It goes over her.'

'Beat to quarters and fire coolly and deliberately at her masts and yards.'

'*Le Généreux* at this moment opened her fire on us', continued Parsons, 'and, as a shot passed through the mizzen stay-sail, Lord Nelson, patting one of the youngsters on the head, asked him jocularly how he relished the music: and observing something like alarm depicted on his countenance, consoled him with the information that Charles XII of Sweden ran away from the first shot he heard, though afterwards he was called 'the Great' and deservedly, from his bravery. "I therefore", said Nelson, "hope much from you in the future."'

At this point the *Northumberland* joined in. 'Down came the tricoloured ensign', said Parsons, 'amid the thunders of our united cannon.' Berry boarded the prize, and received Perrée's sword, but the admiral himself was dying of his wounds. The last time Berry had been aboard *Le Généreux* it had been as a prisoner of war, after the *Leander*'s battle.

> With what joy you must have received the news of his Lordship's success [wrote Sir Alexander Ball to Lady Hamilton]. . . . Fortune smiles wherever he goes. We have been carrying on the blockade of Malta sixteen months during which time the enemy never attempted to throw in great succours until this month. His Lordship arrived off here the day they were within a few leagues of the island, captured the principal ship and dispersed the rest, so that not one has reached the port.
>
> I dined with his Lordship yesterday, who is apparently in good health, but he complains of indisposition and the necessity of repose. I do not think a short stay here will hurt his health, particularly as the ship is at anchor, and his mind not harassed. Troubridge and I are extremely anxious that the French ships (*Le Guillaume Tell* in particular) and the French garrison shall surrender to him. I would not urge it if I were not convinced that it will ultimately add to his honour and happiness.

Ball was right. It was known that *Le Guillaume Tell*, lying under the guns of

Valletta, would attempt escape, and Keith had enjoined Nelson to continue the blockade in person, not to return to the flesh-pots of Palermo. He himself pushed on for Egypt.

But Nelson was of another mind, and after a short stay at Malta he returned to the Hamiltons. Arriving back at Palermo on 16 March, he shifted his flag to a transport, and allowed Berry to resume watch in the *Foudroyant* off Malta without him. His action shocked the captains in his squadron, and did not escape the notice of Lord Spencer, who wrote that he was sorry to feel that Nelson's health allowed him to remain 'inactive at a foreign Court'. The shaft went home, but it was the *Foudroyant*, sailing under Berry as a private ship, together with the *Lion* and the frigate *Penelope*, which had the honour of overcoming the last of Brueys's fleet.

On 30 March, not far from Malta, Blackwood in the *Penelope* sighted the big Frenchman, and repeated the tactics of the *Success* against *Le Généreux*. Berry in the *Foudroyant* was soon up with him, though he sadly missed the presence of his beloved admiral, and kept popping his head into his empty cabin, so he wrote, 'to ask you if we were doing all right'. He added that he was 'praying earnestly for you to fly on board'.

The Journal of the *Foudroyant* describes the action as follows:

> 30 March . . . At daybreak, having all sail set, saw H.M. ships *Lion* and *Penelope* engaging a French line-of-battle ship, with her main and mizzen-topmasts gone. At 6, came up with her, when Sir Edward Berry hailed her, and desired him to strike, but received no answer. An officer shook his sword at him, and a broadside was fired from her, which was immediately returned within half pistol-shot.
>
> Her first broadside cut our rigging very much, and second carried away our fore-topmast and main topsail-yard. Half-past 6 . . . saw a man nail the French ensign to the stump of the mizzen mast. At 7, *Penelope* fired at the enemy in passing under her stern. Half-past 7, spoke the *Penelope*. 5 minutes past 8, shot away the enemy's fore-mast. 10 minutes past 8, all the masts being gone by the board, the enemy struck his colours, and ceased firing.

The *Foudroyant*'s Journal continued on a note which is a very direct echo of the Nile.

> Performed Divine Service, and returned thanks to Almighty God for the victory.

By the time of the capture of *Le Guillaume Tell*, most of the loose ends left after Nelson's victory had been tied up, and it was more than ever time for him to direct his energies elsewhere. 'Discretionary power' had been given to the Commander-in-Chief by the Admiralty to permit him to return home, if such was his wish.

In the circumstances, Nelson allowed himself one more excursion, which was to Malta. On 24 April 1800 he sailed in the *Foudroyant*, with the Hamiltons as his guests, in the hope that the French might surrender during the term of the cruise. The brave defenders under Vaubois were, however, fully capable of sustained resistance, and intended nothing of the sort. In fact, they were in good heart, and Emma Hamilton, always intrepid, thrilled to the scream of shot aimed at the ship by the shore batteries, while even old Sir William felt no disrelish at once again being under fire. It was on this voyage that Nelson and Emma became lovers, and their names were to be linked together for the rest of their lives.

Malta did not fall until September 1800. As for Egypt, it needed a large expedition, transported by Keith and led by Sir Ralph Abercromby, to defeat the French army. Keith's transports anchored in Aboukir Bay on 1 March 1801, and although the British general died of wounds received during a battle fought near Alexandria some weeks later, the French at last met their match, and agreed to withdraw from the country.

Among Keith's squadron were the *Minotaur, Swiftsure, Foudroyant* and *Le Guillaume Tell*, the latter renamed *Malta* and taken into British service. As she came to anchor in Aboukir Bay, the *Foudroyant* fouled the submerged wreck of *L'Orient*. To have been the scene of three battles in less than three years was a strange fate for a stretch of coast which had been quiet for generations.

By the time of Abercromby's success and death, Nelson was once again on active service, this time in the Baltic. He had returned to England overland with the Hamiltons, fêted in Vienna, Dresden, Prague and elsewhere as one of the hopes of Europe. At Vienna, he gave Lady Minto and Lord Fitzharris some final memories of the Nile.

> Without knowing the men he had to trust to [said Nelson], he would not have hazarded the attack: there was very little room, but he was sure each would find a hole to creep in at. [Lord Fitzharris noted down the admiral's actual words at one point in the conversation.] When I saw them [said Nelson], I could not help popping my head every now and then out of the window (although I had a damned tooth-ache), and once, as I was observing their position, I heard two seamen quartered at a gun near me, talking, and one said to the other, 'Damn them, look at them. There they are, Jack, if we don't beat them, they will beat us.' I knew what stuff I had under me, so I went into the attack with a few ships only, perfectly sure the others would follow me, although it was nearly dark and they might have had every excuse for not doing it, yet they all in the course of two hours found a hole to poke in at.
>
> [He added] If I had taken a fleet of the same force from Spithead, I would sooner have thought of flying than attacking the French in their position, but I knew my captains, nor could I say which distinguished himself most.

Nelson landed at Great Yarmouth, in his native county, on 6 November 1800, to be given a rousing welcome by those for whom he had fought.

'Ifs' in history are at best tantalising and at worst extravagant, but there are certain reflections arising from the Battle of the Nile which surprise by contrast. In a sense, it was the most paradoxical of victories. It was resounding; it set a new standard in achievement, yet in sum total the consequences must appear to be disappointing.

Because the battle was fought too late, and in the wrong place, it did not attain its full strategical intention. *If* Nelson had had frigates, *if* he had waited off Alexandria on his first appearance there, he would have fought Brueys at sea, and although the French battle squadron would not have been annihilated, the military expedition could have been ruined, and even Bonaparte might have been captured or killed. It had been the intention of the British Government that Nelson should meet the armada while at sea: that he did not do so was partly owing to chance, and his efforts, consummate though they were, did not ruin the enemy scheme.

Again, the combination which Nelson and the diplomatists, including the brothers Smith, brought about, that of Turkey, Russia and Great Britain, together with

Austria and Naples, effected little in itself, and led to some disasters and much humiliation. Turkey showed poorly at war; Russia's influence in the Mediterranean led to friction with her allies. Malta, which was retained by Great Britain, long remained a bone of contention, particularly with the Tsar, who resented British intrusion there almost as much as French. And when British and Russian forces acted together, as they did in Holland and Italy, the results were rarely satisfactory.

As for Naples, the restoration of 1799 did not prosper, and Ferdinand remained many years an exile in Sicily, hunting and amusing himself to his own satisfaction, and at the last returning with reluctance to his mainland capital.

Even while Nelson was crossing Europe on his way home, Bonaparte was restoring his grip on the Continent, defeating the Austrians first at Marengo and later at Hohenlinden. Only in India was there a clear-cut success. Tippoo Sahib's defeat led to the return of the ancient Hindu dynasty in Mysore, while the rest of his dominions were divided.

It was as an example and an inspiration that the battle had most effect. The Royal Navy had thrown up another tactical genius, the greatest of them all, and it had inspired Europe to continue to resist the limitless lust for power with which Bonaparte seemed to have injected France. Although it took years to overthrow the colossus, Nelson and Sidney Smith had proved that he was not superhuman, while the conduct of the Battle of the Nile itself became a pattern of brilliance which no sea officer forgot. It showed what could be achieved, against equal or superior forces, by preparation, by seizing the moment when it came, and by making the most of opportunity.

Nelson had proved that it was possible to win a resounding victory under sail not through centralised command by written instructions, not even by centralised command through signals, but by broad directives giving scope for independent action by subordinates. It was a revolutionary discovery. If it had been more attended to by later admirals, the history of warfare at sea would have run a different course.

PART IV

Copenhagen

1 *The Mediterranean and the Baltic*

To the peripheral powers, Great Britain and Russia, who were to be the ultimate victors in what had developed by degrees into a world struggle, both the Mediterranean and the Baltic areas were of the first importance. There they touched; there they deployed. The Baltic, besides providing what Peter the Great had called his 'window on the west', gave Russia access to the other seas and continents, and this independently of how strong any country grew to be in the heart of Europe. It was true that during certain months the eastern Baltic was ice-bound, but for much of the year it was open, and Peter's aim of a large navy based on his capital and Kronstadt had been remembered.

To Great Britain, the Baltic lands were not only a traditional source of trade, they provided naval stores of a quality and in an abundance not to be matched elsewhere: timber above all, but also hemp, canvas, pitch, tar, rosin, turpentine, brimstone, copper and iron. Only the metals were readily accessible from home or other sources, while British salt and coal, together with manufactured goods and such commodities as sugar, tobacco and tea, for which she acted as carrier or re-exporter, were almost as vital to the health and economy of the north as the materials which Scandinavia in her turn provided.

To Britain, the Mediterranean was almost equally important commercially as politically, and as her political influence waxed and waned, so did her trade: both were in a low state until, at a comparatively late stage in the struggle, the efforts begun by Spanish patriots to throw off the yoke of France at last began to take effect. To Russia, the direct route to the Middle Sea was barred by the broad band of Ottoman possessions which stretched from Bosnia, south through Greece and Crete to Asia Minor and Palestine. Russian access to the Mediterranean had as a general rule to be by way of the long haul from the Baltic, and her interests were those of policy, not trade. Whenever she was in active alliance with Britain, her ships were to be found in the ports of southern Europe. Whenever she was either hostile to Britain or neutral, they were absent. In essentials, her interests marched so closely with those of Britain that hostility to the principal sea power was in the nature of an aberration. Catherine the Great, under whose rule Russia first observed the war, collaborated actively with George III. Her successor, Paul, did so for a time, until persuaded to change sides. Paul's son, Alexander I, was by turn neutral, foe and friend.

Unhappily for Britain, and sometimes for themselves, the interests of the Baltic powers and Britain did not always coincide. Denmark (which then included Norway),

Sweden, and to a lesser extent Russia, conducted a substantial traffic with Germany, the Low Countries, France and Spain, and these powers in turn were dependent on the northern lands for their naval stores, and sometimes for their grain. Conflict in which Britain was involved, whether or not Scandinavian countries were drawn in, was bound to affect northern interests adversely. Profits might soar, but they could also vanish; markets opened or were barred without warning and often without explanation; shipping was at all times liable to delay, and cargoes to confiscation. So difficult did conditions become at the time of the War of American Independence that, under Russian leadership, principles of Armed Neutrality were enunciated. The same ideas, revived by the same combination of interests, emerged during the progress of the later conflict. Somewhat over-simplified, the idea behind the original association was 'free ships, free goods'—i.e. that neutrals should be allowed to trade as and where they pleased, protected by their flags and as necessary by their navies. It was not one which could be acceptable to a belligerent, and least of all to Britain, one of whose means of imposing her will upon an adversary, and thus of winning her wars, was by controlling sea traffic to her own advantage, and by blockade and embargo.

The first incident which suggested the likelihood of more general complications occurred in January 1798 when a convoy of Swedish merchantmen, bound for the Mediterranean with a frigate as protection, was intercepted in the Channel by a British squadron under Commodore Lawford. The Swedish frigate captain submitted to *force majeure* after formal resistance and vehement protest, and the ships were brought in for adjudication. A few months later Sir William Scott, the Admiralty judge, after considering the official instructions from Stockholm which prohibited the giving of permission to search, pronounced sentence in the case of one of the seized vessels on the general ground that her master had been enjoined to dispute the exercise of what Scott described as 'an incontestable right of the lawfully commissioned cruisers of a belligerent Power'.

With Denmark, issue was joined in even more striking fashion. In December 1799 the captain of a Danish frigate fired on British boats which were attempting to search cargoes under his charge, off Gibraltar. The *chargé d'affaires* at Copenhagen demanded an explanation, and the Danish Government, far from disavowing the proceedings of the captain, defended his conduct and called upon the British for reparation for damages he had received in the course of his duty.

The matter was still under discussion the following July when the Danish frigate *Freja* was captured in the Channel after a smart action, and was brought in, together with the six ships in her convoy. The Danes in this case demanded immediate restitution of the seizure, and prompt satisfaction for what they deemed to be a signal insult to the honour of their flag. Britain's reply was to send Lord Whitworth to Copenhagen, while a fleet, under Admiral Dixon, entered the Sound just to make it clear beyond a doubt that business was intended. A peremptory interchange of State papers ensued, but at length milder counsels prevailed, and on 29 August 1800 a convention was arrived at whereby Britain restored the *Freja* and her charges, and, on her part, Denmark agreed to suspend for the time the grant of convoy. Neither side was

28 Sir Hyde Parker

*From a pastel by
Sir Thomas Lawrence*

29 Captain Edward Riou

From a drawing by J. Jackson

30 The forcing of the Sound: the fleet off Kronborg, 28 March 1801
From a coloured aquatint after Nicholas Pocock

31 The Battle of Copenhagen, 2 April 1801
From an oil painting by Nicholas Pocock

satisfied, and the obvious Danish move was to report the whole proceedings to St Petersburg.

From the Danish point of view, the information was well timed. The eccentric Tsar Paul, though still nominally at war with the French Republic, was becoming ever more enmeshed in Napoleon's diplomatic schemes. Malta—upon which Paul had claims as well as designs, since he had become Grand Master of the Knights of St John—was on the point of falling after its long siege, and it only needed some such spark to start a blaze. On 27 August Paul issued a declaration wherein, after referring to the *Freja* incident, he invited the sovereigns of Prussia, Denmark and Sweden to unite with him in the re-establishment of an Armed Neutrality in full force, and when news arrived of Admiral Dixon's appearance in Baltic waters, he ordered the sequestration of all British property within his dominions.

When Malta fell in September, and it became evident that Britain had no intention of allowing the island to be annexed, Paul imposed an embargo on all British vessels in Russian ports. The crews of two ships having resisted the execution of this decree and made their escape from Narva, Paul ordered a third vessel, which had remained in the haven, to be burnt.

Prussia fell in obligingly with Russian plans and so, for the time, did Sweden. The Swedish sovereign, Gustavus IV Adolphus, had recently celebrated his majority by recalling the Russophil minister Armfeldt. He then hastened in person to St Petersburg, and within a few days Russia, Sweden, Denmark and Prussia were knit together in an association which had the following objects: (1) Every neutral to be free to navigate from port to port and on the coasts of nations at war. (2) Goods belonging to subjects of belligerent powers, with the exception of contraband, to be free on neutral vessels. (3) Blockade, to be recognised, must be exercised by a close watch. (4) Neutrals only to be arrested 'for just cause and in view of evident facts'. (5) The declaration of officers commanding armed vessels accompanying a convoy that the cargoes do not include contraband shall suffice to prevent any visit of inspection.

On hearing of the Russian embargo, Bonaparte forbade any further capture of Russian ships by French men-of-war, declared that he regarded the Republic as already at peace with the Tsar, and attributed only to the great distance which separated the two countries the delay in a formal signature of a treaty. Paul at once despatched a plenipotentiary to Paris, and by the end of January 1801 Bonaparte was already at work devising vast schemes of Franco-Russian co-operation. He still had an army in Egypt, severed though it was from direct communication with the homeland, and as he remarked: 'Peace is nothing in comparison with an alliance which will overcome England and preserve Egypt to us.'

Whatever his other shortcomings, Paul was not far behind Bonaparte in imagination. He asked the First Consul to concert with Spain to obtain the accession of Portugal and the United States to the Armed Neutrality; and he himself proposed a Russian invasion of India. All practical difficulties sank into insignificance in the eyes of the excited Tsar.

In Denmark, origin of the new troubles, the sovereign, Christian VII, who had married the sister of George III, was peace-loving, but his mental powers were uncertain, and the Prince Royal, who exercised effective government, supported his principal minister, Count Bernstorff, in an attitude of increasing stiffness towards Britain. No belligerent could be indifferent to threats from so many new quarters, and the Admiralty, in assembling a squadron stronger than Dixon's for service in Baltic waters, acted none too soon. For on 29 March 1801 Denmark placed an embargo on British vessels in her ports, and on the same day Danish forces entered Hamburg and declared the Elbe closed to British merchantmen. A few days later, Danish troops took possession of Lübeck as part of the process of holding up British trade. All was now set for a clash, and only a miracle, or submission by one side or the other, could have prevented it. As London saw it, the so-called Armed Neutrality was likely to prove nothing less than a direct and substantial augmentation of the French navy. It would range most of Europe against an island which was fighting for survival, and which could afford to pull no punches.

On 13 January 1801, a day of the month which he probably thought appropriate, Vice-Admiral Lord Nelson—his step in rank dated from New Year's Day—separated for ever from Fanny, and left London for Plymouth, where he hoisted his flag in the *San Josef*, the ship he had taken from the Spaniards nearly four years earlier. She was a unit of the Channel Fleet, then commanded by the Earl of St Vincent, who was shortly to be called to Whitehall as First Lord of the Admiralty, and thus to be political, titular and administrative head of the Service of which he was by now the foremost officer.

Nelson was low, and for many reasons. By nature strongly religious and moral, he was in the wrong in the case of his wife, and he even felt estranged from his father, who had always been her champion. He was madly in love with Emma Hamilton, who was not only about to give birth to his child Horatia, but who was goading her adorer into a frenzy of jealousy by pretending that Sir William was shortly to receive the Prince of Wales. Nelson was certain that, if he came, the Prince would make advances to Emma.

As if all this were not enough, Nelson's good eye was troubling him; he found the winter weather a strain after the long spell he had enjoyed in the south; and he was uncertain of his next service. He was soon to be involved in a law-suit over prize-money with a nominee of Lord St Vincent, in which matter he was, incidentally, in the right. Troubridge was now a member of the Board of Admiralty, a fact which Nelson resented, and Nelson also knew full well that both his old friend and his Commander-in-Chief felt that he was making a fool of himself, and that the sooner he was packed off to a scene of activity, the better for his reputation. Although the authorities were right in their diagnosis they were less than just in the new appointment which they chose for their most brilliant tactician. They made Nelson second-in-command to Sir Hyde Parker in the fleet destined for the Baltic. It was a strong fleet, and it was assembled with appropriate speed, but the idea of Nelson serving as subordinate to Parker reminded many of a racehorse harnessed tandem behind an elderly farm animal.

In point of fact Parker was a respectable officer, of a well-established naval family, who had, however, no recent experience of war likely to equip him for the arduous and complicated task of disrupting a dangerous maritime coalition. The first quality needed was enterprise, and the second suppleness of mind. Parker was indolently inclined, as was not unnatural since he was over 60, very comfortably circumstanced, and recently married to an ample young creature known to the irreverent as 'batter pudding'. The prospect of a foray to the Baltic would not, at the best of times, have appealed to him after years in the West Indies and the Mediterranean, and Nelson, for one, could detect in his chief no signs of eagerness for the assignment, or of any disposition towards bustle and stir.

Nelson had no prejudice against Parker, with whom he had served before, and he treated him with the outward deference suitable to age and seniority: but their ways were so different that if Nelson were not to become a cipher—and the notion was ridiculous—Parker would need to accept the fact that he must adapt himself to a man who, although 20 years his junior, knew how a fleet should be handled with aggression and success. Nelson wrote privately to Lord St Vincent:

> Our friend is a little nervous about dark nights and fields of ice, but we must brace up; these are not times for nervous systems. I want Peace, which is only to be had through, I trust, our still invincible Navy.

Parker's attitude to Nelson was, at first, one of extreme caution. He had too much sense to antagonise him, but he had the standards and the outlook of a different age, and beneath his courtesy he seems to have distrusted Nelson's ever-restless activity. Over the past centuries, the Royal Navy had intervened in Baltic affairs on more than one occasion, but it had never engaged in a full-scale fleet action within that sea, and the prospect of being the first admiral to conduct one can have had no appeal to Parker. Mere physical bravery could be taken for granted in a man of his training and antecedents. Strategic wisdom and tactical address were now required, together with a sense of timing.

While on his way to the rendezvous at Great Yarmouth, Nelson exchanged from the *San Josef* into the *St George*, which ten years later was to end her days wrecked on the coast of Jutland in a sensational marine disaster. At Spithead Nelson was joined by Lieutenant-Colonel the Hon. William Stewart, who was to be in charge of some 600 troops earmarked for service in Denmark to form landing parties. Stewart, a Rifleman, was still in his twenties, and he shared Nelson's passionate ardour for war and zeal for his country. As had been the case with Colonel Drinkwater before the Battle of St Vincent, Nelson struck up a friendship with this young soldier, and for his part Stewart, by recording anecdotes of Nelson which might otherwise have been lost to posterity, did him as good service as had Drinkwater.

A little later, a certain Commander Thesiger reported as a volunteer. He had served with distinction in the Russian navy during the wars of Catherine the Great (as had Nelson's old acquaintance James Trevenen of Turks Island), and Thesiger's knowledge of the Baltic was likely to be valuable. In Thesiger Nelson found yet another friend, and as his flag-captain was Hardy, there was a nucleus of officers who could scarcely fail to work notably together.

Parker needed stimulus even to leave Yarmouth, and it was largely as a result of an urgent—and private—appeal from Nelson that the Admiralty sent orders that the fleet should weigh at once. The admiral's mind had been on a ball on which his wife had set her heart, and he was not best pleased that he could not contrive to postpone departure later than 12 March, by which time Nelson was as ignorant of his intentions as he had been before he first called upon his senior to pay his respects.

The fleet included an imposing number of ships-of-the-line, of which Parker's *London* and Nelson's *St George* were three-deckers. The *Edgar, Bellona, Russell, Elephant, Ganges, Monarch, Defiance, Warrior, Defence, Saturn* and *Ramillies* were 74-gun ships, and the *Ardent, Glatton, Isis, Agamemnon, Polyphemus, Raisonnable* and *Veteran* were of 64 guns or of slightly less powerful armament. The frigates included the *Desirée, Amazon, Blanche, Alcmene, Arrow* and *Dart*, and there were bomb-vessels, sloops, cutters, schooners, gun-brigs, fire-ships and even luggers. A newly promoted rear-admiral, Thomas Graves, flew his flag in the *Defiance*, and if one thing was more certain than another, it was that Parker had never before been given mission or equipment approaching the present scale of importance.

Nelson would have noted with pleasure his very first ship, the *Raisonnable*, and the newly repaired *Agamemnon*, which he had made famous in the Mediterranean. Among the captains were many friends of standing such as Fremantle in the *Ganges*, Sir Thomas Thompson in the *Bellona*, and Foley in the *Elephant*. Bligh of the *Glatton* was the victim of the *Bounty* mutiny of 12 years earlier, and as such he is most often called to mind. In point of fact he was the strongest link between the Navy's greatest explorer, Captain James Cook, with whom he had served on Cook's second voyage of circumnavigation, and Nelson, the country's most famous tactician. Whatever his defects of temper, no one ever impugned Bligh's conduct as seaman or fighting officer, for his professional capabilities were exceptional. He wore the King's gold medal for services at the Battle of Camperdown, and Nelson was soon to learn his quality.

In the earlier stages of the sortie, Nelson was not much impressed by the discipline of the fleet. The ships, he noted in a private Journal:

> . . . keep very badly their stations, for although the Commander-in-Chief made the signal for close order of sailing, yet scarcely one have kept their stations and in particular the good going ships.

By 14 March he had had a note from Parker containing something of the admiral's intentions. A fairly well authenticated story gives the credit for at least some of this increased open-ness to a turbot. The fish had been caught by an officer of the *St George*, off the Dogger Bank, and was sent over to the *London* as an offering to Parker.

By 24 March, when the fleet was in the neighbourhood of Elsinore and therefore off the north entrance to the Sound between Denmark and Sweden, the frankness between the two principal officers had become such that Nelson felt able to send Parker a reasoned memorandum of his view of how the approaching operations should be conducted. It had now been made clear by messages delivered by Mr

Vansittart, a Foreign Office official who had been sent ahead to discover the immediate situation at Copenhagen, that Denmark would refuse to detach herself from the Armed Neutrality, and it was plain that a battle could not be avoided, if the expedition was to do its duty.

> . . . the more I have reflected [wrote Nelson], the more I am confirmed in opinion, that not a moment should be lost in attacking the Enemy: they will every day and hour be stronger; we never shall be so good a match for them as at this moment. The only consideration in my mind is how to get at them with the least risk to our Ships. . . . I am of opinion the boldest measures are the safest; and our Country demands a most vigorous exertion of her force, directed with judgment. In supporting you, my dear Sir Hyde, through the arduous and important task you have undertaken, no exertion of head or heart shall be wanting from your most obedient and faithful servant, *Nelson and Brontë.*

There were two ways by which Copenhagen could be approached; directly by way of the Sound, though with the certainty of fire from the batteries mounted at Kronborg Castle (the citadel of Elsinore and incidentally the castle of Hamlet); and possibly from the Swedish side as well, or indirectly, by way of the Belt, where the dangers would be those of navigation rather than of ordnance. On the whole, Nelson favoured the passage of the Sound. He had little personal acquaintance with the Baltic, not having sailed its waters since the days when he had commanded the *Albemarle*, but he knew the reputation of the Belt, which was always hazardous for larger vessels, and there was the added advantage in the case of the Sound that Parker was already at the entrance, and could make the assault on Copenhagen with little or no delay.

Parker, influenced perhaps by Vansittart's account of activity at Copenhagen, and by the views of the pilots, who were mainly seamen from the Baltic trade, unused to shot and shell, at first decided to proceed by the circuitous route of the Belt. Then, after the fleet had proceeded some little way along the coast of Zealand, he changed his mind. He brought the ships to, and sent for Nelson and Captain Murray of the *Edgar*, who knew the Baltic well. Murray was strong for the Sound, and so was Otway, flag-captain in the *London*. When the matter was put to Nelson he exclaimed: 'I don't care a damn by which passage we go, so that we fight them!'

Parker then saw fit to enter into negotiations with the Governor of Kronborg Castle, for he was still hoping against hope to settle matters without bloodshed, but the Governor replied that his orders were to fire on the British fleet if it began the passage of the Sound in strength, and came within reach of his cannon.

At last, early in the morning of 30 March, the wind being fair for the purpose, the fleet set sail direct for Copenhagen. As the *Monarch*, the leading vessel, drew abreast the Castle and hoisted her colours, a heavy fire opened from the Danish batteries, and six bomb-vessels, inshore of the rest, made reply. Most British ships-of-the-line, seeing that the Danish fire would be ineffective, spared their ammunition, the only casualties occurring in the *Isis*, the result of the bursting of a gun. Parker kept the fleet well away from the Danish shore, for the absence of fire from the Swedish side was a welcome surprise. It arose from various reasons, chief among them the general unpopularity of any course which aligned the country's policy with that of Russia, though for the sake of appearances the Swedish Government found it necessary to issue a statement that it had been agreed at conferences at St Petersburg to fix the point of defence at Drogden, which was further south. In point of fact, the batteries at Helsingborg, opposite Kronborg, mounted only eight guns of light calibre.

'More powder and shot, I believe, never was thrown away', wrote Nelson of the Danish bombardment. He himself had once more transferred his flag, this time to the *Elephant*, for the *St George* would be of too deep a draught for service in the 'home stroke' which he expected to deliver at Copenhagen. 'The *Elephant* did not return a single shot', he added. 'I hope to reserve them for a better occasion.'

2 The Order of Battle

Having passed Kronborg successfully, Parker anchored the fleet at about ten o'clock on the morning of 30 March in two lines between the islands of Ven and Amager. He then summoned a party to reconnoitre. This included himself, Nelson, Graves, the Captain of the Fleet, Dommett, and Colonel Stewart. The ship chosen to survey the area of attack was the frigate *Amazon*, Captain Riou, notable for discipline and smartness.

Copenhagen, part of whose residential and dockyard area extends to the nearby, pear-shaped Amager, had her northern approaches guarded by the formidable Trekroner batteries, named after the crowns of Denmark, Sweden and Norway. The twin forts, which were constructed on piles, mounted 30 24-pounder guns and 38 36-pounders, equal to the heaviest artillery carried in a ship's broadside.

Attack on the city from the south required a passage of the Outer Channel between the islands of Amager and Saltholm. That having been achieved, a change of wind was essential, in order to approach inshore by sailing along Amager's eastern side. The feat was rendered difficult by the presence of a shoal, called the Middle Ground, which lay between Amager and the Outer Channel.

If the natural hazards of navigation were considerable, the Danes had already made sure—for they had been given plenty of time—that nature's protection was reinforced in the stoutest way they could contrive. Moored near the Trekroner, in the harbour entrance, were the two-decker hulks *Elephanten* and *Mars*, and above them in the fairway were two 74-gun ships, a large frigate, and two 18-gun brigs, all rigged.

In a narrow channel between the shore and the sands of the Middle Ground lay a line, about one-and-a-half miles long, of 18 men-of-war, armed hulks and floating batteries, covering the east front of the city, and mounting over 600 guns. On shoals behind this line were a number of armed zebecs, while on the shore itself were covering batteries. All the buoys marking the shoals and the Middle Ground had been removed, and it was a sober party which attended the Commander-in-Chief at a Council of War which was called as soon as the survey was over.

Nelson disliked Councils of War. As he wrote later, and out of profound experience: 'If a man consults whether he is to fight, when he has the power in his own hands, *it is certain that his opinion is against fighting*.' The italics were Nelson's, and the dismal history of many eighteenth-century operations supported the view as realistic. His own bravery was extraordinary, but he knew that, in battle, it represented the victory of exaltation over self-preservation, and he knew, moreover, that many of his fellows lacked his vital fire. Never unreasonable, he was at all times prepared to work to a lower margin of safety than men of less combat seasoning than himself. His own view of the Danish defences was that although they looked daunting enough 'to those who are children at war', yet, to his judgment, 'with ten sail-of-the-line I think I can annihilate them; at all events, I hope to be allowed to try.'

As he stepped aboard the *London* for the Council, Nelson realised that a preliminary struggle was before him. It would be one of words. He would need to convince his fellow officers that an immediate attack was practicable; moreover, that it had a fair chance of success. The atmosphere was one of gloom, and that would have to be dispelled. Stewart is the best witness of what followed:

> During this Council [he wrote] the energy of Lord Nelson's character was remarked: certain difficulties had been started by some of the members, relative to each of the three Powers we should either have to engage, in succession or united, in those seas. The number of Russians was, in particular, represented as formidable. Lord Nelson kept pacing the cabin, mortified at everything which savoured either of alarm or irresolution. When the above remark was applied to the Swedes, he sharply observed, 'The more numerous the better'; and when to the Russians he repeatedly said; 'So much the better, I wish they were twice as many; the easier the victory, depend on it.' He alluded, as he afterwards explained in private, to the total want of tactique among the Northern Fleets; and to his intention, whenever he should bring either the Swedes or Russians to action, of attacking the head of their Line, and confusing their movements as much as possible. He used to say: 'Close with a Frenchman, but out-manœuvre a Russian.'

There could be no gainsaying such zeal, backed as it was by recent achievement, and Parker, with a spirit that did him honour, decided to leave Nelson a free hand for the arrangement of the close attack, and gave him 12 ships-of-the-line instead of the ten he had asked for. It was well that he did so, for in the event the wind which helped Nelson frustrated the Commander-in-Chief, whose own part, with the heavier ships, was to prevent any sortie by the enemy within Copenhagen harbour, and gradually to approach the Trekroner in the hope of silencing the fire.

The plan, the close attack from the south and the threat by Parker from the north, was as good as could be devised, but the more difficult role, that of Nelson and the ships of lighter draught, involved fighting of a sort which would have reminded those who had been at the Nile of the apparent strength of Brueys's position: but there were notable differences. For one thing, there was no getting inshore of the Danes, who had made careful and admirable dispositions, possessed great superiority in guns, and were arrayed in defence of their beloved capital, with all the resources of an arsenal-dockyard at call. There were those who continued to think that Nelson's optimism was misplaced, but nothing could shake it.

Nelson's force included his own ship the *Elephant*, in which Hardy of the *St George* was to serve as a volunteer, strengthening the resourceful Foley; there was the *Edgar*, a crack ship, Murray being a close friend, one day to become Nelson's chief of staff in

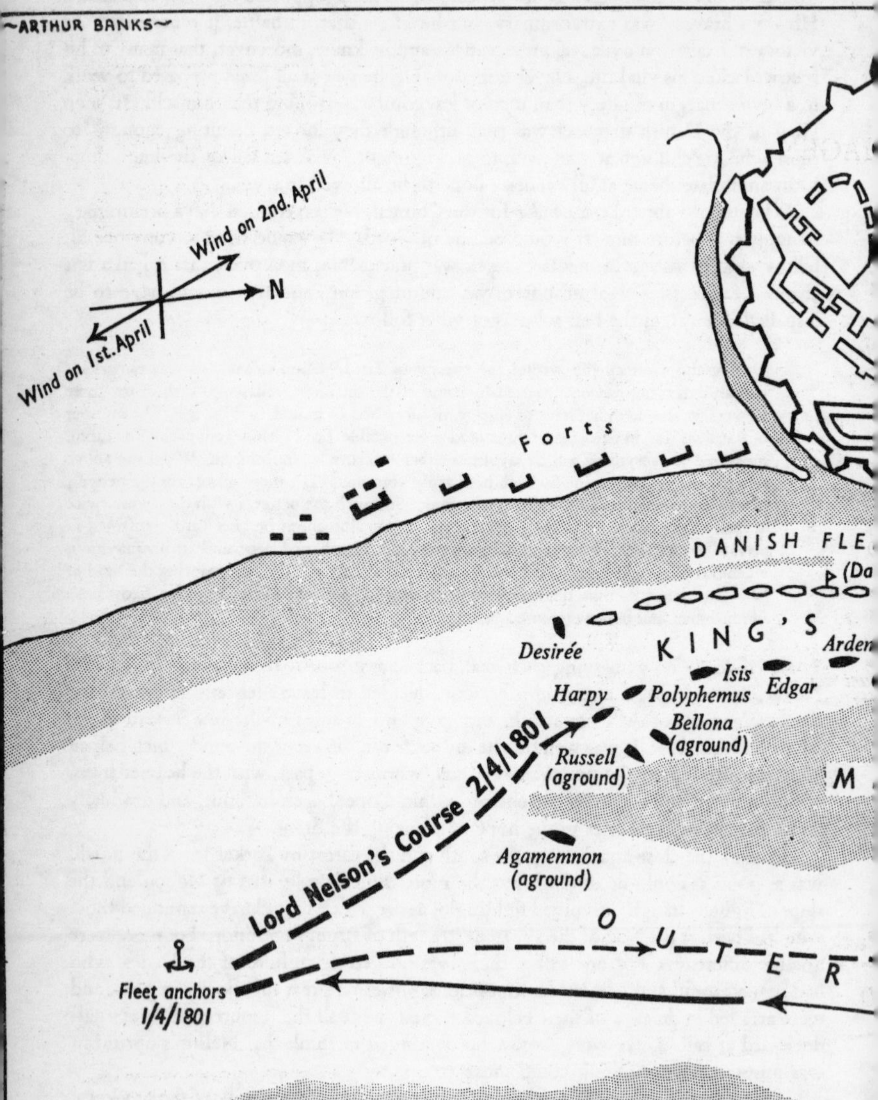

Wind on 2nd.April

N

Wind on 1st.April

Forts

DANISH FLE

(Da

Desirée

KING'S

Arden

Harpy   Isis   Edgar
Polyphemus

Bellona
(aground)

Russell
(aground)

M

Agamemnon
(aground)

Lord Nelson's Course 2/4/1801

O U T E R

Fleet anchors
1/4/1801

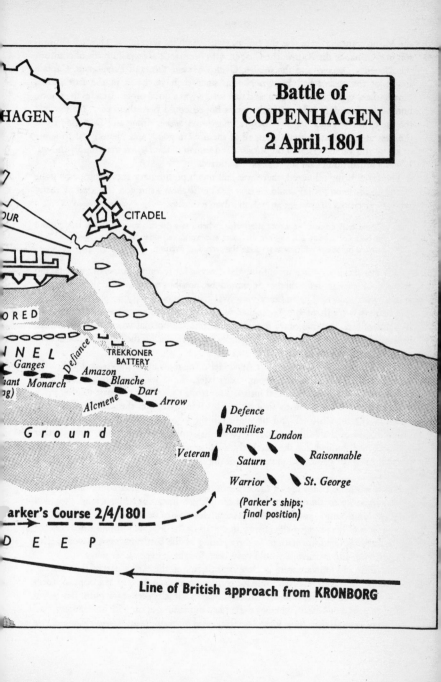

Battle of COPENHAGEN 2 April, 1801

HAGEN

CITADEL

OUR

ORED

NNEL

Ganges

Defiance

TREKRONER BATTERY

Amazon

hant Monarch
(ng)

Blanche

Dart

Alcmene

Arrow

Ground

Defence

Ramillies

London

Veteran

Saturn

Raisonnable

Warrior

St. George

(Parker's ships;
final position)

arker's Course 2/4/1801

DEEP

Line of British approach from KRONBORG

the Mediterranean; there was the *Bellona*, with the Nile veteran Sir Thomas Thompson in command; the *Russell*, the *Ganges*, with Fremantle always a source of comfort, the *Monarch*, *Defiance* and the smaller *Glatton*, *Ardent*, *Isis*, and *Polyphemus*. Captain Bertie of the *Ardent* had known Nelson since their boyhood in the East Indies. Finally there was the *Agamemnon*, and that surely was a good omen. Besides the sloops, bomb-vessels and fire-ships which it was hoped could play their part, Nelson had the use of the frigates *Amazon*, *Desirée*, *Blanche*, *Alcmene*, *Arrow* and *Dart*. Riou was the best of the frigate captains, but all of them were good, and Nelson was to come to know and value Sutton of the *Alcmene* and Inman of the *Desirée* very highly indeed. It was a squadron not far short of Nile standards.

The force being allocated, there was still much preliminary surveying to be done before operational orders could be issued. The *Elephant*'s surgeon was one of many who never ceased to wonder at Nelson's own exertions.

> I could only admire [he wrote afterwards] when I saw the first man in all the world spend the hours of the day and night in the boats, and wondered when the light showed me a path marked by buoys which was trackless the preceding evening.

Parker was also busy, once again using the *Amazon* for reconnaissance, this time taking artillery officers to see whether it would be possible to bombard the docks and arsenal with success. The military view was that it would only be practicable if the line of vessels south of the Trekroner were reduced and removed, not otherwise. In point of fact, contemporary accounts state that the normal work of the dockyard continued not only during the preliminaries but even during the height of the action, a tribute to Danish phlegm!

At 7 o'clock on the morning of 1 April Nelson again went in the *Amazon* to test the depths of the Outer Channel. Four hours later, the work completed, he went on board the *London* to receive final instructions from Parker. At half past two he made the signal to his squadron to weigh. Led by Riou's frigate, the ships passed safely down the Outer Channel, and by night fall the whole force was at anchor off the southern end of the Middle Ground, two miles from the Danish line. The weather had been well judged, for the northerly wind needed for the passage lasted just long enough, then dropped, and gave hope of the southerly breeze needed for the attack next day.

Hardy made splendid use of the first hours of darkness, under cover of which he rowed right up to the nearest ships of the Danish line, 'sounding round', recalled Stewart, 'and using a pole when he was apprehensive of being heard.' He found that the water was deeper near the enemy line than in the Middle Ground side. Had the pilots acted on this information, at the opening of the battle, no vessels would have run aground, and the action would have been fought at even closer range.

Fremantle and Stewart were in close consultation in the earlier part of the evening, for Fremantle was to be responsible for conveying a landing party of troops to storm the Trekroner, if the fire of the squadron should eventually silence the guns. Bertie had earlier enquired of Nelson whether the soldier and sailor got on with one another, and had been assured that they were 'perfect good friends'. The *Ardent*'s captain was also worried about his pilot, who was fidgeting about the depths of water, though as this was the Baltic there was not the added complication of tides. 'I will talk to him', said Nelson, 'but I do not much mind what they say.' His experience was that pilots were over-cautious. It was a quality necessary to their profession, but if Hawke had relied on the pilots at Quiberon, or Nelson considered their point of view at the Nile, two famous victories would never have been won.

How the rest of the night passed is once again best left to Colonel Stewart to describe, for he was there, and aglow at all he saw.

> As soon as the Fleet was at anchor, the gallant Nelson sat down to table with a large party of his comrades in arms. He was in the highest spirits, and drank to a leading wind, and to the success of the ensuing day. Captains Foley, Hardy, Fremantle, Riou, Inman, Admiral Graves and a few others to whom he was particularly attached, were of this interesting party; from which every man separated with feelings of admiration for their great leader, and with anxious impatience to follow him to the approaching Battle.
>
> The Signal to prepare for Action had been made early in the evening. All the captains retired to their respective Ships, Riou excepted, who with Lord Nelson and Foley arranged the Order of Battle, and those instructions that were to be issued to each Ship on the succeeding day.
>
> From the previous fatigue of this day, and of the two preceding, Lord Nelson was so much exhausted while dictating his instructions, that it was recommended to him by us all, and indeed, insisted upon by his old servant, Allen, who assumed much command on these occasions, that he should go to his cot. It was placed on the floor, but from it he still continued to dictate.
>
> The orders were completed about one o'clock, when half a dozen Clerks in the foremost cabin proceeded to transcribe them. Lord Nelson's impatience again showed itself; for instead of sleeping undisturbedly, as he might have done, he was every half hour calling from his cot to these Clerks to hasten their work, for that the wind was becoming fair: he was constantly receiving a report of this during the night. The work being finished about six in the morning, his Lordship, who was previously up and dressed, breakfasted, and about seven made the Signal for all captains. The instructions were delivered to each by eight o'clock; and a special command was given to Captain Riou to act as circumstances might require.

Of the many scenes before battle, extending back to Shakespeare's version of Henry at Agincourt, this is one of the most famous, and not the least characteristic. Nelson's exaltation had already begun. It was this time to continue not only through the action, when he exclaimed: 'It is warm work, and this day may be the last to us at any moment. But mark you! I would not be elsewhere for thousands', but in the taxing negotiations and change in command which followed. 'Joyous, animated, elevated and delighted'—that was how Southey described him on active service, for Nelson added to his valour and energy the magic power, not given to all great captains, of 'electrifying all within his atmosphere.' Stewart himself was proof enough of the truth of these sentences: and as Mahan remarked of the 'heaven-born' admiral: 'It was characteristic that the wind which had been fair the day before to take him south, changed by the hour of battle to fair to take him north: but it is only just to notice also that he himself never trifled with a fair wind, or with time.'

3 Events of the Action

Nelson's method of attack was on the lines of that which he had employed in Aboukir Bay. The part of the Danish line least easily reinforced was to be overwhelmed first. The leading ship, on reaching her allotted berth, was to anchor by the stern. The succeeding ship would pass close along her disengaged side, and anchor in the next berth, and the procedure would continue until the last ship had taken up the farthest berth. The plan was in essence simple, but this was war, and accidents were to be expected: moreover, the time allowed between the receipt of the operational orders and that of their execution must have been the briefest on record for an attack of such intricacy and hazard.

The leading ship, the *Edgar*, was to anchor abreast No. 5 in the Danish line, the two-decker *Jylland*; the *Ardent* was to pass the *Edgar* and anchor abreast the Danish Nos. 6 and 7, the frigate *Kronborg* and a masking floating battery. Bligh's *Glatton* would come-to abreast the large *Dannebrog*, the flagship of the Danish Commodore Fischer. The *Isis* would be abreast of No. 2, a two-decker without masts, and the *Agamemnon* abreast No. 1, the *Proevesteen*. They were to fire in passing to their stations.

The frigate *Desirée* was to follow the *Agamemnon* and to rake No. 2. The remaining ships were to follow in the order *Bellona*, *Elephant*, *Ganges*, *Monarch*, *Defiance*, *Russell* and *Polyphemus*. When the first four Danish ships had been subdued, which was expected to occur early in the day, the *Isis* and *Agamemnon* were to cut their cables, make sail, and take station at the north end of the line, where they would be under fire from the Trekroner, but might expect support from Parker's detachment. The rest of the frigates, sloops and fire-ships were to proceed under Riou's orders, and if all went brilliantly, there might be a chance for Stewart to use his soldiers.

Between eight and nine o'clock on the morning of 2 April, the pilots and masters were summoned to the *Elephant*, when Nelson noticed—without surprise—a degree of hesitation which would have alarmed a less resolute officer. There was doubt about the precise bearing of the west end of the Middle Ground, and about the exact line of deep water in the King's Channel, where the Danish ships were moored, and along which the British would approach. Not a moment was to be lost; the wind was fair, and the signal made for action. At length Mr Briarly, master of the *Bellona*, declared himself ready to lead the squadron in, and others quickly followed his example in zeal. Nelson wrote afterwards, with a touch of asperity: 'I experienced the misery of having the honour of our country entrusted to a set of pilots who had no other thought than to keep the ships clear of danger, and their own silly heads clear of shot.' He was less than fair, as events were soon to show.

The wind had at first been east by south, but by nine o'clock it had veered to south by east, as fair as it could be for the Channel, but likely to carry the smoke of the broadsides of each ship, as she anchored, across the field of view of her next astern. At 9.45 the signal was made to weigh in succession, and the *Edgar* proceeded 'in a noble manner' for the Channel, to the cheers of her consorts. At about the same time the *Defence*, *Ramillies* and *Veteran* of Parker's division weighed and began to beat up towards the Trekroner, to menace the northern end of the enemy line, and to assist disabled ships of Nelson's force if they were beaten from their stations. Within a few minutes the *Proevesteen* had fired her first broadside at Murray's ship, but it was not until eleven o'clock that the *Edgar* was at her berth abreast the *Jylland*, with her guns going full blast. By that time the *Ardent* had opened fire, passed between the *Edgar* and the Danish batteries and anchored ahead of her. The *Glatton* followed, anchoring with Bligh's usual efficiency and precision one cable's length from the *Dannebrog*.

Trouble began when the *Agamemnon* failed to weather the end of the Middle Ground. Warned by a signal of her danger from the *Elephant* she anchored, and tried all day to warp to windward, but without success, owing to the strength of the current. Her situation was the same as that of the *Culloden* at the Nile, and Fancourt, her captain, was as maddened by the event as Troubridge had been three years earlier. The *Isis* took her station. Nelson then ordered the *Polyphemus*, which should have had the northern berth, to place herself astern of the *Isis*. At 11.20 she ran in and anchored abreast of the *Proevesteen*. The *Desirée* placed herself across the bows of the Danish three-decker, and lay there raking her, much as the *Leander* had done with larger French units at the Nile.

The next ship to proceed up the Channel was the *Bellona*, of whose captain Nelson expected much. As Thompson passed the *Isis* he gave the order to open fire, but almost at once found himself aground. The master and the pilot kept too much to starboard. The *Bellona* could use some of her guns, but already Nelson's effective force was reduced to ten, the number with which he believed he could succeed. The admiral himself was close behind his friend. He had already made the *Bellona*'s signal to engage more closely, and now in his desire for a 'home stroke' he kept to port and passed on in safety. The *Elephant* anchored in the berth the *Bellona* should have occupied, just ahead of the *Glatton* and also abreast the *Dannebrog*, which was the most appropriate place.

The distance between the ships at this point was 'nearly a cable's length' but 200 yards was not near enough for Nelson. He could not however persuade his own pilot and master, who dreaded shoaling their water on the port side, to move the ship, and the anchor was dropped. Fremantle in the *Ganges* was close behind, conning the ship himself, for his master had already been killed and his pilot had lost an arm. Nelson himself hailed him when to let go his anchor, close ahead of the flagship.

The *Russell* should have followed the *Defiance*, with Graves aboard, but in complying with the general signal at 10.40 a.m. to make more sail, she got ahead of station, lost touch with her leader in the smoke, and seeing a ship's masthead with which she was coming up fast, lowered her topsails on the cap. She ceased fire on another ship passing, the smoke cleared, and she found herself hard and fast aground astern of the *Bellona*, and tried in vain to heave herself off. At 11.30 she re-opened fire, but already Nelson was one ship short of his requirements.

It was the *Monarch*, Captain Mosse, which had the toughest usage among the British ships, playing a similar part to the *Bellerophon* at the Nile, but facing a fixed battery instead of a French three-decker. Observing the *Russell*'s predicament, Mosse reserved his first broadside till the *Monarch* came up with her, a gesture for which he was rewarded by the cheers of the stranded ship's company. Mosse continued firing all the way down the line, gave Nelson three hearty cheers, and passed on. He did not anchor immediately ahead of the *Ganges*, owing to the absence of the *Bellona* and the *Russell*, and the new berth of the *Polyphemus*, but proceeded north until he was within range of the Trekroner, and then moored head and stern abreast the Danish No. 13, the unrigged two-decker *Sjaelland*. Mosse himself was killed soon after his ship was in position.

At 11.30 the *Defiance*, last of the line, let go her stern anchors with a spring on, abreast the Trekroner, which damaged her main and mizzen and split her bowsprit with the first salvo. Finally Riou led the *Amazon*, *Blanche*, *Alcmene*, *Dart* and *Arrow* past Graves's flagship, and anchored in the berth which should have been taken by the *Polyphemus*, engaging the Trekroner. It was an action typical of Riou. Nelson had given him a free hand, and he had placed his frigate in the forefront of the battle. Towards midday two of the bomb-vessels, the *Discovery and Explosion*, reached a station abreast the *Elephant* and opened fire with their mortars, first on the enemy ships and later on the dockyard. Other small vessels went to the help of the ships aground.

It was clear from the outset that the Danes would fight stoutly, under the immediate eye of the Prince Royal, who took up a position near one of the shore batteries. As men fell at the guns, they were replaced by volunteers, many of whom had known nothing of weapons a fortnight earlier. A small floating battery, commanded by a lad of 17 called Willemoes, got under the stern of the *Elephant*, and fought his guns, despite a heavy fire from small arms, almost until the end of the action. The *Proevesteen* and the *Valkyrien* held out so long, contrary to Nelson's expectations, that the *Isis* and *Polyphemus* were never able to shift their berths.

The *Glatton*, with a special armament of carronades, set the *Dannebrog* alight, and about noon, in consequence of this, the Danish Commodore shifted his pendant to the *Holsteen*. Captain Thura, of the *Indfodstratten*, No. 17 in the Danish line, fell early in the action, and all his officers, except one lieutenant and one marine officer, were either killed or wounded. In the confusion of the day, the colours were either struck or shot away, but the ship was moored athwart one of the batteries in such a way that the British made no attempt to board, and a boat was sent to the Prince to inform him of her situation. He turned to those about him and said: 'Thura is killed: which of you will take the command?' Schroedersee, an officer who had recently resigned on account of ill health, answered at once that he would do so, and went aboard, but he was soon a casualty himself, and a lieutenant who had gone to the *Indfodstratten* with him continued to fight the ship.

Now that by accident and hazard Nelson had been robbed of a quarter of his force, tension rose, and an incident occurred which illustrates his frame of mind. A lieutenant who had reported the grounding of the *Bellona* and *Russell* was sharply reprimanded by Captain Foley, not for the information but for the way in which he conveyed it. Nelson supported his flag-captain in no uncertain terms. 'I think', he said, 'at such a moment the delivery of anything like a desponding opinion, unasked, was highly reprehensible.' No one knew better the value of morale, and the speed at which, in time of acute crisis, it could be weakened. He remembered the salutary example of Jervis before the Battle of St Vincent, who, when more and still more Spanish ships were reported to be in sight, cut the reports short with: 'Enough, Sir, no more of that. The die is cast, and if there are 50 sail I will go through them!'

At 1.30 p.m. when the action had been in progress for over three hours, and was still in full fury, there occurred one of the most astounding incidents in the history of naval warfare. Parker hoisted the signal—'Discontinue the engagement.' It was a decision, based upon imperfect knowledge, for which there was no excuse valid by any rules known to the tactician. It could have led to disgrace and disaster, and it resulted in the loss of Captain Riou. That the consequences were no worse was due to an act of disobedience on Nelson's part as sublime in its courage and assurance as the way he had turned out of the line at St Vincent.

The episode in Jervis's action might have been interpreted as intelligent anticipation, or as what the Commander-in-Chief himself might have done had he been in Nelson's place. The justification for Nelson's action at Copenhagen was that he, not Parker, was at the point of contact, and that he knew the Danes were weakening, despite appearances from Parker's distance away. Added to this was the fact that if the signal was obeyed, every ship, in attempting to rejoin the heavier units in the north, would have to run the gauntlet of the Trekroner, and besides the whole Baltic mission would have been in ruins. Rear-Admiral Graves wrote afterwards to his brother: 'If we had discontinued the action before the enemy struck, we should have all got aground and been destroyed.'

Parker's motives were understandable, but they were not those of a resolute man. At the time, the *London* was about four miles to leeward, beating against an unfavourable wind. Parker could see through his glass that two big ships were aground, and the *Agamemnon* hopelessly out of range, while the Trekroner was bombarding Riou's lightly armed frigates. He had been in an agony of suspense for some time, but Dommet, the Captain of the Fleet, had begged him to postpone the message.

> I will make the signal of recall for Nelson's sake [Parker said at last]. If he is in a condition to continue the action successfully, he will disregard it; if he is not, it will be an excuse for his retreat, and no blame can be imputed to him.
>
> [Later he added] The fire is too hot for Nelson to oppose. A retreat must be made. I am aware of the consequences for my own personal reputation, but it would be cowardly to leave Nelson to bear the whole shame of the failure, if shame it should be deemed.

But the signal was *not* in fact permissive, as the result soon showed, and to place the onus of disobedience on Nelson's shoulders, while it did credit to Parker's knowledge of his subordinate's nature, made no allowance for the fact that it would be read, and acted upon, by the ships at the northern end of Nelson's line. That led to Riou's tragedy.

In point of fact Otway, the flag-captain in the *London*, who agreed with Dommet that such a signal would be misguided, received permission from Parker to make his way by boat to the *Elephant*, with verbal authority from Parker to say that the battle should continue if Nelson saw there was a probability of success, but before Otway could reach Nelson through the shot, Parker, deciding that he could bear the anxiety no more, flew the signal. His was the despondent lieutenant's fault writ large.

Riou in the *Amazon* obeyed at once, and was killed as he turned his ship. The frigate captain, said Stewart:

> ... was sitting on a gun, encouraging his men, when the *Amazon* showed her stern to the Trekroner, and had already been wounded in the head by a splinter. He had expressed himself grieved at being thus obliged to retreat, and nobly observed: 'What will Nelson think of us?' His Clerk was killed by his side, and by another shot, several of the Marines, while hauling on the main-brace, shared the same fate. Riou then exclaimed: 'Come, then, my boys, let us die all together!' The words were scarcely uttered, when the fatal shot severed him in two. Thus, and in an instant, was the British service deprived of one its greatest ornaments, and society of a character of singular worth, resembling the heroes of romance.

Graves in the *Defiance* saw the signal and had to repeat it, but declared that all the halyards had been shot away except that at the cross-jack yard. He hoisted it there, where (since the driver was set) he thought Nelson could not possibly see it. Nor did he cut his cable.

For what happened in the *Elephant*, Stewart is once more the best witness, Nelson, as if expecting some such move, had already said sharply to one of the officers: 'Mr Langford, I told you to look out on the Danish Commodore, and let me know when he surrendered. Keep your eye fixed on *him*.' Presently, the truth became known. Nelson, said Stewart:

> ... continued his walk, and did not appear to take notice of the signal. The Lieutenant meeting his Lordship at the next turn asked 'whether he should repeat it?' Lord Nelson answered, 'No, acknowledge it.' On the Officer returning to the poop, his Lordship called after him, 'Is No. 16 [for close action] still hoisted?'. The Lieutenant answering in the affirmative, Lord Nelson said: 'Mind you keep it so.'
>
> He now walked the deck considerably agitated, which was always known by his moving the stump of his right arm. After a turn or two, he said to me in a quick manner: 'Do you know what's shown on board of the Commander-in-Chief—No. 39.' On asking him what that meant he answered: 'Why, to leave off Action.' 'Leave off action!' he repeated, and then added, with a shrug, 'Now, damn me if I do.' He also observed, I believe to Captain Foley: 'You know, Foley, I have only one eye. I have a right to be blind sometimes', and then, with an archness peculiar to his character, putting the glass to his blind eye, he exclaimed: 'I really do not see the Signal!' This remarkable Signal was, therefore, only acknowledged on board the *Elephant*, not repeated.

It was about the time Parker's signal was flown that the Danish fire began at last to slacken. At two o'clock the floating battery *Nyborg*, No. 4 on their line, cut her cables, and ran for harbour in a sinking state. She tried to take No. 12 in tow, the *Aggershuus*, but both foundered. Then No. 18, the frigate *Hjaelperen*, took the same course, and got away. Half an hour later, the resistance of nearly all the Danish units had come to an end. Though their doughty qualities, the absence from his own line of the *Agamemnon*, *Bellona* and *Russell*, and the delay by wind and current of the *Defence*, *Ramillies* and *Veteran* from Parker's division, had so far prevented Nelson from sending troops to storm the Trekroner, the conditions which the artillery officers had said were

32 *The Battle of Copenhagen*
From an engraving by I. F. Clemens after C. A. Lorentzen

33 The old mast-house at Copenhagen
(*shown above*), as it appears today

34 Danish commanders at the Battle of Copenhagen
From a lithograph by Em Baerentzen & Co.

necessary to enable the bomb-vessels to attack the dockyard and arsenal had almost been fulfilled.

But as the British boats approached to take possession of ships which had struck, or to pick men up out of the water, they were fired upon by the shore batteries, and sometimes from the vessels themselves, either from ignorance of the customs of war, or from a not unnatural confusion. In consequence, the *Elephant* and *Glatton*, whose broadsides were temporarily stilled, were obliged to open fire once more on the *Dannebrog* and other vessels. In a few minutes the Danish flagship was a shambles, and, on the smoke clearing away, she was seen to be drifting helplessly before the wind. About 4.30 she blew up, taking many good men with her.

Seeing ships still firing, though obviously crippled and almost useless, Nelson said that he must either send on shore to stop such unfortunate proceedings, or summon fire-ships to burn them, an action for which he had no taste. The day was his, and he had no wish for the loss of a single unnecessary life.

Going aft to the rudder-head casing, he wrote a note to the Prince Royal, to be taken ashore under flag of truce by Commander Thesiger. This read as follows:

> *To the Brothers of Englishmen, the Danes:*
>
> Lord Nelson has directions to spare Denmark, when no longer resisting; but if the firing is continued on the part of Denmark, Lord Nelson will be obliged to set on fire all the Floating-batteries he has taken, without having the power of saving the brave Danes who have defended them. Dated on board his Britannic Majesty's Ship *Elephant*, Copenhagen Roads, 2 April 1801.
>
> NELSON AND BRONTË, Vice-Admiral, under the Command of Admiral Sir Hyde Parker.

This note was copied, as Nelson wrote it, by Mr. Thomas Wallis, the *Elephant*'s purser, who stood beside him. Mr Wallis's account of the incident is graphic and circumstantial:

> The original was put into an envelope, and sealed with Lord Nelson's Arms. At first I was going to seal it with a wafer, but he would not allow this to be done, observing that it must be sealed, or the Enemy would think it was written and sent in a hurry. The man who went below for a light never returned, having been killed on the way.

'The wax', said Nelson, 'told no tales', and at a little after three o'clock the Danish Adjutant-General, Lindholm, returning with a flag of truce, directed all fire, including that of the still active Trekroner, to be suspended, Stewart reckoned that substantial firing had continued for no less than five hours, 'four of which were warmly contested'. The Prince Royal, in his reply, enquired more minutely into the purport of the message, and was given an answer as follows:

> Lord Nelson's object in sending the Flag of Truce was humanity; he therefore consents that hostilities shall cease, and that the wounded Danes may be taken on shore. And Lord Nelson will take his prisoners out of the Vessels, and burn and carry off his prizes as he shall think fit.

> Lord Nelson, with humble duty to His Royal Highness the Prince of Denmark, will consider this the greatest victory he has ever gained, if it may be the cause of a happy reconciliation and union between his own most gracious Sovereign, and His Majesty the King of Denmark.

Fremantle had been summoned to the *Elephant* from the *Ganges*, and was in no shadow of doubt as to the wisdom, as well as the humanity, of Nelson's proceedings. It was only two days later that he wrote to his wife:

> Every merit is due to Lord Nelson for his policy as well as bravery on this occasion: as soon as the ships abreast of the *Elephant* and *Ganges* had struck, he hailed and desired I would come on board. I found him talking to some Danes in his cabin, and telling them how he longed to see the Russians down; at the same time he was sending an officer with a flag of truce on shore to tell the Prince that if he did not cease firing from the batteries he should be under the necessity of burning all the ships with the people in them. This produced a cessation to the very severe battle, which was certainly as convenient for *us* as the Enemy, as we had several ships on shore and most of the Ships engaged crippled so completely that it was with difficulty they could sail out.

The difficulties in which the British still found themselves were not exaggerated by Fremantle, for no sooner had Lindholm gone off to the *London*, to confirm the truce with Parker, than the *Monarch*, in attempting to weigh, hit a shoal, but was pushed over it by the *Ganges* taking her amidships. The *Glatton* got clear, but the *Defiance* and the *Elephant* also went aground, where they remained until nightfall. Nelson followed Lindholm to Parker, 'low in spirits at the surrounding scene', said Stewart, and saying: 'Well! I have fought contrary to orders, and I shall perhaps be hanged: never mind, let them.'

It is scarcely necessary to say that Nelson's reception by Parker was as enthusiastic as were the congratulations he had received from Jervis after St Vincent. The difference was that whereas, at St Vincent, Nelson knew perfectly well that he could leave the aftermath to his Chief, and to the other senior officers engaged, he had no such consolations with regard to Parker. If he knew anything of his present Chief, the 'follow up', the gathering of the harvest of the battle and the slaughter, would be left to an already weary man, or nothing effective would be done. Nelson's activity immediately after Copenhagen is as astonishing as anything in his career, and proves, if proof were necessary, that he never allowed himself to forget that a battle was not an end in itself, but a furtherance of policy. There is Fremantle's evidence that even before the smoke had cleared, he was thinking of the Russians, just as he had thought of India the moment he had won the Nile. It would be over-straining sympathy to a kindly and generous-minded man to believe that Parker was as eager in pursuit of the greater objects of his mission.

The cost of the action in life and limb was very heavy. Casualty figures for the greater actions of the period vary considerably, but those accepted by Professor Michael Lewis in his *A Social History of the Navy* are, on the British side, 253 killed and 688 wounded, and on the Danish, 790 killed and 910 wounded. Only at the Glorious First of June and at Trafalgar was a higher toll taken from the victors, and, as was always his way, Nelson's first thoughts were for the wounded, whom he visited wherever he could: there was nothing to be done for the dead, except to honour their memory and see that their sacrifice was not wasted.

According to Robert Southey, whose brother Tom was a lieutenant in the *Bellona* and who, when he came to write his life of Nelson, relied on Tom for details of Copenhagen, some of the slaughter was unnecessary, particularly among the troops not directly under Stewart's eye. It had been the mark of a considerate commander, at least since the time of Howe's Relief of Gibraltar during the War of American Independence, to order sailors to lie down when not actually on duty at the guns or otherwise, though the practice had not become universal even by the time of Trafalgar.

> The commanding officer of the troops on board one of our ships [wrote Southey] asked where his men should be stationed. He was told that they could be of no use; that they were not near enough for musquetry, and were not wanted at the guns; they had, therefore, better go below. This, he said, was impossible, it would be a disgrace that could never be wiped out. They were, therefore, drawn up upon the gangway, to satisfy this cruel point of honour; and there, without the possibility of annoying the enemy, they were mowed down.

The troops concerned were detachments of the Rifle Brigade and what later became the Royal Berkshire Regiment, both of which have the battle inscribed on their Colour.

Tom Southey, who supplied what details he remembered to his literary brother, was himself wounded during the action, and the experience of the *Bellona* was doubly unfortunate, since not only did she fail to reach her berth, but she suffered, as the *Isis* had done off Kronborg, from the bursting of some of her guns. She was one of the oldest ships present, having been afloat since 1760, and her cannon were, in some cases, honeycombed with air pockets, the result of faulty workmanship on the part of the ironmaster who cast them.

Briarly, the ship's master, returned to the *Bellona* after offering to lead the fleet in. He was an enterprising man, and he had been master of the *Audacious* at the Nile. His description of the *Bellona*'s misfortunes is typical of the matter-of-fact way in which master's logs and journals recorded incidents which laymen would have been tempted to embroider.

> At $\frac{1}{2}$ past 11 the Captain, standing on the 3rd gun on the quarter-deck, received a shot which took off his left leg. He was carried off the deck, and the 1st Lieutenant, by his directions, took the command . . . At 2, the fourth gun on the lower deck burst, by which there were several men killed and wounded, among the latter two lieutenants and two midshipmen; one of the main-deck beams broke, and part of the main-deck gangway blown up. At 3, the 14th gun on the lower deck burst, by which several men were killed and wounded, a great part of the main deck blown up, and 3 of the main-deck guns disabled aloft and 2 forward.

There is evidence in Southey's letters to his brother that the *Bellona*'s men were well aware of the state of their ordnance, and fully expected such accidents to happen.

Poor Thompson suffered dreadfully. 'For myself,' he wrote three weeks after the action, 'I am lain down, having patiently to wait my cure or dissolution as it shall please God. I am now totally disabled and my career is run through, only at the age of

35.' Nelson had visited him with Fremantle on 4 April, and Fremantle had then, so he told his wife:

> . . . been desired by Sir Hyde Parker to take on the care of removing poor Sir Thomas from his ship to the *Isis*, in which he is to go home; figure to yourself removing a poor man, whose leg is just amputated, from the side of one ship and having him hauled up the side of another, his agonies were great, and it brought to my recollection what I once suffered, and the never ceasing attention you showed me. . . .

Fremantle was thinking of the days in the *Seahorse* after the failure at Teneriffe. 'Thompson', he added, 'is very ill, if anything can support him it is his spirits which are very good.' His spirits saved Thompson's life. He survived for another 26 years, was made a Baronet in 1806, and became Member of Parliament for Rochester.

Rear-Admiral Graves, whom Nelson had expected to be made a Baronet, and who was in fact given the star of the Bath instead, sent off a rousing letter to his brother the very day after the engagement.

> I am told [he said] the Battle of the Nile was nothing to this. I am happy that my Flag was not a month hoisted before I got into action, and into the hottest one that has happened the whole of the war. Considering the disadvantages of navigation, the approach to the enemy, their vast number of guns and mortars on both land and sea, I do not think there ever was a bolder attack . . . In short, it was worthy of our gallant and enterprising little Hero of the Nile. Nothing can exceed his spirit. . . .
>
> Lord Nelson sent for me at the close of the action, and it was beautiful to see how the shot beat the water all round us in the boat.

From the *Monarch*, and from the pen of one of her midshipmen, Millard, came one of the most circumstantial narratives of what occurred in a ship, nearly as old as the *Bellona*—she had been launched on the day of George III's accession in 1760—which suffered more severely than any other British ship in Nelson's line. Millard had a long day.

> The hammocks were piped up at six [he wrote], but having had the middle watch I indulged myself with another nap, from which I was roused by the drum beating to quarters. I bustled on deck, examined the guns under my directions, saw them provided with handspikes, spare breechings, tackles etc., and reported accordingly. . . . As the gunner's cabin, where I usually messed, was all cleared away, I went into the starboard cockpit berth, where I found one of the pilots that had been sounding the night before. He told us that they had pulled so near the enemy's ships as to hear the sentinels conversing, but returned without being discovered.
>
> Our repast, it may fairly be supposed, under these circumstances was a slight one. When we left the berth, we had to pass all the dreadful preparations of the surgeons. One table was covered with instruments of all shapes and sizes, another, of more than usual strength, was placed in the middle of the cockpit. As I had never seen this produced before, I could not help asking the use of it, and received the answer 'that it was to cut off legs and wings upon'. One of the surgeon's men (called Loblolly Boys) was spreading yards and yards of bandages, about six inches wide.

The midshipman was greatly impressed by the spectacle of the approach to battle by the ships-of-the-line: 'a more beautiful and solemn one I never witnessed', he said:

A man-of-war under sail is at all times a beautiful object, but at such a time the scene is heightened beyond the powers of description . . . our minds were deeply impressed with awe, and not a word was spoken throughout the ship but by the pilot and the helmsman, and their communications being chanted very much in the same manner as the responses in our cathedral service, and repeated at intervals, added very much to the solemnity.

When the *Monarch* took up her station, Millard saw Captain Mosse on the poop, his 'card of instructions'—Nelson's Orders—in his left hand, and in his right a speaking trumpet. Millard then went to his place of duty at the aftermost guns, and within a few minutes, Mosse had been killed.

Lieutenant-Colonel Hutchinson, who was in charge of the troops carried in the ship, suggested that the captain's body should not be taken below, as it would damp the spirits of the men. It was therefore placed in the stern-walk, covered by a flag.

At the guns, said Millard, he pulled off his coat, helped to run out the pieces:

> . . . and literally worked as hard as a dray horse. Every gun was at first supplied with a portion of shot, wadding etc., close by it, and when these were expended, we applied to a reserved place by the main-mast. It immediately occurred to me that I could not be more usefully employed than conveying this supply, which would enable the stronger ones to remain at their guns, for the men wanted no stimulus to keep them to their duty, nor any direction how to perform it. The only cautions I remember to have given were hinted to me by the Gunner before the action—viz., to worm the guns frequently, that no fire might remain from the old cartridge, to fire two round-shot in each gun, and to use nothing else while round-shot was to be had.
>
> As I was returning from the main-mast, and was abreast of the little binnacle, a shot came in at the port under the poop ladder, and carried away the wheel, and three out of the four men stationed at it were either killed or wounded, besides one or two at the guns.

The officers with the troops were naturally eager for employment, though they found little enough. One of them, a Lieutenant Dennis:

> . . . had just come up the companion ladder, and was going aft, when splinters shattered his sword, which was in the sheath, into three pieces, and tore off the finger ends of his left hand. This, however, he scarcely seemed aware of, for, lifting up the sheath with his bloody fingers, he called out: 'Look here, Colonel!' On being reminded by Colonel Hutchinson of his wounded hand, he twisted his handkerchief round it, and set up a huzza, which was soon repeated throughout the ship. Dennis, though he could not act against the enemy, found means to make himself useful; he flew through every part of the ship, and when he found any of his men wounded, carried him in his arms down to the cockpit. When the carnage was greatest he encouraged his men by applauding their conduct, and he frequently began a huzza, which is of more importance than might be imagined, for the men have no other communication throughout the ship, but know when a shout is set up, it runs from deck to deck, and that their comrades are, some of them, in good spirits.

Dennis had in fact discovered a cardinal principle in keeping up morale, and had he been in the *Elephant* he would certainly have been applauded by Nelson. For his part Colonel Hutchinson, seeing no immediate prospect of being ordered away under Stewart to storm the Trekroner:

> . . . begged I would employ him if I thought he could do any good. I was at that time seated on deck, cutting the wads asunder for the guns, and the Colonel, notwithstanding the

danger attending his uniform breeches, sat himself down and went to work very busily. Indeed, afterwards I was often obliged to leave the charge of my guns to the Colonel, for I was now the only midshipman left upon the deck, and was therefore employed by Mr Yelland, the commanding officer, as his aide-de-camp, and dispatched occasionally into all parts of the ship. On my return, the Colonel made his report of what had passed in my absence.

Millard himself escaped fairly lightly. Two other midshipman had had to go below with bad splinter wounds, and then his own turn came.

> When the wheel was shot away [he said], I was in a cloud, but being some little distance away, I did not receive any of the larger pieces. When I passed backwards and forwards between my quarters and the main-mast, I went on the opposite side to that which was engaged, and by that means probably escaped a severe wound, for as I was returning with two shot in one hand and a cheese (or packet) of wads in the other, I received a pretty smart blow on my right cheek.
> I dropped my shot, just as a monkey does a hot potato, and clapped my hand to the place, which I found rather bloody, and immediately ran aft to get my handkerchief out of my coat pocket. My friend Colonel Hutchinson came to me immediately . . . and seemed really afraid lest my jaw was broken; however, after having felt it and found it all right, he let me return for my burden.

Later still, Millard had to go to the main-deck on some errand. There he found:

> . . . not a single man standing the whole way from the main-mast forward, a district containing eight guns on a side, some of which were run out ready for firing; others lay dismounted, and yet others remained as they were after recoiling. . . . I hastened down the fore-ladder to the lower deck, and felt really relieved to find somebody alive; from thence I reached the fore cockpit, where I was obliged to wait a few minutes for my cargo, and after this pause, I own I felt something like regret, if not fear, as I mounted the ladder on my return. This, however, entirely subsided when I saw the sun shining and the old blue ensign flying as lofty as ever. I never felt the genuine sense of glory so completely as at that moment, and if I had seen anyone attempt to haul that ensign down, I could have run aft and shot him dead in as determined a manner as the celebrated Paul Jones. I took off my hat by an involuntary motion, and gave three cheers as I jumped on to the quarter-deck.

The blue ensign was flying by reason of the fact that Nelson, commander of the squadron, was at that time a Vice-Admiral of the Blue, and Millard's reference to 'the celebrated Paul Jones' referred to a well-known episode off Flamborough Head, at the time of the War of American Independence, when Paul Jones defeated Captain Pearson of the *Seraphis*, having dealt with a certain amount of insubordination in his own ship during the course of the action:

Lieutenant Yallard, who had taken over on Mosse's death:

> . . . expressed great satisfaction at seeing me in high spirits and so active [said Millard]. The brave veteran had taken care to have everything clean and nice before we went into action. He had dressed himself in full uniform, with his cocked hat set on square, his shirt-frill stiff starched, and his cravat tied under his chin as usual. . . . How he escaped unhurt seems wonderful. Several times I lost sight of him in a cloud of splinters; as they subsided I saw first his cocked hat emerging, then by degrees the rest of his person, his face smiling, so that altogether one might imagine him dressed for his wedding day.

One or two details have been remembered about Captain Bertie of the *Ardent*, who was among the officers Nelson visited personally as soon as he could after the battle, this time with Hardy, whose ship, the *St George*, Nelson had by then rejoined. When the *Glatton* set the *Dannebrog* on fire, Bertie sent an officer over in the *Ardent*'s launch with orders to save as many of the crew as possible, but not to go alongside, in case the boat should be swamped or overset. By that time Fischer had shifted his pendant, and Bramme, the captain of the Danish ship, who was severely wounded, hailed the launch to find out the name of the captain who had sent over. On receiving the necessary information, Bramme paid a handsome compliment to Bertie, and added that he should make a point of acquainting the Prince Royal with his 'generous attention and humanity'. The launch picked up some 23 Danes, but a great many more were lost, probably as many as 200, when the *Dannebrog* blew up later.

On 4 April Bertie visited the *London*, taking with him one of the Danish captains who had been made prisoner, and the lieutenants of four ships which had struck to the *Ardent*, together with their swords, which Bertie wished to return. Sir Hyde Parker naturally did not oppose such chivalry, and Bertie made the gesture the occasion of expressing what everyone felt, admiration for the able and gallant conduct of the defence. A 'preventative' war against the Danes was a very different matter from a campaign against the godless French. So thought Nelson, and his feelings were shared throughout Parker's fleet. It was now up to the victors to contrive to win by diplomacy a greater success than had been gained by arms, and once again it was Nelson who was ordered to the point of contact.

4 Nelson and the Prince Royal

The very day after the battle, Nelson went ashore to visit the Danish Prince Royal, who was to succeed to the throne in 1808 as Frederick VI, and who, even as a very young man, had exercised authority on behalf of his father. On landing, the Admiral was received, according to a Danish account, 'neither with acclamations or with murmurs; the people did not degrade themselves with the former, nor disgrace themselves with the latter. Nelson was received as one brave enemy ought ever to receive another—with respect. A carriage was provided for his lordship, which, however, he declined, and he walked amidst an immense crowd of persons, anxious to catch a glimpse of the hero, to the palace of the Prince Royal.'

Nelson breakfasted with Fremantle soon afterwards, and Fremantle wrote off to the Marquis of Buckingham, giving rather a different account of the immediate reception. 'He was hailed with cheers by the multitude', says the letter, 'who came to receive him at the waterside, and "Viva Nelson" resounded until he got to the palace, much to the annoyance, I believe, of His Royal Highness and his Ministers. During dinner, the people were allowed to come in and look at him, and on going down to the boat, again he was saluted the same way, The populace are much in our favour and the merchants already feel the total want of commerce.' The truth is likely to be somewhere between the Danish version and that of Fremantle. Stewart merely said that 'the populace showed a mixture of admiration, curiosity and displeasure.'

Certainly the *entente* with Russia can have had little more popular appeal in Denmark than in Sweden, but the royal houses in the respective countries were then in fact as well as in name at the head of affairs, and their decision had been for Paul.

Nelson wrote a full and careful account of his interview with the Prince for the information of Henry Addington, who had recently succeeded Pitt in the office of Prime Minister. It is a document of the highest interest and importance, not only for itself, but for its illustration of Nelson's grasp in negotiation.

> I own [said Nelson] I do not build much hope on the success of negotiation, as it appears clearly to me that Denmark would at this moment renounce all her alliances to be friends with us, if fear was not the predominating consideration. Sir Hyde Parker thought that probably some good might arise, if I went ashore to converse with his Royal Highness; I therefore went yesterday noon, had a conversation of two hours alone with the Prince (that is, no Minister was present), only his Adjutant-General, Lindholm, was in the room.

Nelson must have blessed the royal command of English, since languages had never been among his own accomplishments.

> His Royal Highness [continued Nelson] began the conversation by saying how happy he was to see me, and thanked me for my humanity to the wounded Danes. I then said it was to me, and would be the greatest affliction to every man in England, from the King to the lowest person, to think that Denmark had fired on the British flag, and become leagued with her Enemies. His Royal Highness stopped me by saying that Admiral Parker had declared war against Denmark. This I denied, and requested His Royal Highness to send for the papers, and he would find the direct contrary, and that it was furthest from the thoughts of the British Admiral.

Nelson then asked if he might speak his mind freely, and on leave being granted, he 'stated the sensation which was caused in England by such an unnatural alliance with, at the present moment, the furious enemy of England'. The Prince replied that it was for the protection of their trade, and that Denmark would never be the enemy of England, and that the Emperor of Russia was not the enemy of England when the association was formed, in fact, 'that he would never join Russia against England, and his declaration to that effect was the cause of the Emperor sending away his Minister: that Denmark was a trading nation, and had only to look to the protection of its lawful commerce'.

The discussion then turned to the subject of contraband, and the Prince explained that 'to be subjected to be stopped—even a Danish fleet, by a pitiful privateer, and that she should search all the ships, and take out of the fleet any vessels she might please—was what Denmark would not permit'. To this Nelson answered: 'What occasion for convoy to fair trade?' To which the Prince answered that no commander could tell what contraband goods might be in his convoy, 'and as to merchants, they would always sell what was most saleable; that as to swearing to property, I would get anything sworn to which I pleased'.

Nelson then said: 'Suppose that England, which she never will, was to consent to this freedom and nonsense of navigation. I will tell Your Royal Highness what the result would be—ruination to Denmark, for the present commerce of Denmark with the warring powers was half the neutral carrying trade, and any merchant in Copenhagen would tell you the same. If all this freedom was allowed, Denmark would not have more than the sixth part; for the State of Hamburg was as good as the State of Denmark in that case, and it would soon be said "We will not be stopped in the Sound"—our Flag is our protection, and Denmark would lose a great source of her present revenue, and that the Baltic would soon change its name to the Russian Sea.' The Prince said that this was a delicate subject, to which Nelson answered that he had been permitted to speak out. His reference to the Sound had been to the fact that for centuries the Royal House of Denmark derived a large income from dues from all ships making use of the Sound, a privilege which was to continue for many years to come.

The Prince then said: 'Pray answer me a question—for what is the British Fleet come into the Baltic?' Nelson answered: 'To crush a most formidable and unprovoked coalition against Great Britain. . . .' The Prince replied that it was a misunderstanding, that his uncle (George III) had been deceived 'and that nothing should ever make him take a part against Great Britain, for that it could not be his interest to see us crushed, nor, he trusted, ours to see him', to which Nelson agreed. Nelson then said: '. . . there could not be a doubt of the hostility of Denmark, for if her fleet had been joined with Russia and Sweden, they would assuredly have gone into the North Sea, menaced the coast of England, and probably have joined the French, if they had been able.' The Prince said that his ships never should join any Power against England, 'but', said Nelson, 'it required not much argument to satisfy him that he could not help it.'

'In speaking of the pretended union of the Northern Powers', continued Nelson, 'I could not help saying his Royal Highness must be sensible that it was nonsense to talk of a mutual protection of trade, with a Power that had none'—the reference was to Russia, whose maritime traffic was indeed very small—'and that he must be sensible that the Emperor of Russia would never have thought of offering to protect the trade of Denmark, if he had not had hostility against Great Britain.' The Prince said repeatedly: 'I have offered today, and do offer my mediation between Great Britain and Russia.' Nelson said: 'A mediator must be at peace with both parties. You must settle your matter with Great Britain. At present you are leagued with our enemies, and are considered naturally as a part of the effective force to fight us.'

'What must I do to make myself equal?' asked the Prince, meaning how could he put himself into the true condition of a mediator. Nelson side-stepped the issue by saying: 'Sign an alliance with Great Britain, and join your fleet to ours.' 'Then', said the Prince, 'Russia will go to war with us, and my desire, as a commercial nation, is to be peace at with all the world.' Nelson said that the Prince knew Great Britain's wishes for Denmark, either to join forces, or to disarm. 'I pray,' said the Prince, 'what do you call disarming?' Nelson's answer was that he was not authorised to give an opinion on that subject, but 'I considered it as not having on foot any force beyond the customary establishment.' 'Do you consider the guard-ships in the Sound as beyond the common establishment?' 'I do not', said Nelson. 'We have always had five sail-of-the-line in the Kattegat and coast of Norway', continued the Prince. Nelson said he thought that such a force would not be allowed. 'When all Europe is in such a dreadful state of confusion,' said the Prince, 'it is absolutely necessary that States should be on their guard.' 'Your Royal Highness knows', said Nelson, 'the offers of England to keep twenty sail-of-the-line in the Baltic.' The Prince then said he was sure that his intentions were very much misunderstood, and asked Nelson what immediate conditions would satisfy the British. Nelson could not say exactly, but the Prince pressed him for his own opinion.

'First,' said Nelson, 'a free entry of the British Fleet into Copenhagen, and the free use of everything we may want from it.' Before Nelson could continue, the Prince quickly replied: 'That you shall have with pleasure.' 'The next,' said Nelson, 'while this explanation [i.e. negotiation] is going on, a total suspension of your treaties with Russia. These, I believe, are the foundation on which Sir Hyde Parker only can build other articles for his justification in suspending his orders, which are plain and positive.'

The Prince requested Nelson to repeat what he had said, and thanked him for his 'open conversation'. Both men then apologised for anything they might have said which was too warmly expressed, and Nelson concluded that his reception 'was such as I have always found it, far beyond my deserts'.

Before leaving, the admiral had the chance of a word with Count Bernstorff, the pro-Russian Danish Minister, '. . . and could not help saying he had acted a very wrong part in my opinion, in involving the two countries in their present melancholy situation, for that our countries ought never to quarrel'. He also noted that he 'found all the country hate both the Russians and Swedes'. Returning to Bernstorff in a later note to Addington, Nelson said bluntly: 'I hate the fellow.'

Nelson paid a second visit to the Prince, on Parker's behalf, to settle the matter of a formal Armistice. This time, Stewart went ashore with him, and recalled that he had by then already made himself known among the Danish fleet, where he had found an old friend, Muller, whom he remembered in the West Indies. His reception on board the *Elephanten*, and his politeness to her officers was such that he 'left as much admired by his enemies, as he had long been by those who were his intimate friends in his own fleet'.

Ashore, when the delegation landed, the crowd was as immense as ever, and, said Stewart, 'they showed more satisfaction on this occasion than on the preceding one'. This was to be expected, since the battle was by then less visibly in evidence.

The most difficult point in the negotiation was the duration of the Armistice, which the British wished to be for 16 weeks, Nelson assuring them, 'with a degree of candour not quite customary in diplomacy, that his reason for requiring so long a term was that he might have time to act against the Russian fleet, and then return.'

> The point not being acceded to on either side [continued Stewart], one of the Danish Commissioners hinted at the renewal of hostilities. Upon which Lord Nelson, who understood French sufficiently to make out what the Commissioner said (for the parley was conducted in this tongue), turned to one of his friends with warmth, and said: 'Renew

hostilities! Tell him that we are ready in a moment; ready to bombard this very night.' The Commissioner apologised with politeness, and the business went on more amicably. The duration of the Armistice could not, however, be adjusted, and the conference broke up for reference to the Prince.

A levee was consequently held in one of the State Rooms, the whole of which were without furniture, from the apprehension of a bombardment. His Lordship then proceeded to a grand dinner upstairs, the Prince leading the way. Nelson, leaning on the arm of a friend, whispered, 'Though I have only one eye, I see all this will burn very well!' He was even then thinking more about the bombardment than about the dinner.

In the end, 14 weeks was agreed upon, the other terms stipulating that the Armed Neutrality should be suspended by Denmark, that Copenhagen should be unmolested, that the British fleet should be free to purchase provisions in Denmark, and that the coasting trade should be safeguarded. The tricky clause, No. 7, ran as follows:

This Armistice is to continue uninterrupted by the contracting Parties for the space of fourteen weeks from the signature hereof; at the expiration of which time, it shall be in the power of either of the said Parties to declare a cessation of the same, and to recommence hostilities, upon giving fourteen days' previous notice.

The document was ratified by the Prince, and by Parker on board the *St George* on 9 April, after which Stewart sped to England as official messenger from the Commander-in-Chief, and as unofficial public relations officer to his friend Lord Nelson.

Not that Nelson needed much help in this respect, for he was a master of self-advertisement as well as of war. On 12 April, the day he sailed from Copenhagen, he sent ashore to Captain Sneedorff, who was then at the head of the Danish Naval Academy, which had been founded exactly a century before, to educate the Corps of Naval Cadets which dated from the reign of Christian IV. Nelson enclosed one of the gold medals which his prize agent, Alexander Davison, had had struck in commemoration of the Battle of the Nile, and the letter which accompanied it concluded with the words:

I send you also a short account of my life, it cannot do harm to youth and may do good, as it will show that perseverance and good conduct will raise a person to the very highest honours and rewards. That it may be useful in that way to those entrusted to your care is fervent wish of your most obedient servant, NELSON AND BRONTË.

It is certainly not surprising that Sneedorff cherished the missive as a curiosity, and that it is still preserved in Denmark.

5 *Nelson Replaces Parker*

Battle and Armistice concluded, both of which were Nelson's work, lethargy appears to have regained its ascendancy over Parker, and for the first time in their intercourse, at least since the dalliance off Yarmouth, Nelson became openly critical of his chief. Loyalty and discipline prevented him from voicing his feelings except among close friends, but in his letter and memoranda he grew increasingly and justi-fiably impatient.

> I am tired to death [he confided to Lord St Vincent]. No man but those who are on the spot can tell what I have gone through, and do suffer. I make no scruple in saying that I would have been at Reval fourteen days ago; that without this Armistice the Fleet would never have gone but by order of the Admiralty, and with it, I dare say, we shall not go this week. . . . Think for me, my dear Lord, and if I have deserved well, let me retire; if ill, for heaven's sake supersede me, for I cannot exist in this state.

A little later, when he felt called upon to justify his having sent a flag of truce ashore during the battle, which some ill-informed critics had described merely as a ruse, Nelson added a memorandum, addressed to Addington, on the Armed Neutrality in general, which put his view, and that of all thinking strategists, in a nutshell.

> I look upon the Northern League to be like a tree, of which Paul was the trunk, and Sweden and Denmark the branches. If I can get at the trunk, and hew it down, the branches fall of course; but I may lop the branches, and yet not be able to fell the tree, and my power must be weaker when its greatest strength is required. If we could have cut up the Russian Fleet, that was my object. Denmark and Sweden deserved whipping, but Paul deserved punish-ment. . . .

Nelson spoke of Paul in the past, for it was by then known in the British fleet that, by one of the ironies of history, an event at St Petersburg had already laid the Baltic policy of the Northern Powers in ruins, and rendered the battle superfluous. On the night of 24 March, Tsar Paul had been strangled by some of his own people, and by the time the news had spread, his son and successor Alexander was already in process of revising some of the more misguided decisions of the dead man. Even so, it was not Denmark's fate to remain long in any state approaching amity with Britain, and once again, in 1807, her fleet and capital were to suffer attack. Even before Nelson left the area, there were indications of the future trend of her policy.

Sweden was an altogether different matter. The active young monarch, Gustavus IV, had gone impulsively far ahead of what his countrymen in general would have approved, in supporting so warmly the cause of the traditional enemy, Russia. He deserves some sympathy. Heir to a man of brilliant gifts and intelligence who had been murdered less than ten years earlier (and with far less reason than Paul), the young ruler's ambition was to emulate the heroes of what Swedes know as their *stormaktstid*, their age as a Great Power under Gustavus Adolphus, Charles X, and his grandson Charles XII. Gustavus IV was fated to end his reign in humiliation and exile, and Sweden was never to fire a shot in anger against Britain, for the silence of the guns at Helsingborg as Parker's fleet passed the entrance to the Sound was both symbolic and prophetic. Sweden, despite some periods of reversal of policy due to matters over which she had no direct control, was among George III's most constant friends during the Napoleonic era, and it was to be left to Nelson's second-in-command at the Nile, Sir James Saumarez, to exercise supremacy in the Baltic during the most critical years of the long struggle.

There was, in fact, an immediate Swedish scare, for after Parker had at last started on his way to Reval, where he expected to find a strong Russian fleet, he had news that a Swedish squadron was at sea, and he proceeded to the northern extremity of the Danish island of Bornholm, in a position to intercept: the Swedes, however, returned to their base at Karlskrona, from which they did not stir, though they fortified the entrances.

Nelson, who had been left to follow the Commander-in-Chief as soon as he had concluded some necessary business at Copenhagen with regard to the destruction of prizes, flew to the scene when he heard that there was the prospect of another battle. The St George drew too much draught to negotiate the channels to Bornholm with any ease, and some of her guns had been put aboard a merchantman, but according to Briarly, the master of the Bellona, the St George was nothing to Nelson so long as he could be up with the advance units of the fleet. Briarly had something of a reputation as a teller of stories, but his account of Nelson tallies with other incidents in his career. The moment that word was received that the Swedes might be out, said Briarly:

> . . . he ordered a Boat to be manned, and without even waiting for a boat-cloak (though you must suppose the weather pretty sharp here at this season of the year), and having to row about twenty-four miles with the wind and current against him, jumped into her, and ordered me to go with him, I having been on board the St George till she had got over the Grounds.
>
> All I had ever seen or heard of him could not half so clearly prove to me the singular and unbounded zeal of this truly great man. His anxiety in the Boat for nearly six hours (lest the Fleet should have sailed before he got on board one of them, and lest we should not catch the Swedish squadron) is beyond all conception. I will quote some expressions in his own words.
>
> It was extremely cold, and I wished him to put on a great-coat of mine which was in the boat: 'No, I am not cold; my anxiety for my country will keep me warm. Do you think the Fleet has sailed?' 'I should suppose not, my lord.' 'If they are, we shall follow them to Karlskrona, by God!'
>
> The idea of going in a small boat, rowing six oars, without a single morsel of anything to eat or drink, the distance of about fifty leagues, must convince the world, that every other earthly consideration than that of serving his country was totally banished from his thoughts.
>
> We reached our Fleet by midnight, and went on board the Elephant, Captain Foley, where I left his Lordship in the morning, and returned to my ship.

The scare being over, Parker anchored in Kioge Bay, immediately to the south of Copenhagen, acting on the principle he had guided himself by ever since the fleet had entered the Baltic. He would not allow an undefeated enemy, in this case the Swedes, to menace his rear. Nelson thought nothing of this precaution. As he had already told St Vincent at the Admiralty, he would himself have gone straight to Reval. It was therefore in Kioge Bay that Parker and Nelson received new instructions and heard of the generous terms in which the victory had been praised in both Houses of Parliament. As early as 23 April Nelson was able to write to a friend that Sir Hyde had had information from the Russian Minister at Copenhagen 'that his Master will not go to war with us', but he was not yet fully convinced. Meanwhile, praise was balm.

The way in which the news of events in the Baltic was greeted at Westminster indeed reflected the general feeling of the country towards Nelson, and of the many who spoke words of admiration, some have become household names. St Vincent himself, as head of the naval administration, naturally reaped credit; the Duke of Clarence, once a fellow captain with Nelson in the West Indies, and best man at his wedding, spoke of his friend's 'courage and intrepidity, which Fortune seemed to back in any enterprise in which he was engaged'; Lord Hood spoke of Parker and Nelson in the warmest terms, as officers he had once had under his own command.

In the House of Commons, Addington turned a graceful sentence by observing 'that Lord Nelson had shown himself as wise as he was brave, and proved that there may be united in the same person, the talents of the Warrior and the Statesman'. The great William Pitt came up from Walmer, where he was enjoying a spell in the honorific post of Lord Warden of the Cinque Ports, to praise an old friend. Sheridan, characteristically, hoped that Captain Mosse's widow and six children would be the subject of Royal bounty, and Wilberforce, the great champion of the abolition of slavery, who had, incidentally, found enthusiasm for his cause in Denmark, added his voice to the chorus. Shortly afterwards Nelson was made a Viscount, an event which made his worldly clerical brother William, who hoped to inherit the title, dance a jig in the Hamilton's dining-room, to the astonishment of old Sir William.

The new orders from the Admiralty anticipated the change which in fact soon took place in the relationship of Britain with the Northern Powers, and they were dated 17 April. The Commander-in-Chief was enjoined to suspend for the time any attack on the Russians, but a flag of truce was to be sent to Reval to enquire 'whether the embargo laid on British ships by the late Emperor had been taken off, and their crews released'. If the answer was in the affirmative, hostile proceedings were to be suspended 'without limitation of time or other conditions'. But if, contrary to expectation, no order should have come from the new Tsar, the squadrons at Reval and Kronstadt should if possible be prevented from uniting, and 'it should be further understood that hostilities may be commenced by either party at the expiration of twelve hours after they shall have given a notice in writing to that effect.' The Admiralty were taking no chances, and although the orders were in the first place addressed to Parker, Lord St Vincent wrote directly to Nelson in the following terms:

My dear Lord,

It is impossible for me to describe the satisfaction expressed by His Majesty, his confidential Servants, and the whole body of the People, at the conduct of your Lordship, and the Officers, Seamen, Marines and Soldiers, who served under your auspices on the 2nd instant: and all are equally well disposed to give credit to your zeal as a negotiator. You cannot have a stronger proof, than in your appointment to succeed Admiral Sir Hyde Parker in command of the Baltic Fleet, on the conduct of which the deepest interests of this nation depend; and although the death of the late Emperor of Russia appears to have made a material change in the politics of the Court of Petersburg, it is absolutely necessary to be prepared for the sudden changes which too frequently happen in the political hemisphere.

I will seize the first opportunity to convey to the King the high estimation in which you hold our friend Colonel Stewart; he is the bearer of this and will, I am persuaded, be of great use to you, both in negotiating and fighting, if there should again be occasion. That the same Divine influence which has hitherto prospered all your Lordship's exertions in the cause of your Country, may continue to hover over you, is the fervent prayer of your truly affectionate, ST VINCENT.

This letter expressed a change in St Vincent's whole attitude towards Nelson. He had always believed in him, but hitherto he had regarded him as a zealous, skilful and fortunate tactician—what he termed a 'partisan', splendid in action, but less certain in council. By his whole conduct in Denmark, Nelson had proved to St Vincent that he had grown in stature, that he was fitted for the highest posts. Whatever might be the disorder of his private life, upon which the First Lord of the Admiralty looked askance, Nelson was a man who rose to events, and of these there are few enough in any generation.

Before news of the change reached the fleet, Nelson more than once bemoaned Parker's inactivity, and his apparent predilection for the waters of Kioge Bay. He had time for a correspondence, which began acrimoniously, about Danish versions of the battle which were beginning to appear, and which were eventually rewritten, nearer to the strict evidence of events, largely through the tact of the Prince Royal's Adjutant-General, Lindholm, with whom Nelson was now on the best of terms. He also wrote to the mayor of Great Yarmouth, of which town he was a Freeman, thanking him for a letter of congratulation which had been among the first to be received, since the news from Denmark was known in the seaport many hours before it reached London. Nelson wrote on 27 April in higher spirits than usual, telling the mayor that:

> . . . the spirit and zeal of the Navy I never saw higher than in this Fleet, and if England is true to herself, she may bid defiance to Europe.

In the same letter he let fall some sentences which deserve to be remembered, since they are as true and as important today as when they were penned.

> The French have always, in ridicule, called us a Nation of shopkeepers—*so*, I hope, we shall always remain, and, like other shopkeepers, if our goods are better than those of any other country, and we can afford to sell them cheaper, we must depend on our shop being well resorted to.

Just over a week later, Stewart rejoined the fleet with despatches from England, with news of the reception in London of the victory, and with various private letters for Nelson, of which St Vincent's was the most important. The mail directed to the Commander-in-Chief was bulkier though not so pleasant, for Parker expected no such shock as he received.

His thoughts regarding his supersession by the Admiralty, in favour of Nelson, were noted in his Journal under the date of Tuesday, 5 May.

> A.m.—At 1, the Hon. Lieut.-Col. Stewart came on board with dispatches from England, by whom I received the King's and their Lordships' approval of the armistice with the Danes; but what was my astonishment and surprise at reading the next paragraph of the letter, which was an order to resign the command of the fleet to Lord Nelson, and shift my flag on board a frigate or a two-decker, and return to Yarmouth Roads.
>
> At 9, sent Captain Otway on board the *St George*, to communicate these orders to the Vice-Admiral (who was to have sailed this day in the *Blanche* for England, with my leave, for the recovery of his health). At noon, waited on his Lordship, and delivered up all my public and secret instructions, unexecuted orders, &c, &c. Ordered the squadron to put

themselves under his Lordship's command, and follow his orders for their further proceedings. Left with him the remains of stationery, &c. Ordered the Vice-Admiral to take them under his command.

P.m.—Fresh breezes and clear. At 3, went on board the *Blanche*, when my flag was immediately hoisted, and struck on board the *London*. At ½ past 4, weighed and sailed.

The *Blanche* was a new frigate, and this was her first service. It was Sir Hyde's last, and his final years—he survived until 1807—were undistinguished by further employment. He had the sympathy of many in the fleet, not least among Nelson partisans such as Fremantle, who in the past had owed much to his indulgence. Fremantle's comment on the episode was in fact very severe. He wrote to his wife from Bornholm a few weeks later:

> . . . the attention I receive from Lord Nelson is flattering beyond what I can name. [But, he added] . . . the insult of the Admiralty to my friend Sir Hyde is scarcely to be named without feeling detestation to the person who occasioned his recall in such a way as *Treason only* could have rendered necessary.

Fremantle's thoughts were much the same as Nelson's own, about the *manner* of Sir Hyde's dismissal. In the middle of June he had occasion to write to Alexander Davison about some private matters, and he added a postscript to the letter which he headed 'Secret'.

> They are not Sir Hyde Parker's real friends who wish for an enquiry [wrote Nelson]. His friends in the Fleet wish everything of this Fleet to be forgot, for we all respect and love Sir Hyde; but the dearer his friends, the more uneasy they have been at his *idleness*, for that is the truth—no criminality. I believe Sir H.P. to be as good a subject as his Majesty has.

As was his way, Nelson summed the whole matter up succinctly, and with truth. There was no enquiry, and Sir Hyde has passed into history as the second senior admiral—Lord St Vincent being the first—who gave Nelson a free hand, and saw what a master of war could accomplish.

Nelson had bemoaned his health to Parker, and his situation had been viewed so sympathetically that, as the admiral noted in his Journal, written permission had been given for him to go home. His private worries were now added to by the severe illness of his brother Maurice, an official in the Navy Board. Maurice had always been a favourite with Nelson, and even his strict partiality for Fanny, the wronged wife, never clouded their relationship—for that matter, Captain Hardy and others felt much the same. Maurice actually died when Nelson was in the Baltic, at a time when he was nearly at the top of his particular ladder of promotion, but Nelson knew little of his brother's financial circumstances, only that he left a poor blind woman who passed as his wife, and of whom Nelson, for the future, took particular care.

If Nelson's own health did not markedly improve as a result of his new responsibilities, at least he could be active. Stewart, once more among his naval friends, was delighted at the reinvigoration which he felt around him. As became an officer still young, though destined to rise high in the army, and with considerable campaign experience already behind him, Stewart loved Nelson's economy of time, his early

35 The *Victory* at Trafalgar

Detail of the engraving (1858) by J. Burnet after the painting by J. M. W. Turner

36 Captain Fremantle
From a contemporary tinted drawing

37 Lord Barham
From a chalk portrait by J. Downman (1809)

start to the day, which was like St Vincent's, his eagle eye on every concern of the fleet, even to such matters as victualling, and the fact that all the paper work was finished by breakfast time. That, felt Stewart, was how to get things done.

> The first signal which Lord Nelson made as Commander-in-Chief [he wrote] was to hoist all launches, and prepare to weigh. This at once showed how different a system was about to be pursued; it having been intended that the Fleet should await at anchor fresh instructions from England relative to the state of Northern affairs.
>
> Lord Nelson, who foresaw every bad consequence from this inactive mode of proceeding, owed his bad health to chagrin more than to any other cause. The joy with which the signal was received not only manifested what are the customary feelings on those occasions, but was intended as peculiarly complimentary to the Admiral.
>
> On 7 May the Fleet left Kioge Bay, and, proceeding towards Bornholm, anchored, in blowing weather, off that island. The greater part was here left to watch the motions of the Swedes; and with a chosen squadron, consisting of his best-sailing 74's, two frigates, a brig and a schooner, Lord Nelson sailed for the Port of Revel. He wished for further satisfaction respecting the friendly disposition of the Russians, and thought that the best method of putting this to the proof would be to try how he should be received in one of their Ports. He sincerely desired peace, but had no apprehension of hostilities. Exclusive of a wish to show the activity of his Fleet, he had two other objects in view; personally to wait on the Emperor, and congratulate him on his accession to the Throne, and also to promote the release of the British Merchant Seamen who had been detained by the Emperor Paul.

Sir Hyde had already sent Fremantle on a mission to St Petersburg in the *Lynx*, where he arrived on the day that Nelson took over command. Soon after his return to the *Ganges*, Fremantle wrote to his wife to give her some idea of his experiences.

> I was exceedingly well received by Count Panin, the Court Minister [he said], and Prince Korakin, the Vice-Chancellor. With the former I dined twice, with the latter once, during the four days I remained at Petersburg; I saw the whole of the Winter Palace, the Hermitage, where the Museum and all the fine paintings are . . . and the Palace of St Michael where the late Paul was strangled; to relate you all the modes he had found out to torment and tyrannize over his subjects will fill a folio volume, and I am only surprised to think he was suffered to live so long.

Fremantle found that the Russians still 'stickle a great deal about this Armed Neutrality', and although he felt sure there would be a Treaty, he was not able to report that the detained ships and seamen had been released.

Nelson himself had no doubt that the Russian difficulties would be removed before long, and his view that the young Emperor should be allowed the initiative in policy showed a sound reading of his character and position, but he himself had every intention of making the British position clear; his country would stand no equivocation. He had already anticipated the official orders he was soon to receive with regard to the Swedes—that he should prevent any possibility of their admiral joining forces with the Russians in the Gulf of Finland. On their own, they were not much more than a theoretical danger: in combination, they might be more formidable.

Nelson wrote to St Vincent, with whom his public relations were never more cordial (though their litigation in the matter of prizes was already pending), that he thought another fortnight would see all principal matters settled, when he would like to return home. He also gave his opinion to Nicholas Vansittart, who had been concerned with the unsatisfactory negotiations before the battle, that he thought Sir Hyde's notion of staying in the Kattegat, 'and there wait the time when the whole naval force of the Baltic might choose to come out and fight', a suggestion he had with difficulty been able to counter, would have been 'a measure, in my opinion, disgraceful to our Country'.

To the Swedish commander at Karlskrona he wrote in unambiguous if undiplomatic terms on 8 May:

> I should be sorry that any event could happen which might disturb for a moment the returning amity (I hope) between Sweden and Great Britain. I beg leave, therefore, to apprise your Excellency that I have no orders to abstain from hostilities, should I meet the Swedish Fleet at sea, which, as it lies in your power to prevent, I am sure you must take this communication as the most friendly proceeding on my part. . . .

The missive had exactly the effect which was intended. While Swedish trading vessels continued unmolested, the fleet remained behind the Karlskrona defences.

Off Reval, where Nelson arrived on 12 May, he was disappointed to learn that a Russian squadron which had wintered there, taking advantage of the early breaking up of the ice, had made its way to Kronstadt, and he experienced a little comedy which confirmed his opinion of Russian ways.

> We came to anchor in the outer bay [said Stewart], and a friendly message was sent on shore to the Governor, General Sacken, enquiring whether a salute was intended to be fired. Lord Nelson stated his being ready to return the same, and assured him of the friendly objects which he had in view in entering a Russian port.
>
> Cordial declarations of amity were returned, and a salute promised; this, however, being neglected, the Admiral again sent on shore, and was informed that the delay had arisen from the misconduct of the Officer commanding the Artillery, who had been put under arrest in consequence, and that the salute should be given. This was accordingly done, but at so late an hour that our salute was not returned until next morning.

Nelson went ashore next day, to be greeted with every attention. He was able to send messages to St Petersburg, and to provide his ships with fresh meat and vegetables. On 14 May the General returned the visit.

> He was accompanied [noted Stewart] by young Pahlen, the Minister's son, who commanded a regiment of hussars in garrison there, and by other military commanders. They were shown over part of the *St George* by Lord Nelson, and it was observable that the Cossack officers gave infinitely more attention to what they saw, than did any of the Russians.

The ships remained off Reval until 17 May, when Nelson sailed out of the Gulf of Finland and cruised for a time off Gotland, the Swedish island once famed as a centre of the Hansa trade, and then as always celebrated for its roses; next he moved southeast to Rostock, where he hoped for good German provisions. There, a Russian lugger brought a flattering communication from Tsar Alexander. The Emperor did not welcome the prospect of a British fleet, for which he saw no occasion, but he invited Nelson to visit the capital in person, 'in whatever mode might be most agreeable to himself'. Stewart noted that the lugger:

> . . . on leaving our fleet with Lord Nelson's answer to this gracious letter, fired a salute, an act which implies much more in the Russian service than in many others. . . Lord Nelson

observed: 'Did you hear that little fellow salute? Well, now, there is peace with Russia, depend upon it: our jaunt to Reval was not so bad, after all.'

Back in Copenhagen, however, matters were not in good shape. One or two of the junior officers had got themselves into trouble and were publicly reprimanded, and Nelson saw every indication that the Armistice would soon be regarded as a dead letter. His uneasiness was well founded. Bonaparte told a British officer, many years later, that France began to receive masts through Denmark within a very short time of the battle. Nelson's new view was that 'generally speaking, the Danes hate us. . . . In the nation we shall not be forgiven for having the upper hand of them: I only thank God we have, or they would try to humble us to the dust.'

There was, in fact, some reason for the fresh wave of dislike, for word had just come to the north of Europe that an expedition under Rear-Admiral Duckworth and General Trigge had seized the Danish West Indian islands, and that the terms granted in the capitulation did not err on the lenient side.

Nelson's work was now done, and Lieutenant-Colonel Hutchinson, who had served so usefully in the *Monarch* during the battle, was this time the means of informing Lord St Vincent, when he went home with despatches, that the Admiral's ill health was not feigned, and that the sooner he was relieved the better for his future prospects. St Vincent had already taken the necessary measures—it was his way— and Admiral Pole was half way to the Kattegat when the First Lord sent a letter to Nelson which would have warmed the heart of the most stony, so generous was its praise.

> I have the deepest concern [wrote the Earl] at learning from Lieutenant-Colonel Hutchinson that your health has suffered in so material a degree. To find a proper successor, your Lordship well knows, is no easy task; for I never saw the man in our Profession, excepting yourself and Troubridge, who possessed the magic art of infusing the same spirit into others, which inspired their own actions, exclusive of other talents and habits of business, not common to naval characters . . . Your Lordship's whole conduct, from your first appointment to this hour, is the subject of our constant admiration. It does not become me to make comparisons: all agree there is but one Nelson. That he may long continue the pride of his Country, is the fervent wish of your Lordship's truly affectionate ST VINCENT.

As soon as Pole arrived, Nelson made arrangements for a passage home to Yarmouth in the Brig *Kite*. His last public act in the Baltic was to invest Rear-Admiral Graves with the insignia of Knighthood of the Bath, a ceremony which he was authorised to perform on behalf of the King as an encouragement to the fleet.

This, alas, was as far as encouragement went. When next he was received in audience in London, the King whom Nelson reverenced made no allusion to his victory, and no gold medals were awarded to the captains who had taken part. No doubt it was thought that this would be too invidious to Parker's division, most of which had scarcely fired a shot.

For the rest of his life, Nelson remained indignant at the lack of general recognition of his 'brave fellows', and in the November following the battle he wrote a letter to the Lord Mayor of London which can have left that dignitary in no doubt as to his feelings.

> From my own experience [said Nelson], I have never failed seeing that the smallest services rendered by either Navy or Army to the Country have never missed being noticed by the great City of London with one exception—I mean, my Lord, the glorious 2nd of April—a day when the greatest dangers of navigation were overcome, and the Danish force (which they thought impregnable) totally taken or destroyed by the consummate skill of the commanders and by the undaunted bravery of as gallant a band as ever defended the rights of this Country.
>
> For myself I can assure you that if I was only personally concerned, I should bear the stigma now first attempted to be placed upon my brow with humility. But, my Lord, I am the natural guardian of the characters of the officers of the Navy, Army and Marines, who fought and so profusely bled under my command on that day. In no sea action this war has so much British blood flowed for their King and Country. . . . Never was the glory of this Country upheld with more determined bravery than upon that occasion; and if I may be allowed to give an opinion as a Briton—then I say that more important service was never rendered to our King and Country.

The patriotic eloquence had no effect, and as the omission was never repaired, Nelson refused a proposed Vote of Thanks to himself, at a later date, for his services in defence of the Channel. His country had shown in no undecided terms that insistence on her interests in the Baltic, vital on strategic and economic grounds, which she would continue to make clear until all danger from enemies on the Continent was past. It was Nelson's belief that the Corporation of London should have been among the first to recognise the importance of the mission on which he had been engaged. More than four-fifths of her imported grain came from lands washed by the Baltic to an island partly dependent on such traffic.

When Nelson landed at Yarmouth on 1 July 1801, it was to revisit his native county for the last time, and he made sure of seeing, and where possible relieving, such wounded as were to be found in the local hospitals. His prestige and abilities were such that he could not long be unemployed, and even before the end of the month he was given charge of the seaward defences of the south and south-east coasts of England, a task which occupied him for the rest of the year. It brought him one of his failures. This was the repulse of an attack which he had planned, but which he did not lead in person, on the invasion flotillas massed at Boulogne. They were too well secured by chains and other defences to permit of capture or destruction.

The remarks of the First Lord, and of Nelson himself, were, on this as on other occasions, thoroughly characteristic. St Vincent wrote to Nelson:

> It is not given to us to command success; your Lordship and the gallant officers and men under your orders most certainly deserved it, and I cannot sufficiently express my admiration of the zeal and persevering courage with which this gallant enterprise was followed up, lamenting most sincerely the loss sustained in it. The manner in which the enemy's flotilla was made fast to the ground, and to each other, could not have been foreseen: the highest praise is due to your Lordship, and all under your command, who were actors in this glorious attempt.

Nelson wrote to his subordinates:

The Vice-Admiral begs to assure them that the Enemy will not have long reason to boast of their security, for he trusts ere long to assist them in person, in a way which will completely annihilate the whole of them. Lord Nelson is convinced that if it had been possible for man to have brought the Enemy's Flotilla out, the men that were employed to do it would have accomplished it. The moment the Enemy have the audacity to cast off the chains which fix their vessels to the ground, that moment, Lord Nelson is well persuaded, they will be conducted by his brave fellows to a British port, or sent to the bottom.

Soon afterwards, the preliminaries to a Treaty with France were concluded, and Nelson was able to spend the ensuing months of peace at a property he had bought at Merton in Surrey, which he shared with the Hamiltons. This was an idyllic spell, the happiest in all his life, but it was short. Early in 1803 private and public events affected all his plans. Sir William died in April, and in May Nelson was appointed Commander-in-Chief of the Mediterranean Fleet, a post which, as St Vincent said, required 'an officer of splendour'.

On 16 May 1803 Nelson hoisted his flag in the *Victory*. With the war reopened, the train of events began which was to end, nearly two and a half years later, off the shoals of Trafalgar.

Sailor (1807)

PART V

Trafalgar

1 *The News Breaks*

For its issue dated Thursday, 24th October 1805, the *Gibraltar Chronicle* was presented with one of the biggest scoops in newspaper history—first news of Trafalgar. This came in the form of a letter from Vice-Admiral Collingwood to General Fox, Governor of the Rock, which ran as follows:

Euryalus, at Sea, October 22

Sir,

Yesterday a Battle was fought by His Majesty's Fleet, with the Combined Fleets of Spain and France, and a Victory gained, which will stand recorded as one of the most brilliant and decisive that ever distinguished the British Navy.

The Enemy's Fleet sailed from Cadiz, on the 19th, in the Morning, Thirty-Three sail-of-the-line in number, for the purpose of giving Battle to the British Squadron of Twenty-Seven, and yesterday at Eleven A.M. the contest began, close in with the Shoals of Trafalgar.

At Five P.M. Seventeen of the Enemy had surrendered, and one (*L'Achille*) burnt, amongst which is the *Sta. Ana*, the Spanish Admiral Don D'Alava mortally wounded, and the *Santissima Trinidad*. The French Admiral Villeneuve is now a prisoner on board the *Mars*; I believe Three Admirals are captured.

Our loss has been great in Men; but, what is irreparable, and the cause of Universal Lamentation, is the death of the Noble Commander-in-Chief, who died in the Arms of Victory; I have not yet any reports from the Ships, but I have heard that Captains Duff and Cook fell in the Action.

I have to congratulate you upon the Great Event, and have the Honor to be, etc., etc.

C. COLLINGWOOD.

In those days the paper was, on great occasions, printed in two parallel columns, English and French. Below Collingwood's letter were some further details, much less accurate.

In addition to the above particulars of the late Glorious Victory, we are assured that 18 Sail-of-the-Line were counted in our possession, before the Vessel, which brought the above dispatches, left the Fleet; and that three more of the Enemy's Vessels were seen driving about, perfect Wrecks, at the mercy of the Waves, on the Barbary Shore, and which will probably also fall into our hands.

Admiral Collingwood in the *Dreadnought* led the Van of the British Fleet most gallantly into action, without firing a shot, till his yard-arms were locked with those of the *Santissima Trinidad*; when he opened so tremendous a fire that, in fifteen minutes, she was completely dismasted, and obliged to surrender.

Lord Nelson, in the *Victory*, engaged the French Admiral most closely; during the heat of the action, his Lordship was severely wounded with a grape-shot, in the side, and was obliged to be carried below. Immediately on his wound being dressed, he insisted upon being again brought upon deck, when, shortly afterwards, he received a shot through his body; he survived, however, till the Evening, long enough to be informed of the capture of the French Admiral, and of the extent of the Glorious Victory he had gained.—His last words were, 'Thank God I have outlived this day, and now I die content!'

There were a number of curious features about this earliest printed report. The first was how quickly Collingwood had been faced with the onerous process of writing despatches, once the guns had ceased to fire, in addition to managing the command to which he had succeeded. He was occupied to the same manner, without respite, for many weeks. Even the comparatively full reports which he sent to the Admiralty, and which appeared in *The Times* on 7 November, were not the end of the business, nor were the details wholly correct. A comprehensive picture emerged only gradually.

Another remarkable fact about the news was that, in spite of its immediacy, how much of it was wide of the mark; yet it had the merit of illustrating how hard it is to describe a battle until long after firing has ceased, and until those who survive, on both sides, have had the chance to compare notes. Collingwood, as was his way, was as precise as he could be, from the very first, though he was wrong about D'Alava, who not only recovered, but even preserved his flagship, which was recaptured in a sortie from Cadiz.

The supplementary details, no doubt supplied verbally by the captain of the vessel which brought the letter to the Governor, were wildly wrong. Collingwood, who did not lead the 'Van' but the 'Rear' (as he described it in his fuller account—it was really the 'Lee' line), was not in the *Dreadnought* but the *Royal Sovereign*, another three-decker. He transferred his flag to the frigate *Euryalus* because the masts of his own ship were shot away, and because the signalling in the *Euryalus*, commanded by Captain Blackwood, was the most efficient in the fleet. He did not first engage the *Santissima Trinidad*, which probably figured in the early news simply because she happened to be the largest battleship then afloat. Finally Nelson, once he had received his wound, which was from a bullet, never returned to the upper deck of the *Victory*, and his last words were not quite as reported, though the printed version was in character.

Actually, when Collingwood began his despatch, not everyone even in the victorious fleet knew that Nelson was dead; Captain Harvey of the *Téméraire*, for instance, who had been closest in support of the Commander-in-Chief, and whose ship was very near indeed when Nelson was struck down, did not learn the news for three days, and then it came by signal from a captain in Collingwood's division.

Nevertheless the ship that brought the tidings to Gibraltar had done well enough. She had conveyed the full momentous *effect* of the battle. There was evidence enough to give Governor Fox excuse to fire salutes, to order illuminations and to prepare to receive the victors with tempered jubilation for their achievement in adding 'a ray of Glory to His Majesty's Crown', to use a later phrase by Collingwood. It was one which he hoped would 'be attended with public benefit to our Country'.

Out in the Atlantic, beyond the Strait's mouth, a gale was blowing, and ship after ship, scarred, dismasted and leaking, was trying to claw away from a lee shore, sometimes without success. There could be no pause for thanksgiving. Nothing but incessant work, performed with skill in the face of near-exhaustion, enabled the victors to bring in even the few prizes they were able to save—four in all. Perhaps the most remarkable result of the encounter was that not a single British ship was lost, in spite of the ravages of shot and weather. Frenchmen found this hard to believe.

It was fitting that it was to Gibraltar that the news first came of the greatest fleet action of the Napoleonic War, and one of the last in history to be fought under sail. Gibraltar was at the door of the Mediterranean, and it was because of Villeneuve's intention to return to that sea that Nelson had been given the chance to bring him to battle. Trafalgar marked the end of the career of the most illustrious admiral in his country's history, fulfilled his wish for the annihilation of his opponents as a coherent force, and secured for the Royal Navy a supremacy which was unchallenged for more than a century.

That was enough for one autumn day.

2 The Campaign

A favourite analogy, used of the process which follows when a land-power engages in warfare against a sea-power, is to describe the matter as a tussle between an elephant and a whale. But in more recent English history what has invariably happened is that the whale has turned amphibian, while the elephant has never crossed the stretch of sea which matters most, the English Channel. The elephant has threatened; it has never been able to strike the final blow. The whale, on the other hand, while retaining mastery in its own element, has gone ashore, with aid from allied creatures, and has at last forced the elephant to come to terms.

The tussle is painful, clumsy and wasteful, like warfare in general. The classic instance occurred during the protracted war with France, and the campaign which led to Trafalgar may be said to have begun when the French decided, for the second time, to mass an army on their own side of the Channel. It was, therefore, concerned with a project for invasion, since that idea was at one time dominant in Napoleon's mind. But neither the campaign nor its culminating engagement saved England from the threat, because its realisation was in fact never likely. Channel supremacy, at least temporarily, was essential to success, and that supremacy remained British. Before Trafalgar was fought Napoleon, despairing of his seamen, had faced his army about, and had engaged in operations which led to French triumphs at Ulm and Austerlitz, deep in the heart of continental Europe.

Yet in order to understand both campaign and battle, it is necessary to follow the threads of Napoleon's scheme, to trace the countermeasures, and to perceive how the retention of sea supremacy turned what appeared to be a defensive campaign into one which broke the Franco-Spanish navy, forced Napoleon into maritime guerrilla warfare which could irritate but which could not be decisive, and enabled Great

Britain to retain that foothold in the Mediterranean which was one of the principles of her strategy.

Trafalgar did not save England: she was always inviolate while her fleet remained undefeated. It reinforced her naval 'combat supremacy'—to use a well-known phrase of Admiral Mahan's—and it ensured that she retained a springboard in the Mediterranean, in far-away Sicily, from which Napoleon himself could be threatened. It was an offensive, not a defensive success.

A plan for invasion had been in Napoleon's mind at least since the year 1798, when he had paid a brief visit to Dunkirk and the Flemish coast. He had then concluded that the idea was too hazardous to be attempted, except as a last desperate measure.

> Whatever efforts we make [he reported to the French Government], we shall not for some years gain the naval supremacy. To invade England without that supremacy is the most daring and difficult task ever undertaken. . . . If, having regard to the present organisation of our navy, it seems impossible to gain the necessary promptness of execution, then we must really give up the expedition, be satisfied with keeping up the pretence of it, and concentrate all our attention and resources on the Rhine, in order to try to deprive England of Hanover and Hamburg . . . or else undertake an eastern expedition which would menace her trade with the Indies. And if none of these three operations is practicable, I see nothing else for it but to conclude peace. . . .

Napoleon's career was an illustration of the truth of his report. The plan for invasion, which he then judged impracticable, was a threat which would always engage a high proportion of England's resources; the matter of British interests in Germany was one which, in due time, a successful French policy could determine; while he himself led the 'eastern expedition' which gained him Egypt, and might have taken him to the gates of India had not Nelson destroyed his fleet at the Nile, isolated his troops and left them to become the victim of one of the earlier amphibious triumphs of the war.

Despite his low view of the prospects of success, Napoleon revived the scheme of invasion in the spring and summer of 1801, and assembled flotillas and an army at Boulogne to train for the attempt. Nelson, fresh from the campaign in the Baltic, was given command of a force of small vessels, stationed at strategic points from Orfordness to Beachy Head, which were to destroy the enterprise should it ever leave France.

Never defensively minded, on 15 August 1801 Nelson made a bold attempt at capturing the French craft as they lay in harbour.

> When any boats have taken one vessel [so ran his orders], the business is not to be considered as finished, but a sufficient number being left to guard the prize, the others are immediately to pursue the object by proceeding to the next, and so on until the whole Flotilla be either taken or wholly annihilated, for there must not be the smallest cessation until their destruction is completely finished. . . .

The orders typify Nelson's whole attitude to war. The only way to fight Napoleon was to be as ruthless as he was, and equally skilful.

In the event, however, the assault was repulsed with loss, to the mortification of Nelson and the jubilation of the enemy—but the gallantry with which it was carried out gave the French a shrewd notion of what they might expect if they ever put to sea in force.

The army remained massed at Boulogne until the signing of the Treaty of Amiens in 1802. When the conflict was resumed, Napoleon detained every male Briton aged between 18 and 60 who happened to be in France, an act which caused a general outcry throughout the civilised world, since hitherto any non-combatant overtaken by hostilities in enemy territory had been safe from molestation. He also concentrated much of his powerful energy on a renewal of the threat upon the island which he could see so plainly from his northern cliff-tops.

He pushed forward preparations in all available dockyards of France, Holland and northern Italy. The great mole which had been planned to shelter the roadstead at Cherbourg was continued, and the entire littoral, from the Seine to the Rhine, became 'a coast of iron and bronze'. Troops were withdrawn from distant frontiers and encamped along the shores of Picardy; others were stationed in reserve at St-Omer, Montreuil, Utrecht and elsewhere, while concentrations were made at Ghent, Compiègne and St Malo. Bodies of men at Boulogne, Étaples, Wimereux and Amble-teuse formed the spearhead of the Grand Army with which Napoleon proposed to conquer the stubborn islanders. England might well have trembled, since she could see gigantic preparation and was battered with incessant propaganda: actually she did nothing of the sort. She rearmed, she prepared, she waited. The idea of invasion was an old one: Philip of Spain had tried it with his Armada in 1588; the Dutch had boldly sailed up the Medway in the following century; it had been a recurring project with the French.

> But the most remarkable feature of the time [wrote Sir Henry Bunbury, who was then serving as an army officer] was the flame which burst forth and spread its light over the whole of Britain. It was not merely the flame of patriotism, or of indignation at the bare idea that England should lie at the proud foot of a conqueror; it appeared to be fed and rendered intense by a passionate hatred of Napoleon personally.

It was hatred that the writer emphasised, not alarm. 'Never fear the event!' That had been Nelson's summing up in 1801. 'Mark the end!' he wrote on one of Napoleon's letters. If pressed, he would probably have agreed with a famous remark of Lord St Vincent. 'I don't say the enemy cannot come; I only say they cannot come by sea!'

Although such optimism was justified, yet while the French fleet remained unde-feated in battle, the threat of a descent by the Grand Army hung like a distant cloud. To meet the enemy at sea was a major object in the Trafalgar campaign.

Admiralty dispositions to counter Napoleon's land concentration were traditional; experience had proved them effective. Facing the army of invasion from the Texel to Havre was a swarm of sloops and gun-vessels, rendering the passage of flotillas impossible without the support of ships-of-the-line. A small battle-squadron under Lord Keith, with his headquarters in the Downs, and with secondary bases at Great Yarmouth and the Nore, provided a covering force. There was an independent cruiser squadron under Saumarez, based on the Channel Islands, which not only

38 *Admiral Villeneuve*
From a contemporary engraving

prevented the passage of hostile transports from that quarter, but acted as a link between Keith and the main British fleet. This fleet was Cornwallis's western squadron, whose purpose was to contain the enemy at Brest, to secure the entrance to the Channel, and to provide a focal point for outlying squadrons watching ports such as Rochefort.

Cornwallis's force was the core of Britain's defence. It exercised a close blockade of Brest: its other duty was trade protection, and guardianship of the whole Channel position. Until the enemy defeated Cornwallis, invasion was impossible. If any of his outlying ships were forced to retreat by the appearance of an independent or an escaping squadron superior in numbers, it was the duty of the commanding officer to join the nearest British detachment, and to await reinforcement, remembering always that the key position was the western approach to the Channel. 'We are aware that many circumstances may occur to which these instructions are inapplicable, and for which no provision is made.' So ran the orders to Cornwallis. 'In these cases you must use your discretion and judgment for your guidance, giving us the earliest information of your proceedings. . . .' The principles of maritime strategy in home waters were so well understood that latitude could be allowed; they held good for the entire campaign.

On renewal of war Nelson kept continual though generally distant watch on Toulon throughout the later part of the year 1803 and the whole of the following year, often with meagre forces, never setting foot ashore, and without the excitement of a general action. Before the close of 1804 Napoleon had secured an ally in Spain, which country brought him a nominal increase of 32 ships-of-the-line. With the Dutch fleet also arrayed against Britain, the Navy's margin of strength was then barely superior.

It was in fact questionable how much additional strength the Spanish would afford the enemy at sea. Their ships were well-built but ill-manned, and their war record, in the earlier stages of the struggle, had been indifferent. Nevertheless one of the first steps taken by Pitt's Government after the advent of the new combination had been to form a 'Spanish Squadron' under Sir John Orde, whose sphere was to be between the Straits of Gibraltar and Cape Finisterre, with the particular duty of watching Cadiz. For various reasons, this was annoying to Nelson. Orde was senior to him, and he was in the best possible position to gather prize-money; moreover, the new disposition divided Nelson's command, which by tradition extended as far as Cape St Vincent. The appointment itself was reasonable enough, in view of Nelson's application for leave to come home on account of his health, an application which had actually been granted. But the entry of Spain into the war determined him not to leave his station. New dangers and difficulties revived his spirits. The bigger the problem, the more his mind rejoiced in finding a solution. It was not long before he was faced with the first of many, for in January 1805 Villeneuve escaped from Toulon.

On 17 January 1805 the French put to sea with 11 of the line and nine frigates. No one knew their intended destination, which was in fact the West Indies, Admiral Missiessy having also escaped from Rochefort under orders to make his way thither. Napoleon's scheme at this time may have been an expedition against British possessions in the Caribbean, not a concentration to be formed with the object of returning to Europe and ensuring a chance of invasion. For the moment invasion plans were dormant.

Two British frigates shadowed the enemy until they were in the latitude of Ajaccio. There they made for the Maddalena anchorage at the northerly tip of Sardinia, which was Nelson's rendezvous. They reported that they had left the enemy standing south-south-west.

Nelson, in common with most of Europe, considered that Napoleon's immediate object was the subjugation of all Italy, and he knew that the security of sea communications in the Mediterranean hung largely upon the integrity of Sicily. In the dead of night, and in a north-westerly gale, he led his fleet through the perilous Biche Passage and down the eastern coast of Sardinia, in order to bar Villeneuve's way east.

Having reached the southern end of Sardinia, Nelson was faced with a heavy westerly gale which held him there until the 26th, when his frigates began to come in from renewed searches. They brought no news except that at least one of Villeneuve's ships had been disabled by heavy weather. Nelson now felt sure that the French had either put back to Toulon, or, favoured by the weather, had swept round him to attack Greece or Egypt. These countries were second only to Naples, Sardinia and Sicily in the defensive function that had been assigned to him, and he therefore held away eastwards. In Greece all seemed quiet, but there was information that the French ambassador had just been recalled from Constantinople, which might indicate that Villeneuve's destination was Egypt. Nelson therefore carried on to Alexandria. Once again there were no signs of the enemy.

Villeneuve, meanwhile, had found that his ships, manned with inexperienced seamen and encumbered with troops were unable to face the heavy weather. All was havoc aloft, the fleet began to scatter, and the French admiral, oppressed with the consciousness that wherever his enemy might be he would be spoiling for a fight, felt it madness to proceed. He consulted General Lauriston, who was in command of the troops, and together they decided to turn back. 'Finding ourselves observed from the first night of our getting out by the two English frigates,' Villeneuve wrote to the Emperor, 'which could not fail to bring down upon us the whole force of the enemy, and it being out of our power to make much sail with the ships so much maltreated, we agreed to return.'

By 21 January the French were once more snug in Toulon, while Nelson, cleared for action, was waiting for them to the south of Sardinia. Although Villeneuve had succeeded in getting away, he had failed to profit by it, and Napoleon immediately informed Missiessy that his operations, henceforward, were independent. Nelson's vain search had depressed his spirits, though he found some consolation in the efficiency of his ships. When the alarm was over he wrote to his friend Collingwood: 'Bonaparte has often made his brags that our Fleet would be worn out by keeping the sea—that his was kept in order and increasing by staying in port; but now he finds, if Emperors hear truth, that his Fleet suffers more in one night, than ours in one year.'

No informed person blamed Nelson for the fact that Villeneuve had got away—he always insisted that this was his wish, since it gave him the chance to defeat him in the open sea, preferably at some distance from his base. 'I beg to inform your Lordship', he once wrote to the Lord Mayor of London, 'that the port of Toulon has never been blockaded by me, quite the reverse—every opportunity has been offered to the enemy to put to sea, for it is there that we hope to realise the hopes and expectations of our country. . . .' What had foiled him was the fact that both his lookouts had been driven off at the same time, due to the number and activity of the enemy's light forces. But he still held command of the Mediterranean.

Thwarted in one plan by the failure of Villeneuve, Napoleon quickly embarked on another, which has become known as his grand design for the campaign. He had been encouraged by the energy which Spain had shown in her preparations for war, and to the Spanish Government he gave an early indication of his scheme.

On 27 February 1805 Missiessy, in the West Indies, was ordered to stay where he was at least until the end of June, and then to be in immediate readiness to join other forces which would in due course appear off Martinique. On the same day Admiral Gourdon, who commanded a French force at Ferrol, was told to be ready to come out with such Spanish ships as were prepared for sea, and to combine with a squadron which would appear before the port. This squadron was to be Ganteaume's, the admiral who held the command at Brest.

Ganteaume was ordered to embark some 3,000 troops over and above those already serving as marines, and to sail at the earliest possible moment with 21 of the line, six frigates, and two store-ships carrying provisions for Gourdon.

He was to make straight for Ferrol, driving away the blockading squadron under Sir Robert Calder. He was then to summon Gourdon by signal, and proceed with him to Martinique, where he would find Missiessy and Villeneuve awaiting him. Ganteaume was to reinforce the Martinique garrison with a thousand troops, and, with the 40 sail-of-the-line which he would by then have collected under his command, he was to return at once to Europe. Off Ushant he was to overwhelm any British force he might find there, and push on to Boulogne, where he would be expected by about the middle of July. In the event of Villeneuve failing to leave the Mediterranean, Ganteaume was to wait 30 days, and then, though he would have only 25 of the line instead of 40, he was still to try to fight his way through to Boulogne. If for any reason he found himself with less than this number, then he was to rendezvous off Ferrol, where there would be a concentration of all the French and Spanish naval forces in Europe. He was then to make for the Channel.

Villeneuve's orders, when he had broken out of the Mediterranean, were to relieve the blockade of Cadiz, to release the Spanish ships in that port, and proceed with them to Martinique. Once there he was to hold his squadron for 40 days in readiness to come out on a signal from Ganteaume. At the end of that time, if Ganteaume had not appeared, he was to land his troops in the French islands, do what harm he could to British interests, and take station off the Canaries, on the route to the East Indies. Possibly Ganteaume might meet him there, but if Ganteaume did not appear within 20 days, then Villeneuve was to return to Cadiz, where he would be given further orders. In Villeneuve's case no provision was made for the concentration at Ferrol, but possibly it was Napoleon's intention to arrange for this when the situation had developed further.

The idea was simple and admirable on paper, but it was that of a soldier. What his admirals thought of it is not on record, which is perhaps as well. When, during the present century, the scheme came to be scrutinised by the French general staff they concluded: 'Such a plan would be unworthy both of Napoleon and his genius, if we could discover nothing deeper in it.' What can be discovered 'deeper' is a way whereby a dictator could save his face. If his combinatiŏns failed, the blame would not be upon his own head, but on that of his navy. 'Englishmen with judgment unoppressed by the Napoleonic legend', says Sir Julian Corbett, 'will see in it the work of a self-confident amateur in naval warfare, the blindness of a great soldier to the essential differences between land and sea strategy, and something perhaps of the exasperated despot who refused to own himself beaten.' Napoleon blithely ignored the winds, and the obvious counter-moves by the enemy. In fact he dismissed the possibility of serious opposition until a combination of his squadrons presented themselves in overwhelming superiority. He could admire the neatness of his own scheme, unbothered by any problems of practical application. These were a matter for the sailors; his part was to give them orders.

'It is grievous to me to know the naval profession,' wrote Decrès, the French Minister of Marine, to his imperial master, 'since this knowledge wins no confidence, nor produces any result in Your Majesty's combinations.' Poor Decrès put the matter neatly. Napoleon's assumptions were outrageous, but no-one was in a position to tell him so, and if they had been it would have made no difference. It almost appeared as if he was bent on sacrificing his navy, and incidentally that of Spain, for the slender chance of bringing about an invasion in which he had himself begun to lose hope.

In point of fact Napoleon had reason to hold the British Navy in less regard than did his admirals. He had made a name for himself as a young artillery officer by helping to drive Hood's ships and men from Toulon. He had sailed the Mediterranean at the centre of a strong fleet, taking Malta on the way to his successful landing in Egypt. Although his flagship and all but two of his battle-squadron had been sunk by Nelson, he, himself, months later, had successfully evaded the British blockade, sailing back to France in a frigate commanded by Ganteaume. As for Villeneuve, he credited him with being lucky: not only had he escaped from the holocaust of the Nile with his 80-gun ship, *Le Guillaume Tell*, but he had shown that it was possible to elude Nelson's watch. If his luck held, he might do this again.

The Admiralty in London at first suspected nothing of the scope of the grand design, but from every blockade port there came signs of activity. Off Ferrol, Calder had news that the enemy squadron was ordered to be ready to sail by 22 March. On 26 March Ganteaume was seen to be moving from the inner harbour at Brest. Cornwallis himself was on sick leave, but Sir Charles Cotton, who had been left in charge, immediately closed in. Ganteaume sent to Napoleon to say that it was impossible to sail without an action, but that, as the signal stations could only count 15 British ships-of-the-line, he wanted to risk one. 'Success is not doubtful', he urged. 'I await your Majesty's orders.' Napoleon answered: 'A naval victory in existing circumstances can lead to nothing. Keep but one end in view—to fulfil your mission. Get to sea without an action.'

With these ideas in mind Ganteaume moved his force outside the Goulet into the Bertheaume anchorage, which had been heavily fortified to help his escape. All he now wanted was a spell of thick weather, and it soon came. He signalled to weigh anchor, but just as he was about to make sail the fog lifted, and the signal stations announced that the British were in the offing. Bound by his orders Ganteaume directed the fleet to moor where it was, while Cotton held on to within five miles of his opponent. Fearing an attack at anchor, and a repetition of the Battle of the Nile, Ganteaume prepared to make sail, but Cotton tacked and stood out again, hoping the French would follow. A fine chance of mauling Ganteaume had been missed. It was one which was never to recur, though Cotton was not blamed for his prudence in preferring to fight the enemy in the open sea. Soon the wind came fresh from the south-west, and the French had to run back into Brest for safety.

It so happened that the British fleet was itself at this time ordered to provide cover for an expeditionary force. This was commanded by Sir James Craig, and was puny by continental standards, but it consisted of good material, destined for the Mediterranean. By the end of March the troops, 300 light dragoons and six battalions of infantry, had been embarked at Portsmouth, and on 19 April they put to sea.

Craig's task was manifold. He was to leave two battalions at Gibraltar, and with the rest of his force he was to proceed to Malta, where his arrival would free some 8,000 seasoned troops for service elsewhere. There were 45 transports, with an escort of the three-decker *Queen*, and a 74-gun ship, the *Dragon*, which the admiral, John Knight, was taking out to reinforce Orde before Cadiz.

'It being of the utmost importance that Sicily should not fall into the hands of the French,' so ran Craig's orders, 'the protection of that island is to be considered as the principal object of that expedition.' When in Italy, Craig was to co-operate with a Russian army, a new treaty of alliance with the Tsar Alexander being by then almost concluded. Admiral Knight was in a responsible position. Not only had he to convoy Craig's force but he had charge of several hundred ships bound for the East and West Indies, which—as was usual—proceeded in company as far as the latitude of Cape St Vincent. The Admiralty, acutely sensitive to the importance of troop movements, looked to Knight to defend transports against attacks by light forces, and to the blockading squadrons for stronger cover.

The fact that Ganteaume had returned to Brest meant that there would be no danger from that quarter and no concentration at Ferrol. Only at Toulon was there any change. Villeneuve's luck held. On the evening of 30 March he put to sea in his 80-gun flagship *Bucentaure*. He had with him three other ships of the same rating, seven 74's, eight frigates, and over 3,000 troops. He had learnt that Nelson had been seen off Barcelona, and in order to give that place a wide berth he had laid his course so as to pass to the eastward of the Balearics.

On his first day out Villeneuve found himself shadowed by two British frigates, whose captains were cheered by the fact that the course he was steering was likely to bring him within striking distance of Nelson's secret position. This was the Gulf of

39 'Lord Nelson from Life'
From the pastel by Schmidt (Dresden, 1800)

40 Collingwood
*From a bracelet formerly in the Royal United
Service Institution*

41 Magon
From an engraving by Maurin (1837)

42 Lucas
From an engraving by Maurin (1837)

43 Sir Thomas Hardy

From the portrait by Lemuel Abbott

44 'The *Victory* to leeward of the *Santissima Trinidad*

From an aquatint by J. Jeakes after T. Whitcombe (1806)

Palmas, at the southerly tip of Sardinia. Villeneuve then had one of the greatest pieces of luck in his entire cruise. He spoke to a neutral merchantman, who told him exactly where Nelson was. During the night Villeneuve altered course to pass inside the Balearics. This movement caused the frigates to lose touch, and the French were able to run clear down the coast of Spain, and right out of Nelson's ken. Nelson's counter-action was to spread his forces to bar Villeneuve's way east, and to wait for certain news. His principal duty, then as always, was guardianship of the Mediterranean.

Although only a part of Napoleon's plan, and that the most doubtful, seemed to have succeeded, the campaign of Trafalgar was well and truly under way. On 7 April, while Nelson was waiting near Ustica, Villeneuve was becalmed off Barcelona. There he could see a Spanish squadron of six of the line under Salcedo, who would have been willing enough to have had his company to Cadiz if the French could have waited for Salcedo to receive positive orders to move, and given him time to get his powder on board. But in the evening an easterly breeze sprang up, ideal for a run to the Straits of Gibraltar, and Villeneuve, uncertain where Nelson was, dared not wait. He left the Cartagena squadron isolated, and made for the Atlantic, which he entered on 9 April.

At Cadiz Admiral Gravina, with 15 of the line, was waiting for the French, but only a proportion of his ships were ready for sea, and he was watched by Orde, though with an inferior force. The first news that Orde had of Villeneuve's escape was from Sir Richard Strachan in the *Renown*. He came under press of sail to say that he had actually seen the French off Gibraltar. Had it not been for this warning, Orde, who was provisioning, believed that he would have been surprised and des-troyed.

Orde had by then heard of Ganteaume's activity at Brest and shrewdly guessed that what was in Napoleon's mind was a massing of his squadrons at some distant rendezvous. He himself had not the force to remain off Cadiz, and as he moved away he sent an urgent appreciation to the Admiralty. 'I am persuaded', he said, 'the enemy will not remain long at Cadiz, and I think the chances are great in favour of their destination being westward, where, by a sudden concentration of several detach-ments, Bonaparte may hope to gain a temporary superiority in the Channel, and, availing himself of it, to strike his enemy a mortal blow.' Orde intended to follow traditional strategy by falling back towards the western squadron. 'In bringing to England the larger ships under my command', he said, 'I shall afford an opportunity to dispose of them anew; by which little can be risked, and much might be gained if the enemy's blow is aimed at England or Ireland.' He ordered his cruisers to warn blockaders in the northerly positions, sent off a ship to the West Indies with informa-tion that the French were at large in the Atlantic and arranged for the *Amphion*, a fast sailer, to keep in touch with the enemy.

Late on 9 April the French were off Cadiz, and Villeneuve signalled Gravina to come out. In his eagerness to hide his tracks Villeneuve dared not sacrifice the darkness of a single night, and after waiting less than four hours, he held away, leaving his allies to straggle out as best they could. The movement was so speedy that the *Amphion* had no chance to begin her watch.

Villeneuve and Gravina were gone, and from the moment they left Cadiz were lost to British eyes. They had the world before them, and only off Ushant was there a force capable of bringing them to battle successfully. When messengers from Spain sped to Napoleon with the news of the first powerful joining of squadrons, the Emperor had every reason to be pleased. He had been right in his faith in Villeneuve. He had misled the most dreaded of his opponents, and had evaded the others. It must have seemed to Napoleon that at no time, since he had first contemplated the idea of invasion, had it had a better prospect of success.

Only one thing could have been calculated to please Napoleon as much as Villeneuve's escape, and that was the existing state of affairs in London. There, in spite of an impassioned defence by Pitt, his friend Lord Melville had been forced from office after the revelation that serious irregularities had been permitted in the handling of Admiralty funds, for which, as First Lord, Melville was responsible. For a time the Admiralty was without a head, and that at a crisis in the war.

Pitt would have been in desperation had there not been an officer capable of taking the helm, though it was improbable that the appointment could be of long duration. Sir Charles Middleton, the man in question, had made a high reputation as Controller of the Navy. Although nearly 80, he was prepared in the emergency to serve as First Lord, and was most fitted to do so. He was raised to the peerage as Lord Barham, and at once took over strategical control of the fleet. It was not a moment too soon. Craig was at sea, Villeneuve was out, and no squadron had yet received orders to cover the passage of the transports. Knight with his two ships-of-the-line could have put up no serious defence if the French appeared in strength, and the capture or destruction of Craig's army would have been felt as a national disgrace.

The first news Barham received that the combined French and Spanish squadron was at large came through the alertness of Lord Mark Kerr, a frigate captain who had been refitting at Gibraltar when Villeneuve passed through the Straits. It came on 25 April, just a week after Craig had sailed. On the same day there issued a series of prescient orders from Barham.

First to be warned was Sir Alexander Cochrane in the West Indies. If he could concentrate all the detachments already in that area at Fort Royal, Jamaica, there would be 11 of the line, including one three-decker, which was a force strong enough to hold the combined fleet in check until reinforcements could arrive. Preliminary orders were followed by others, which are best described as contingent. A military force was in process of passing through seas where no decision had as yet taken place. The chain of covering squadrons had been disrupted, therefore the expedition itself must be withdrawn, unless it had already passed the danger point. If, however, the enemy movement was found not to endanger it, it must be assumed that the threat was aimed at the point of greatest stress. That point was the western end of the channel, the permanent focal point of strategy.

During all this time nothing had been heard from Nelson, and Sir Richard Strachan's conjecture that he had once more gone to Egypt was accepted, for want of other news. In fact, in his perplexity, Nelson had resolved not to go to the eastward of Sicily or

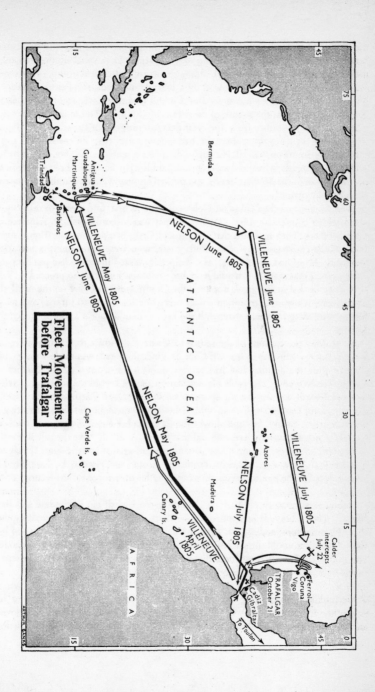

Fleet Movements before Trafalgar

ATLANTIC OCEAN

AFRICA

Bermuda

Trinidad
Barbados
Antigua
Guadaloupe
Martinique

Cape Verde Is.

Canary Is.

Madeira

Azores

Ferrol
Coruna
Vigo
Cadiz
Gibraltar

To Toulon

NELSON June 1805
VILLENEUVE May 1805
NELSON June 1805
VILLENEUVE June 1805
NELSON May 1805
NELSON July 1805
VILLENEUVE July 1805
VILLENEUVE April 1805
NELSON June 1805

Calder intercepts July 22

TRAFALGAR October 21

ARTHUR BANKS

the westward of Sardinia until he knew something positive of the enemy. Then he heard, for the first time, about Craig and his army. His official notification of its movements had been delayed, and, although at first Nelson had nothing to go upon but rumour, this was soon followed by a letter from Elliot, the British Minister at Naples, which confirmed the news. But if it was true that Craig was at sea, then the true danger zone was the mouth of the Straits of Gibraltar. To increase his dilemma, persistent heavy weather from the west delayed progress in that direction. Finally through one of his own cruisers, he had certain news that Villeneuve had passed through the Straits on 8 April. His cup of disappointment was full; but at least he was no longer uncertain what his own course should be. He disposed a light squadron for the protection of the Mediterranean, and pushed his way westward at the best pace his ships could manage.

Even when he reached Gibraltar Nelson did not, at first, find it easy to make up his mind where to take his ships. His first instinct was to head north, to reinforce the Channel Fleet. Then he heard that Knight and Craig had put into the Tagus, somewhat to the embarrassment of the Portuguese, who were maintaining a precarious neutrality. News had come—false, as it happened—that Villeneuve had put back into Cadiz, and if that was so, it would have been madness for Craig to proceed.

No one landed in Portugal, not even the Commander-in-Chief on the usual visit of courtesy, while as a precaution a plan was made for troops to surprise and seize a fort commanding the main channel, if the French should appear at the approaches to Lisbon.

By 10 May the rumour of the return to Cadiz was shown to be groundless, and the expedition again put to sea. Off Cape St Vincent contact was made with Nelson. By that time the admiral had had private information from an English officer in Portuguese service of the probable destination of the combined squadron. Nelson directed Knight to take the transports wide of Cadiz and Tarifa, and then to run straight along the Moorish coast into Gibraltar. Despite his relative inferiority to his prospective enemy, he handed over the three-decker *Royal Sovereign* to reinforce Craig's escort. He knew it was essential that the army should have the fullest possible protection, whilst on passage in the Mediterranean, against a sortie from Cartagena. 'He seems to have acted most handsomely,' wrote Lord Hardwicke, 'as indeed he always does for the public service, in weakening his own force for the security of the country.'

Nelson then bore up on his long chase westward, with ten of the line and three frigates. On 14 May, as he approached Madeira, he wrote to the Admiralty giving them his intentions, adding that even if Villeneuve was not where he supposed him to be, little harm could come from his own course of action. As he said, if his opponent was not in fact in the West Indies, 'the squadron will be back again by the end of June—in short before the enemy can know where I am.'

Meanwhile all had not gone smoothly with French plans. Missiessy, who had begun his West Indian foray in hope, had met with no sister squadrons to his own, and by 20 May he had returned to Rochefort, sick and dispirited. He had done some damage to British interests in the Caribbean, and Cochrane had missed encountering him, but, though he had tried, he had not removed the thorn and shame of the Governor of Martinique. This was a rugged cone, barely a mile from the south-west point of the principal French island, which had been captured in 1803 by Samuel Hood, and been fancifully placed in the Navy List as H.M. sloop *Diamond Rock*. The cone had been manned for two years by a party of seamen under Commander James Maurice, who had led an adventure-story existence, raiding, cutting-out and proving themselves a running sore to garrison and shipping. Missiessy's failure, during the weeks of his cruise, to dispose of Maurice exasperated Frenchmen from Napoleon downwards. 'I choked with indignation', wrote the Emperor to his Minister of Marine, 'when I read he had not taken the Diamond.'

It was left for Villeneuve to remove the menace. The combined squadron appeared off Martinique on 14 May—with a month's start of Nelson. Maurice's greeting was to entice one of the Spanish ships-of-the-line close to the rock by hoisting French colours, a legitimate ruse of war, and to salute her with shot. Villeneuve then set about him in earnest, with two ships-of-the-line, three frigates, gunboats and a force of troops. Maurice held out until 6 June, by which time he had not a cartridge or a drop of water left. His defence had given time for pursuers to close up; it had also enabled a fast ship to arrive with orders from Paris. Her captain reported that Ganteaume, though hourly expected to leave Brest, had not yet done so, that Nelson had 'gone to Egypt' and that, although Missiessy had vanished, two of the line and 800 soldiers had left Rochefort under Magon and should be near at hand. Villeneuve was ordered to stay for 30 days after Magon's arrival, then, if Ganteaume had not come, he was to return to Ferrol. Meanwhile, he was not to waste time, but to operate against the British colonies.

The day after Diamond Rock fell Magon appeared, but Nelson, with his ten of the line, was by then off Barbados. Returning to the West Indies after 18 years it seemed at first that he had the chance of a battle on the scale of Rodney's famous action in 1782. But luck was still with Villeneuve. Nelson, it is true, was joined by Cochrane with two of the line, which brought his numbers up to 12, but he also had news from General Brereton, commanding at St Lucia, that Villeneuve had been seen on a course which would take him to Trinidad. Nelson, though his own instinct was to disbelieve the intelligence, dared not disregard evidence from an officer whom he had known of old, and trusted. He headed his ships south. The news seemed to be confirmed next day by word from the *Curieux* brig, which was scouting ahead.

As he came within sight of Trinidad Nelson was himself mistaken for the enemy; outposts fired their block-houses behind them, and Nelson pushed through into the Gulf of Paria believing that he had before him a second Battle of the Nile, with the French and Spaniards caught embayed. He found nothing.

The tragi-comedy of mistaken identity was soon cleared up, and Nelson, casting all 'intelligence' to the winds, acted on his own judgment, and once more hurried back north. He had scarcely left Trinidad when he had news from Maurice that the combined squadron were still at Martinique. Maurice had been told by his captors that the Ferrol squadron had recently joined them; but about this Nelson felt doubts, since Maurice himself would surely have seen them. 'Powerful as their force may be,' he wrote to the Governor of Barbados, 'mine is compact, theirs must be unwieldy, and although a very pretty fiddle I don't believe that either Gravina or Villeneuve know how to play upon it.'

The next authentic item of news was that Villeneuve had also headed north—he had been seen off Guadeloupe. 'Whether the enemy's object is to attack Antigua or St Kitts', said Nelson, 'or to return to Europe, time will show.' He himself carried on, under press of sail, in the same general direction. He was not able to prevent the one further success of Villeneuve's cruise, the capture of 14 merchantmen, homeward bound, under the escort of a single schooner, but the gap between the squadrons was closing.

At Antigua Nelson, knowing that his active presence had ensured the safety of the British islands and the bulk of the shipping, formed the opinion that the enemy were returning to Europe. The matter was clinched by the arrival of the schooner which had accompanied the luckless convoy. Having escaped his pursuers, her captain was able to report the course and strength of the combined squadron, and Nelson knew that he was now only three or four days behind his opponent. At once he made ready to re-cross the Atlantic, ordering the *Curieux* to proceed ahead at her best speed, with the latest news for the Admiralty. On her way Bettesworth, her captain, sighted Villeneuve on a northerly course, evidently making for the Bay of Biscay rather than the Straits of Gibraltar.

Bettesworth anchored his brig at Plymouth on 7 July, reported to the local admiral and at once posted to London. He reached the Admiralty at eleven o'clock on the night of the 8th, to find that Barham had retired. No one dared disturb him. In the morning, when he heard who had arrived, the First Lord was furious that even an hour had been wasted. Without waiting to dress, he issued instructions to dispose the fleet to meet the return of the enemy. It was likely that a clash might take place off Cape Finisterre, so Sir Robert Calder, who was then off Ferrol, must be reinforced. The squadron off Rochefort was ordered to his support, and Cornwallis, who was back from sick leave, was told to 'stretch with the Fleet under your immediate command' in a south-westerly direction, an order which he had already anticipated.

These moves, to divide the fleet, were stigmatised by Napoleon as *insigne bêtise*— stupidity of a remarkable kind. They certainly opened Brest, which was watched only by a cruiser squadron, and they allowed a vigorous new commander, Allemand, the chance to escape from Rochefort; one which he duly took. Now, if ever, was the time for Ganteaume to act swiftly. He should make at once for Boulogne—so said Napoleon. 'There all is prepared, and there, master of the sea for three days, you will enable us to end the destiny of England. . . . When you receive this letter we shall be in person at Boulogne, and all will be on board and moored alongside.'

But before Ganteaume could make ready, Cornwallis, having run his 'stretch' without sight of Villeneuve, was back in position. The Brest fleet was held fast within its port, and it was Calder who, on 22 July, met the combined squadron in what could have been a dress rehearsal for Trafalgar, or what could even have made that battle unnecessary.

Calder's action, fought in a mist and therefore in increasing confusion, was inconclusive. The admiral himself described it as 'very decisive', while, for his part, Villeneuve reported 'cries of joy and victory are heard from all our ships!' In fact Calder, facing a fleet superior in numbers, captured two Spaniards, inflicted otherwise more damage than he sustained and prevented Villeneuve, at least for the time, from gaining Ferrol. But it was not enough. He had achieved little more than a creditable brush in the old style of encounter.

It was a poor result for being directed to the right place at the right time. For his failure to make every possible effort to renew action next day, and 'to take and destroy every ship of the enemy', Calder was reprimanded. But by the time judgment was delivered Trafalgar had been fought and won, and a new standard established, so that Calder may be said to have fought within one tradition and to have been censured within a greater. He himself was pained at the disappointment felt in England after the action. In fact it had wrecked Barham's careful plans. The enemy fleet was still together: two prizes weighed not a straw in his consideration, and the crisis of the campaign had not yet been resolved. Villeneuve, who had made for Vigo, might still move north or south, towards the Channel or the Mediterranean, and Barham's irritation at Calder's idea that his services should be publicly recognised was, in the circumstances, natural enough.

'It is, as Mr Pitt knows, annihilation that the country wants, and not merely a splendid victory . . . honorable to the parties concerned, but absolutely useless in the extended scale to bring Bonaparte to his marrow bones. . . .' The words were Nelson's, but he belonged to a school of thought to which bravery by itself was not enough. Bravery was taken for granted in such men as Calder. Napoleon's conception was Total War: it was one with which Nelson had long been familiar, and one for which he had prepared ever since the conflict opened.

Making for Cape St Vincent in case Villeneuve's destination should be Cadiz, Nelson reached the coast of Spain, as he had hoped, before the enemy. On 20 July he set foot ashore, at Gibraltar, for the first time in almost two years. Though he remained baulked of his quarry, he had at least some news to cheer him. The Mediterranean was safe, and he found Collingwood off Cadiz, in command of a watching squadron.

In Nelson's absence Collingwood and Bickerton between them had ensured Craig a safe passage to Malta; the transports had in fact anchored at Valletta three days before Nelson reached the Straits, though it was weeks before he knew it. It was Collingwood's view that Villeneuve's object was to bring out the Ferrol squadron and make for Ushant. Nelson was unsure. He redisposed what ships there were in the Mediterranean to give greater safety to Malta, and had scarcely sent off his orders when a sloop, fresh from England, brought news of what the *Curieux* had reported. Nelson could no longer be in doubt. If Villeneuve had been making for the Bay, then to the Bay he would go. Winds forced him to a westerly course, and he met nothing. Leaving the greater part of his squadron to reinforce Cornwallis, he himself, with the worn-out *Superb* in company, made for Spithead, where he anchored on 18 August, very doubtful of the reception he would meet from his countrymen. He had guessed wrong more than once, and he could scarcely have been surprised (though he affected to be pained) that Barham sent for the *Victory*'s journal. When the old seaman read the day-to-day particulars of Nelson's chase, any questions as to the soundness of his conduct were fully answered—though Nelson's luck was another matter. His professional reputation remained where it had stood since the Nile. As for his countrymen, their joy at his return, their respect for his zeal and devotion over the weary and frustrated months at sea, made it almost seem as if he had won a victory.

The atmosphere was prophetic, for at five o'clock on the morning of 2 September, when Nelson was at his country house at Merton, conveniently close to the road from Portsmouth to the Admiralty, a post-chaise drove up to the door bringing Captain Henry Blackwood of the frigate *Euryalus*. Nelson was already dressed, and on seeing Blackwood, who had served him with distinction on earlier occasions, he exclaimed, 'I am sure you bring me news of the French and Spanish fleets, and I think I shall yet have to beat them!'

It was true enough. What Blackwood had to tell him was that Villeneuve had struggled from Vigo to Ferrol, where, with the Spaniards, he mustered a combined force of 30 of the line. He had later, it seemed, attempted to obey his master's orders by heading for Brest, but had met with a strong north-easter, and had turned his ships for Cadiz. His action killed the last remaining hope of invasion. Napoleon, realising at last the futility of his grand design, made preparations to break up his camp, and to employ his army in a land campaign.

Villeneuve, who had left Ferrol on 13 August, was off Cadiz a week later, his force increased by the Spanish ships already blockaded in that port. Collingwood, who at the time was in no strength to prevent it, having but three of the line with him, allowed the enemy undisputed entry, but at once returned to a watching position. 'They are in the port like a forest', he wrote calmly to his sister. 'I reckon them now to be thirty-six sail-of-the-line and plenty of frigates. What can I do with such a host? But I hope I shall get a reinforcement, suited to the occasion and, if I do, well betide us!' He knew that, once fresh ships reached him, Villeneuve could not drive through the Straits without challenge, and, given fair conditions, not at all.

Collingwood did not have long to wait, for Cornwallis made a new disposition which would certainly have ranked, in Napoleon's eyes, as a further *insigne bêtise*, and a detachment under Calder arrived before Cadiz only eleven days after the Combined Fleet.

Of the French squadrons, only Allemand's was now at large, but his force, though sufficient for a raid, and brilliantly used in commerce destruction, could not affect the great issue. Decision would be reached off Cadiz. If his luck changed, Nelson might yet have the chance for which he had waited, and Collingwood, his old and experienced friend, would be with him.

He followed Blackwood to London, accompanied by Emma Hamilton and his two sisters. It was not long before Emma had a note, written after an interview with Lord Barham, telling her that a message had been sent to the *Victory* by the shutter-telegraph which, on a clear day, sent messages from hill-top to hill-top to Portsmouth.

The Ship was to make ready for sea. Nelson asked Emma that everything should be prepared against his own departure.

Crowded and happy as his interlude ashore had been, Nelson could not find it in himself to refuse the request of the Government that he should once more resume his command. As it was the Mediterranean which was now threatened, it was fitting that the man who had served in that sea with such sustained credit should continue its guardian.

In the late evening of 13 September Nelson bade farewell to Emma Hamilton, to his daughter Horatia, and to those of his family who remained at Merton. Once more, as so often before in his life, he took the Portsmouth road.

3 The Scene is Set

On the night he left home Nelson wrote in his private diary:

At half-past ten drove from dear, dear Merton, where I left all I hold dear in this World, to go to serve my King and Country. May the Great God whom I adore enable me to fulfil the expectations of my Country, and if it is His good pleasure that I should return, my thanks will never cease being offered up to the Throne of His Mercy. If it is His good providence to cut short my days upon Earth, I bow with the greatest submission, relying that He will protect those so dear to me, that I may leave behind. His Will be done: Amen, Amen, Amen.

At six o'clock in the morning of Saturday, 14 September, he arrived at Portsmouth. 'Having arranged all my business,' his diary continued, 'embarked . . . with Mr Rose and Mr Canning at two; got on board the *Victory* at St Helens . . . preparing for sea.' Rose was an old friend, Canning a new one, and they were his guests at dinner. Both men were in office, Rose as Vice-President of the Board of Trade, Canning as Treasurer of the Navy.

It was an unforgettable moment when the boatswain piped the admiral over the side for the last time. All had indeed been memorable since early morning, when Nelson made his quarters at the George Inn, conducting his affairs from that convenient place. He took 'a by-way to the beach' and entered his barge from a spot where bathing machines then stood, his idea being 'to elude the populace'. The scene as he left England as told by Southey, a contemporary, is as follows:

. . . a crowd collected in his train, pressing forward to obtain sight of his face: many were in tears, and many knelt down before him, and blessed him as he passed. England has had many heroes, but never one who so entirely possessed the love of his fellow-countrymen as Nelson. All men knew that his heart was as humane as it was fearless: that there was not in his nature the slightest alloy of selfishness or cupidity; but that, with perfect and entire devotion, he served his Country with all his heart, and with all his soul, and with all his strength; and therefore they loved him as truly and as fervently as he loved England. They pressed upon the parapet to gaze after him when his barge pushed off, and he was returning their cheers by waving his hat. The sentinels, who endeavoured to prevent them from trespassing upon this ground, were wedged among the crowd; and an Officer who, not very prudently upon such an occasion, ordered them to drive the people down with

their bayonets, was compelled speedily to retreat; for the people would not be debarred
from gazing till the last moment upon the hero—the darling hero of England!

There is, alas, no firm evidence for this set-piece, the local story being that Nelson
was helped into his barge, off Southsea beach, by a one-legged fiddler; but it has
established its place in the admiral's legend, as has the remark that he is said to have
made to Hardy, his flag-captain: 'I had their huzzas before—I have their hearts now!'

As the great three-decker made her majestic way down Channel she had only the
Euryalus in company, but that was fitting, for if the *Victory* carried the commander
and genius of the fleet, Blackwood and the frigates would give it eyes.

By 16 September Nelson was off Portland; next day he was off Plymouth, where he
picked up the *Ajax* and *Thunderer*; and by the 23rd Cape Finisterre was in sight. On
the 25th he was off Lisbon, and on the 28th, the day before his forty-seventh birthday,
he wrote in his diary: 'Nearly calm. In the evening joined the Fleet under Vice-
Admiral Collingwood, Saw the Enemy's Fleet in Cadiz, amounting to thirty-five or
thirty-six Sail-of-the-Line.' He had caught up with Villeneuve at last.

He had already sent orders ahead that he was not to be accorded the usual commander-in-chief's salute of gun-fire, since this would have given immediate notice of
his presence to the enemy, but his arrival was almost ecstatically welcomed. There
was a double reason for this. Nelson had always been loved by those who served with
him, whatever the circumstances, while it was a fact that the fleet before Cadiz was
restive and bored. 'For Charity's sake, send us Lord Nelson, ye men of power!' That
was the prayer of Codrington of the *Orion*, and it was echoed by Fremantle of the
Neptune and by other officers of standing.

Nelson's command was made up of ships from diverse squadrons. There were the
veteran captains who had shared the long watch off Toulon and the chase to the
West Indies; there was Collingwood's flying squadron, and there were ships which
had fought under Sir Robert Calder in the previous July. Others would soon arrive
from home, among them Sir Edward Berry, in Nelson's famous old ship, the *Agamemnon*. There were no fewer than four flag-officers besides Nelson—Vice-Admirals
Collingwood and Calder; Rear-Admirals the Earl of Northesk and Louis.

Nelson had brought orders with him to recall Sir Robert Calder for the court-
martial arising from his summer action, for which he had himself asked, and he
intended to take with him such captains as were willing to give evidence at the trial.
One other admiral was about to be detached, with ships whose supplies were low, in
order to water and provision at Tetuan and Gibraltar, and to convoy merchantmen
through the Straits. The lot would fall upon Louis, a particular friend of Nelson's.

Of the four subordinate admirals, Collingwood was not merely the senior, he was
the most experienced and distinguished. A Northumbrian, and some ten years older
than his chief, he had been a close friend of Nelson's since they had served together as
lieutenants in the West Indies in the 1770s. Austere, reserved, and something of
a martinet, Collingwood's severe discipline had taxed the patience of the blockaders:
but Collingwood was a man whom to know was to admire, and Nelson, who

had long since pierced through to the essential man, loved him dearly. Not only was Collingwood a thoughtful student of war, he was as brave as a lion, as he had already shown in action under Howe at the Glorious First of June, and under Jervis at Cape St Vincent. Collingwood knew more about the conditions of blockade service off the coast of Spain than most men, and it was well that Nelson and he were so close, or Collingwood might have chafed at the appearance of a senior admiral. But Collingwood had long since clarified his judgment of Nelson. He was peerless.

Sir Robert Calder was a different type of man altogether. Socially inclined, he had many friends in the Navy, though Lady Nelson once wrote to her husband that 'his love of money is great', and the fact must always have been evident. An older man even than Collingwood, he was then 60, and he had taken part as a midshipman in the capture of the *Hermione*, the richest prize on record. His share had been no less than £1,800. He had fought at St Vincent as Jervis's First Captain, and was said to have shown some jealousy at Nelson's part in that encounter. He had been knighted immediately afterwards, an honour which was followed within a year by a baronetcy.

There were those who said that Calder, with prize money in mind, had taken too much care to guard his captures after the action off Finisterre, at the expense of more important considerations. Nelson and Collingwood in fact both sympathised with him in the trial which was before him, though Nelson, kindly as he was, thought him 'too wise' to take sensible advice about the whole matter. Nelson had been ordered to send him home in a frigate, but with extraordinary generosity, which may well have been misguided but which certainly showed no lack of feeling, he disobeyed, and allowed Calder to stay in his splendid three-decker, the *Prince of Wales*, until another ship of comparable size arrived from England, and then to sail back in her.

If, in Nelson, the decision was generous, it was shocking in Calder even to have contemplated allowing the fleet to be weakened by such a powerful unit, and that solely on account of *amour-propre*. Nelson had urged Sir Robert to stay with him a few days longer, being convinced that the enemy would soon make their sortie, since the season was advanced. Calder did not agree, and indeed he did not hold his opinion alone, for Fremantle and others took much the same view. So in due time he sailed home, running the not inconsiderable risk of being engaged and captured by the Rochefort squadron, whose whereabouts was then uncertain. And what he next did should have robbed him of every particle of sympathy. 'What do you think of Calder's modesty', wrote Collingwood to his sister, after Trafalgar had been fought and won. 'The first thing he did on his arrival at Portsmouth was to write to me signifying his claim to *share*. There was a great indelicacy in it under all circumstances, and not a little portion of ignorance.' Calder's astounding claim was a 'share' in the prize money which he knew would accrue from Nelson's victory. Never was kindness more greedily betrayed.

When Calder had departed, Rear-Admiral the Earl of Northesk became third-in-command. He was a Scot, and the son of a sailor. He had learnt his seamanship under Rodney, and was a few months older than Nelson, though he had no opportunity, during his service life, to distinguish himself in a general action. His flagship was the *Britannia*, the oldest and one of the largest units in the fleet, but she was a slow sailer, and it was only Lord Northesk's determined handling which enabled her to take an active part in the battle. Neither Nelson nor Collingwood seems to have known Northesk at all well, but they soon came to a sound understanding, and made up an harmonious chain of command.

Nelson's methods differed radically from those of Collingwood. He worked by frankness and confidence. 'The reception I met with on joining the Fleet', he wrote, 'caused the sweetest sensation of my life.' Greeting old acquaintances with infectious warmth, he soon made it his business to get to know and to enthuse everyone who had not served with him before. And then there was his 'Plan' to unfold. 'I believe my arrival was most welcome not only to the commander of the Fleet', he wrote to Emma Hamilton, 'but also to every individual in it; and when I came to explain to them the "Nelson touch" it was like an electric shock. Some shed tears, all approved. "It was new—it was singular—it was simple!" and, from Admirals downwards, it was repeated—"It must succeed, if ever they will allow us to get at them! You are, my Lord, surrounded by friends whom you inspire with confidence."' 'As soon as these emotions were past,' he told another correspondent, 'I laid before them the Plan I had previously arranged for attacking the enemy, and it was not only my pleasure to find it generally approved but clearly perceived and understood.' The Plan thus referred to, and spoken of as 'the Nelson touch', was afterwards formally issued to the captains as a Secret Memorandum, which is one of the classic documents of its kind. Its essence had already been conveyed to Captain Keats of the *Superb*, in a conversation which he recorded as follows:

> One day, walking with Lord Nelson in the grounds of Merton, talking on naval matters, he said to me: 'No day can be long enough to arrange a couple of fleets and fight a decisive battle, according to the old system. When *we* meet them (I was to have been with him), for meet them we shall, I'll tell you how I shall fight them. I shall form the Fleet into three Divisions in three Lines. One Division shall be composed of twelve or fourteen of the fastest two-decked ships, which I shall always keep to windward, or in a situation of advantage; and I shall put them under an Officer who, I am sure, will employ them in the manner I wish, if possible. I consider it will always be in my power to throw them into Battle in any part I may choose; but if circumstances prevent their being carried against the Enemy where I desire, I shall feel certain he will employ them effectually, and perhaps in a more advantageous manner than if he could have followed my orders.
>
> 'With the remaining part of the Fleet formed in two lines, I shall go at them at once, if I can, about one-third of their line from their leading Ship.' He then said, 'What do you think of it?' Such a question I felt required consideration. I paused. Seeing it, he said: 'But I'll tell you what I think of it. I think it will surprise and confound the Enemy. They won't know what I am about. It will bring forward a pell-mell Battle, and that is what I want.'

The Secret Memorandum, though more elaborate, expressed exactly the same idea, though in action it was seriously modified by the fact that Nelson had under the command a smaller force than he had assumed, and had therefore to make his attack in two columns, not three. The main features were as follows. 'The Order of Sailing is to be the Order of Battle.' 'The Second-in-Command will, after my intentions are made known to him, have the entire direction of his line to make the attack upon the Enemy, and to follow up the blow until they are captured or destroyed.' 'Something

Memo   'Victory off Cadiz 9 Octr 1805'

Thinking it almost impossible to bring a fleet of forty Sail of the Line into a Line of Battle in variable winds thick weather and other circumstances which must occur, without such a loss of time that the opportunity would probably be lost of bringing the Enemy to Battle in such a manner as to make the business decisive.

I have therefore made up my mind to keep the fleet in that position of Sailing (with the exception of the first and Second in Command) that the order of Sailing is to be the order of Battle, placing the fleet in two Lines of sixteen Ships each with an advanced Squadron

45 *The 'Fighting Memorandum'*

must be left to chance; nothing is sure in a Sea Fight beyond all others. Shot will carry away the masts and yards of friends as well as foes; but I look with confidence to a Victory before the Van of the Enemy could succour their Rear.' Perhaps the most memorable sentence was an echo of Lord Hawke, whose fighting tradition Nelson had inherited: '. . . In case Signals can neither be seen or perfectly understood, no Captain can do wrong if he places his Ship alongside that of an Enemy.'

It may seem surprising that a document so apparently simple should have appeared with the effect of an 'electric shock' to veteran captains; but they, like their enemies the French and Spaniards, had been brought up in a rigid and formal school of tactics, one which had been built up, over the centuries, with the object of strengthening mutual confidence. Nelson, who gave his captains just such confidence, soon taught them to believe that mutual support was given best by getting alongside the enemy rather than by keeping station in a line of bearing.

Writing on 9 October to Collingwood, Nelson said:

> I send you my Plan of Attack, as far as a man dare venture to guess at the very uncertain position the Enemy may be found in. But, my dear friend, it is to place you perfectly at ease respecting my intentions, and to give full scope to your judgment for carrying them into effect. We can, my dear Coll, have no little jealousies. We have only one great object in view, that of annihilating our Enemies, and getting a glorious Peace for our Country. No man has more confidence in another than I have in you: and no man will render your services more justice than your very old friend NELSON AND BRONTË.

While Nelson was infusing the watching fleet with his own gay confidence, what of the enemy, apparently impregnable and snug in Cadiz?

The Combined Fleet had reached the southern port by 21 August, to find itself little better off than at Ferrol. Cadiz, together with the surrounding countryside, had not recovered from an epidemic which had ravaged half Andalusia. There was little food; dockyard supplies were inadequate for a large force; and the ill-feeling which at the best of times was active beneath the surface between the navies of France and Spain had been roused by the fact that both ships which Calder had captured in July had been Spanish. Their comrades-in-arms believed them to have been 'deserted in action and sacrificed' by their allies, and although there was no adequate reason for this view, it did nothing to ease an always tricky relationship. At first Villeneuve was actually refused supplies, and it took a peremptory order from Madrid before he could get his essential stores. Even so, the authorities of the port greatly disliked having to accept French paper money, or drafts on Paris. In view of the financial reputation of the French Government, this was not surprising.

The personalities of the leaders of the Combined Fleet were as strongly contrasted as those of their opponents. Admiral Pierre de Villeneuve himself was a Provençal of aristocratic lineage. Like many of his kind who were prepared to serve the Revolutionary Government, he had been given quick promotion. He was a rear-admiral by the age of 33, and at the time of Trafalgar was actually some years younger than Nelson, who had himself attained a flag rank before the age of 40. Villeneuve, like his colleague and friend Decrès, had been a pupil of Suffren, the greatest tactician the French navy produced. Suffren's five engagements in the East Indies against Sir Edward Hughes were among the most stubborn ever fought, and were a fine school of discipline for a young officer.

The French second-in-command, Rear-Admiral Dumanoir le Pelley, was even younger than his chief. Thirty-five years old, he too had worn the King's uniform in the time of the old régime, and again, like Villeneuve, he was of an aristocratic family. So was Magon, the next in command, who had had more battle experience than most of his fellow officers. A Breton, he had fought off Ushant against Keppel, and in the West Indies against Rodney, and he had experienced a spell as a prisoner-of-war in England. One of Napoleon's entourage, who knew all the commanders concerned, gave it as his view that had Magon been in Villeneuve's place the Emperor's orders would have been obeyed, and the invasion of Britain attempted. He was impetuous and daring, and possessed all the certainty and assurance which Villeneuve lacked.

Of the French captains, Cosmao, another Breton, was the most outstanding, and his ship, the *Pluton*, was one of the best-manned in the fleet. It was Cosmao who had taken Diamond Rock, and he had saved at least one Spanish ship in Calder's action. Infernet of the *Intrépide* was another able officer, though his ship was an indifferent sailer. Gourrège of the *Aigle* and Maistral of the *Neptune* were also dependable. Villeneuve spoke of Maistral as 'a pattern to the fleet'. Gourrège was a rough-and-ready Breton merchant skipper brought into the navy by the Revolution; Maistral was yet another survivor from the older service. Other good captains were Lucas of the *Redoutable*, a man of humble origin, but one whose pupilage derived from Suffren, and Baudoin of the *Fougueux*.

As for the Spanish officers, they had both advantages and handicaps as compared with their allies. By and large they were older men, and their service had not suffered political disruption, at any rate on the scale of the French Revolution, but their sea experience had been more limited and, on the whole, less varied. Neither the French nor the Spanish had any living tradition of successful fleet encounter, which was in fact the gravest disadvantage under which any such a body as theirs could labour. If they were not beaten before they put to sea, yet even their bellicose Emperor did not envisage that they could cope with odds, which to the British seaman gave a spice to any fight.

Don Federico Gravina, the senior Spanish flag-officer, had been a sailor since boyhood. At 49 he was one of the most respected men in his country's service. He had been anxious not to continue under Villeneuve, but had been persuaded by his Government to remain in his command, at any rate until the immediate crisis had been resolved. His war experience went back to the days of the great Siege of Gibraltar, and he had been second-in-command of the fleet which had co-operated with Hood at Toulon, at the opening of the Revolutionary War, before his country had changed sides.

Vice-Admiral Álava, or D'Álava, second in the Spanish hierarchy, was three years older than Gravina, with whom he had served in earlier days at Gibraltar. Supporting these senior officers were Rear-Admiral Cisneros, who had taken part at the Battle of Cape St Vincent; Rear-Admiral Escano; Commodore Churruca of *San Juan de Nepomuceno*, a highly intelligent tactician who had no opinion of the French commander-in-chief; Commodore Galiano; and Valdez of the *Neptuno*. Valdez, who was not yet 35, was one of the most popular officers in the Spanish service, for it was he who, more than any other, had been responsible for saving the towering *Santissima Trinidad* from capture off Cape St Vincent, on that memorable day in 1797 when Nelson had won a Knighthood of the Bath.

One of the Gravina's captains was an Irishman, carrying on a well-established tradition of employment in the armed forces of continental countries. He went by the name of Don Enrique Macdonell, and was in command of the three-decker *Rayo*. He too had served the Spaniards at the siege of Gibraltar, in the Regimento de Hibernia, a corps originally raised among Jacobite refugees to Spain three-quarters of a century earlier. Transferring later to the navy, he had actually retired, but on hearing of Gravina's desperate need for trained officers had volunteered his services. As the *Victory*, together with many other British ships, had French names in her muster-book through most of the Napoleonic War, a mixture of nationalities was not in the least uncommon in navies where men were always hard to get.

At the end of September, when Nelson arrived off Cape St Vincent, Napoleon, having abandoned his invasion, solved the problem of how to induce the Combined Fleet to leave Cadiz by ordering it to sail forthwith to Naples, and thence, after landing troops for employment in Italy, back to Toulon. He still believed that his strategy had scattered the British, and that the force outside Cadiz was not a strong one.

The orders which he issued on 18 October through Decrès gave the French admiral discretion not to risk a battle unless circumstances were favourable, but although the Emperor knew, as early as 20 September, that the blockade had been reinforced, he left Paris three days later for his land campaign without modifying his orders. Thus, almost carelessly, did he throw away his fleet.

On hearing the Emperor's wishes, Gravina went on board Villeneuve's flagship and announced that 14 of his ships were almost ready for sea. Soldiers had been ordered to fill the deficiency in sailors. On the same evening, signal stations on the coast reported that a three-decker and two 74-gun ships were joining Collingwood from the westward. It was not then known that it was Nelson himself who had arrived, but the addition of strength caused Villeneuve uneasiness.

The embarkation of troops for service in Italy was completed by 2 October, but on the evening of that day Gravina had news from Lisbon which gave everyone disquiet. It was said that Nelson had indeed arrived, 'with four of the line and great projects for attacking, bombarding and bombing the Combined Squadron'. The effect was startling: the news itself was only too likely to be true, and a defence flotilla was hastily organised consisting of gun-boats, bomb-vessels and other small craft, manned by officers and men from the fleet. And now, instead of being able to get the ships-of-the-line into the Bay as and when they were ready, the fear of an impetuous attack, such as Nelson had made on Boulogne, kept them crowded in the harbour out of harm's way. But despite the alarm, Villeneuve continued to proclaim his intention of sailing the moment he had a fair wind.

At Cadiz, in fine autumn weather, there is often a land breeze at night from the east, favourable for ships to leave the harbour. Outside, in the morning, a westerly wind is usually fair for a run to the Mediterranean. On the evening of 7 October an easterly breeze sprang up, and the signal was made to prepare to weigh. It was quickly annulled, for the wind increased to such an extent as to threaten to carry the ships, once they were in the Bay, 'diametrically contrary to the course they had to make', in Villeneuve's own words. In fact, he had been increasingly affected not only by his pervading fear of Nelson, but by the new disposition of the blockading force. Nelson's custom differed from that of Collingwood, who believed in visibility. Nelson withdrew his main fleet right out of sight, some leagues into the Atlantic, leaving only the watching frigates inshore, with a communicating squadron of fast ships-of-the-

46 'The *Victory* breaking the Line'

From a watercolour by Nicholas Pocock

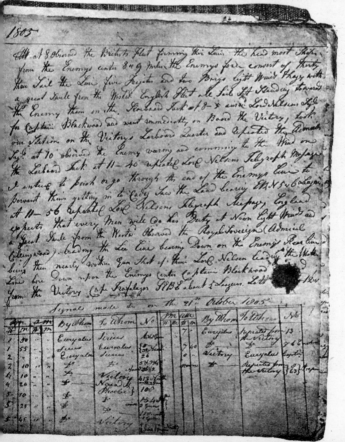

48 H.M.S. *Victory*: the lower gun deck

line, few of which were ever simultaneously in sight from the Spanish signal stations. Nelson might be there, but in what his strength consisted, and how it would be exercised, no one could be certain.

Villeneuve's next act was to summon a Council of War. The French and Spanish officers met aboard the *Bucentaure* on 8 October. Seven French and seven Spanish commanders were present: Villeneuve had his two flag-officers, Dumanoir and Magon, together with Captain Cosmao, Maistral, Lavillegris of the *Mont Blanc*, and Prigny, who acted as Chief of Staff. Gravina brought with him admirals Álava, Escano and Cisneros, and three commodores, Galiano, Macdonell and Hore.

The Spaniards had come to the meeting with a prepared and unanimous opinion. After Villeneuve had told them his orders, they rose one by one to dissent from the view that they should sail at once. Delay, they argued, was in their favour, for the British could hardly remain much longer where they were, if only for lack of supplies. Moreover the new levies badly wanted a few weeks of further training. When they had all spoken, Prigny urged the same opinion as the Spaniards. 'They', he said of the British, 'have kept the seas without intermission since 1793, while most of our fleet have scarcely weighed anchor for eight years.' Prigny favoured the employment of the defence flotilla, and suggested that no orders could bind them to attempt the impossible.

Such words from a fellow-Frenchman were too much for Magon, who not only roundly contradicted his colleague, but used some expressions which wounded Spanish honour. His speech caused a scene, and Commodore Galiano, his hand on his sword-hilt, seemed about to challenge Magon to a duel. Villeneuve calmed things down for a while, but even he was not at his most tactful in dealing with his allies. This time Gravina himself took up the cudgels, and said that only a madman would think of sailing in the present circumstances.

'Do you not see, sir,' he said to Villeneuve, 'that the barometer is falling?' 'It is not the glass, but the courage of certain persons that is falling', replied the French commander-in-chief. The sneer was too much for the courtly Gravina. 'Admiral,' he said, and looked Villeneuve straight in the face, 'whenever the Spanish fleet has gone into action side by side with allies, it has ever borne its part valiantly, and led the way, the foremost under fire. This, as you must admit, we fully proved at the battle off Finisterre.'

The Council ended with the customary formal vote. The result was a decision 'to await the favourable opportunity . . . which may arise from bad weather that would drive the enemy away from these waters, or from the necessity which he will experience of dividing the force of his squadron in order to protect his trade in the Mediterranean and the convoys that may be threatened by the squadrons from Cartagena and from Toulon. . . .'

As the Minutes of the Council would be scrutinised in Paris, they ended: 'The Admirals concluded . . . by renewing the orders to be in readiness to weigh, so as to be able to set sail at the first signal without losing a single instant.'

Whilst the Allies were in Council at Cadiz, reinforcements were gradually reaching

Nelson. On 7 October the *Defiance* joined from Portsmouth, and the *Amphion* frigate from Lisbon. The *Amphion*'s captain was William Hoste, one of Nelson's favourite pupils. Hoste had been with his chief as early as 1793, and had served in several of his battles. The *Amphion* had to be detached shortly before Trafalgar for service in the Mediterranean, and the order nearly broke Hoste's heart. He felt he would miss the fight, and so he did.

By contrast, the captain of the *Defiance*, Philip Durham, was one of the luckiest men in the Navy. He had been trained under Howe, had served in battle with Rodney, had survived the foundering of the *Royal George* at Spithead, fought in Calder's action, and been just in time to catch Nelson on one of his flying visits to the Admiralty. The pair met in a waiting-room. Nelson said: 'I am just appointed to the Mediterranean command, and sail immediately: I am sorry your ship is not ready, I should have been very glad to have you.'

Durham answered: 'Ask Lord Barham to place me under your Lordship's orders, and I will soon be ready.' Nelson did so, and left Durham the necessary orders at Portsmouth.

When the *Defiance* joined the fleet Durham brought out 750,000 dollars with him, for the garrison at Minorca. On paying his respects, Nelson said: 'Durham, I am glad to see you, but your stay will be short, for Sir Robert Calder sails tomorrow and takes with him all the captains who were in his action, to give evidence at the court-martial.' He added: 'The wind is at north-east, and the enemy will soon be out.' It was like turning a knife in the wound.

But when Durham went on board the *Prince of Wales*, Calder's ship, he found that the order to the captains was permissive. They were to go home 'if willing'. Durham was not. He longed to see action under Nelson, which was the wish of every active officer, and he did not love Sir Robert Calder, who owed his first sighting of the Combined Fleet to the alertness of the *Defiance*, but who gave the ship no special credit in his despatch. Moreover Durham sent some signals to Sir Robert next day which the admiral was pleased to term 'over-zealous', and altogether Durham was glad of a change of command.

Nelson forgot about the dollars, and when Durham sought to remind him, jocularly said: 'If the Spaniards come out, fire them at them, and pay them back in their own coin!' In fact, they were sent in to Gibraltar just before the action.

On 8 October the *Royal Sovereign* reported, as did the *Naiad* frigate from Gibraltar. The *Royal Sovereign* was an important addition of strength. Nelson knew her quality of old. A splendid three-decker, she had fought with Howe at the Glorious First of June, 11 years earlier, and had taken part in the watch on Toulon. Newly coppered and repaired, she was a heartening sight.

Collingwood, who was flying his flag in the *Dreadnought*, soon transferred to her, at first with some misgiving, but with increasing pleasure as he grew to learn the ship's qualities. The change was to have two consequences in battle: the first was that, as was the case with the *Victory*, Collingwood's ship outsailed the rest of his line; the second was that the *Dreadnought*, though a slow sailer, had been so well exercised in Gunnery by Collingwood that, when she was at last able to join the mêlée, her fire-power was exceptional, even for her large size. The appearance of the *Royal Sovereign* enabled Nelson to send Calder home in the *Prince of Wales*.

Rear-Admiral Louis had been detached, on 2 October, to Gibraltar and Tetuan for water and provisions, and had taken with him the *Queen*, the *Canopus*, *Spencer*, *Zealous* and *Tigre*—tried ships, all but the first of which had been with Nelson on his chase to the West Indies. The *Donegal*, another veteran, followed them on 17 October. Louis, like Hoste, had been regretful at the order, but Nelson did not expect the enemy to come out until after Louis had rejoined. He detached these particular ships first, so that they should have every chance of being there at the day of battle. No one knew their quality better than Nelson.

On 13 October the *Agamemnon*, Captain Sir Edward Berry, arrived from England, and made no little stir in the fleet. 'When she was signalled,' so a contemporary reported, 'Nelson exclaimed with glee: "Here comes Berry! *Now* we shall have a battle!"' Both ship and captain recalled much in Nelson's life. Between 1793 and 1796 Nelson had made his name, as a Mediterranean man, in the *Agamemnon*, while Sir Edward Berry had been his flag-captain at the Nile, and had served with him earlier still, at Cape St Vincent. He had been foremost in Nelson's boarding-party in that battle. Afterwards, at Court, when George III had remarked on the loss of Nelson's right arm, Nelson had answered at once by presenting his 'right hand', Berry, to his Sovereign.

Berry was indeed the stormy petrel of the Navy. He had already been in several, general actions, and was to survive two more. He had left England on 2 October, and, when eight days out, had been chased and all but taken by Allemand's powerful detachment. Berry had then had one of the narrowest shaves of his life.

On 14 October the *Africa*, which, like the *Agamemnon*, was a 64-gun ship, joined from home, and the Trafalgar fleet was complete. On the same day Blackwood in the *Euryalus* signalled that the Combined Fleet was at the harbour's mouth. Nelson now placed the *Defence* and *Agamemnon* 'from seven to ten leagues west of Cadiz', and the *Mars* and *Colossus* 'five leagues east of the Fleet', adding: 'by this chain I hope to have a constant communication with the frigates off Cadiz.'

Nelson's use of the *Mars* for this special service delighted her Scots captain, George Duff, who had not met Nelson earlier in his career. Duff was a favourite with Collingwood, and had a smart ship. He had a kinsman of the same name acting as his first lieutenant, and a son of 13, called Norwich, among his 'younkers'. His letters to his wife illustrate the Commander-in-Chief's effect on such a man. He wrote on 1 October: 'I dined with his Lordship yesterday, and had a very merry dinner. He certainly is the pleasantest admiral I ever served under.' Nine days later he said: 'He is so good and pleasant a man, that we all wish to do what he likes, without any kind of orders. I have been myself very lucky with most of my admirals, but I really think the present the pleasantest I have ever met with: even this little detachment is a kind thing to me, there being so many senior officers to me in the Fleet, as it shows his attention, and wish to bring me forward; but I believe I have to thank my old friend Collingwood for it, as he was on board the *Victory* when I was sent for.' And three days before Trafalgar: 'You ask me about Lord Nelson, and how I like him. I have already answered that question as every person must do that ever served under him.' The later story of Duff and his ship belongs, appropriately enough in view of her name, to the battle itself.

A few days before the enemy engaged, Nelson became worried about Hardy. The flag-captain's health was poorly, and he was forced for a time to keep to his cabin, Nelson at times refusing to eat, now that the friend who usually did this service for him was not there to cut up his meat.

When Hardy recovered he asked Nelson if the *Victory* might spend a night away from the Fleet, repairing sails. The request was at first refused, but later granted, Nelson realising that it would make a difference to the speed of the ship in action. But the admiral was sleepless all the time the repairs were being done, and when Dr Beatty asked him in the morning how his head was, Nelson having complained of pains, he snapped: 'Heads and tails be damned! I care nothing about them. I wish I were back with the Fleet.'

Very soon, they were.

By the time of the issue of his orders of 18 September for the Combined Fleet to proceed to the Mediterranean, Napoleon had decided to replace Villeneuve by Admiral Rosily. In its way, this was a desperate step, for although Rosily was at the head of the vice-admirals list, he had not served afloat for many years, having been engaged in purely administrative posts. Decrès at first hesitated to tell his old friend the Emperor's decision in plain terms, and when he heard rumours of a change in command, Villeneuve hoped that he would be allowed to act as Rosily's second.

On 12 October, four days after the Council of War, Rosily reached Madrid. The Spanish posting system had broken down, and the roads beyond Cordoba were infested with brigands. Rosily was advised by the French ambassador not to proceed on his way until arrangements had been made for him to travel in safety. It was a ten days' journey from Madrid to Cadiz, but in half that time Villeneuve, already unhappy both at his prospects in battle and at the deliberations of his Council, had learnt of his successor's advent, and had guessed that he had lost the Emperor's favour.

On 18 October, without saying a word to anyone, Villeneuve suddenly ordered Magon to sea with seven of the line and a frigate. Magon was to try to capture Blackwood's squadron, and to find out the strength behind it. But before the order could be carried into effect, Villeneuve had news by telegraph of Louis's appearance at Gibraltar, where there were already two British ships-of-the-line. Villeneuve's natural inference was that Nelson must be in the weakest relative position he would ever be likely to find him. The combination of news was decisive. He gave orders for the fleet to prepare to weigh anchor.

'Enemy have their topsails hoisted.' The news came from the frigate *Sirius* early in the morning on 19 October. An hour later word came: 'The enemy ships are coming out of port or getting under sail.' In ten minutes Blackwood passed it out to the *Phœbe*, which he kept to the westward. As the light strengthened, they got the message through to the *Mars*, and by half-past nine Nelson himself had it. The *Victory* was then nearly 50 miles to the westward of Cadiz. Without waiting to form order of sailing, he signalled: 'General chase, south-east', and shortly afterwards made the signal to prepare for battle. His course was for the Straits of Gibraltar.

What had in fact happened to the enemy was that Magon, with nine of the line and three frigates, had cleared the entrance to Cadiz by seven o'clock in the morning, when the wind suddenly dropped. Blackwood instantly sent a sloop to Gibraltar to warn Louis. Magon's ships lay becalmed until the early afternoon, when a breeze sprang up from west-north-west. They then stood to the northward, shadowed by the *Euryalus* and *Sirius*, while the *Phœbe* and *Naiad* kept touch with the *Defence*, which was ten miles to the westward and in touch with other ships. Owing to the delay in getting out of the harbour, any hope the French had of finding the British scattered had disappeared. There was no chance of capturing the ever-alert Blackwood, and as the wind in the bay was still southerly, Magon could not get in again. Villeneuve decided that he now had no choice but to sail the whole Fleet.

While the enemy were in process of coming out, men of the British Fleet remembered those at home.

> What think you, my own dearest love ? [wrote Blackwood to his wife]. At this moment the Enemy are coming out, and as if determined to have a fair fight; all night they had been making signals, and the morning showed them to us getting under sail. They have thirty-four Sail-of-the-Line, and five Frigates. Lord Nelson, I am sorry to say, has but twenty-seven Sail-of-the-Line with him; the rest are in Gibraltar, getting water. Not that he has not enough to bring them to close Action; but I want him to have so many as to make the most decisive battle of it that ever was, which will bring us a lasting Peace, I hope, and some prize money. Within two hours, though our Fleet was at sixteen leagues off, I have let Lord N. know of their coming out, and I have been enabled to send a vessel off to Gibraltar, which will bring Admiral Louis and the ships in there out.

Blackwood's message in fact arrived too late to bring Louis back in time. He was already some distance into the Mediterranean, covering the passage of supply-ships for Craig. The letter continued:

> . . . At this moment we are within four miles of the Enemy, and talking to Lord Nelson by means of Sir H. Popham's signals, though so distant, but repeated along the rest of the Frigates of this Squadron. You see also, my Harriet, I have time to write to you, and to assure you that to the last moment of my breath, I shall be as much attached to you as man can be, which I am sure you will credit. It is very odd how I have been dreaming all night of my carrying home despatches. God send so much good luck! The day is fine; the sight, of course, beautiful. I expect, before this hour tomorrow, to have carried General Decrès on board the *Victory* in my barge, which I have just been painting. God bless you. No more at present.

The writer had heard the rumour of a change in the command of the Combined Fleet, and had assumed that it was Napoleon's Minister of Marine who was to replace Villeneuve.

As for Nelson, as soon as Blackwood had conveyed his momentous tidings by means of Sir Home Popham's newly issued and improved signal-book, he wrote to Emma Hamilton as follows:

Victory, October 19, 1805, Noon. Cadiz, E.S.E.
16 Leagues.

My dearest Beloved Emma, the dear Friend of my Bosom, the Signal has been made that the enemy's Combined Fleet are coming out of Port. We have very little wind, so that I have no hopes of seeing them before tomorrow. May the God of Battles crown my endeavours with success; at all events, I will take care that my name shall ever be most dear to you and Horatia, both of whom I love as much as my own life. And as my last writing before the Battle will be to you, so I hope in God that I shall live to finish my letter after the Battle. May Heaven bless you prays your

NELSON AND BRONTË.

As darkness fell on 19 October he wrote in his private diary:

Directed the Fleet to observe my motions during the night, and for *Britannia*, *Prince* and *Dreadnought*, they being heavy sailers, to take their stations as convenient; and for *Mars*, *Orion*, *Belleisle*, *Leviathan*, *Bellerophon* and *Polyphemus* to go ahead during the night, and to carry a light, standing for the Strait's mouth.

Next day, Nelson added a paragraph to his letter.

October 20th—In the morning we were close to the Mouth of the Streights, but the wind had not come far enough to the Westward to allow the Combined Fleets to weather the Shoals off Trafalgar; but they were counted as far as forty Sail of Ships of War, which I suppose to be 34 of the Line, and six Frigates. A group of them was seen off the Lighthouse of Cadiz this morning, but it blows so very fresh and thick weather, that I rather believe they will go into the Harbour before night. May God Almighty give us success over these fellows, and enable us to get a Peace. . . .

These were the last words he ever wrote to the woman he loved. He also sent a short note to Horatia, telling her he was sure of her prayers for his safety, conquest, 'and speedy return to dear Merton and our dearest good Lady Hamilton'.

'I have not a thought except on you and the French fleet', he had written to Emma Hamilton earlier in his command. 'All my thoughts, plans and toils tend to those two objects, and I will embrace them both so close when I can lay hold of either one or the other, that the Devil himself should not separate us.' Such dedication deserved its reward.

The 20th of October, which was a Sunday, was no day of rest: it was one of manœuvre, though in any fleet commanded by Nelson religious observance would have been as usual.

In the early morning there was a light wind from southward, and this enabled Villeneuve to get his fleet to sea without confusion. By about seven o'clock all the Allied ships had left Cadiz, and at first stood to the westward. As they cleared the bay, the wind began to freshen, with strong gusts and heavy rain. Some of the Spaniards split their topsails in reefing, and fell away to leeward.

The *Sirius*, which had given the earliest news of enemy activity, intercepted an American vessel, and found that she was out of Belfast, bound for Gibraltar. While the boarding party were still away, the frigate came under fire from a distant broadside, which might be considered as the first shots of Trafalgar. A little later the *Sirius* saw the same French battleship which had fired at her send over a party of investigation. The American was the only neutral recorded to have seen the preliminaries to battle.

Daylight was scarcely clear when the *Euryalus*, ever alert, reported Sir Edward

Berry in a typical incident. The *Agamemnon*, with a brig in tow, was standing, apparently unconscious of her danger, straight for the enemy. 'Made the signal to the *Agamemnon*', noted the master of the frigate in his log. 'Repeated it with many guns before it was noticed.' Captain Blackwood, having at last held Berry's attention, ordered him to repeat the Allied numbers to Nelson.

At eight o'clock, whilst at the mouth of the Straits and still hoping to meet with Louis, Nelson ordered the *Victory* to be hove-to. Shortly afterwards Collingwood, together with the captains of the *Mars*, *Colossus* and *Defence*, came on board and conferred with the Commander-in-Chief for about an hour. These captains, Duff, Morris and Hope, were ordered to keep in touch with the frigates, supporting them whenever necessary, and affording a reliable chain of communication.

'In the afternoon', wrote Nelson in his private diary, 'Captain Blackwood telegraphed that the enemy seemed determined to go to the westward, and that they shall *not* do if in the power of Nelson and Brontë to prevent them. At 5 telegraphed Captain B. that I relied upon his keeping sight of the enemy.' Bruce, the *Euryalus*'s signal midshipman, and Soper, the signal hand, would have no rest till the fleets were in contact, and very little then.

While Nelson had been cruising out of Villeneuve's sight, Blackwood had seen the Allied Commander-in-Chief make the signal for his fleet to form order of sailing in three columns, his apparent intention being to make enough westing to ensure, later, a quick passage through the Straits by a change of course. Admiral Gravina took station to windward, he being in command of the Squadron of Observation. His duty was to keep the British frigates at a distance, and to discover the numbers and movements of Nelson's fleet, of the composition and formation of which Villeneuve was still unsure.

At about four o'clock the weather cleared, and the wind flew round to west, taking the Combined Fleet aback, and throwing it into disorder. Villeneuve signalled a new course for his columns—south-south-west—and as darkness fell, the ships were still trying to take up their new stations. At half-past seven, signalling with flares, rockets and gunfire was seen and heard ahead, and at half-past eight the brig *Argus* came under the flagship's stern and her captain hailed that, some two hours earlier, the *Achille* had sighted 18 British ships-of-the-line in the direction of the Straits.

Fearing to be caught in an order of sailing in which only one of three squadrons could fire without risk to friends, Villeneuve made the signal to form a single line of battle on the leewardmost ship, without regard to sequence. It was the simplest direction he could have given, under the circumstances, but it led to further confusion. The ships to leeward omitted to hoist the distinguishing lights which they should have shown, and each took station as best she could. The squadrons became mixed together, and the duller sailers dropped astern. By daylight, no true line of battle had been evolved, though the Allied Fleet was beginning to assume the appearance of what Collingwood was afterwards to describe as 'a curve, convexing to leeward'.

Nelson, meanwhile, continued to close the enemy, but signalled that the fleet would come to the wind on the starboard tack at the close of day: in effect, this was marking time. The action placed the British some ten miles to windward and some five miles in advance of the enemy during the hours of darkness, ready to act upon any movement the frigates might report, and, if the wind held, ready to force an action when daylight discovered the disposition of the enemy. Nelson does not seem to have contemplated a night action, and he knew that if he waited, the further the Combined Fleet would move from Cadiz, and the more difficult it would be for Villeneuve to make good a retreat to his port of refuge.

At four in the morning, Nelson ordered his fleet to stand north by east. The movement placed him, at daylight, nine miles directly to windward of his opponent. Just before six o'clock, it was light enough to see the Combined Fleet silhouetted against the dawn.

4 The Battle

Nelson may be held to have been lucky in one respect: he had always realised exactly what he was fighting for, and why he lived and might die in the nation's service. When he wrote 'King . . . Country . . . Enemy . . .' he saw precisely what he wrote: the actual George III; the Norfolk fields; and men whose political principles he detested.

He was indeed happier than those, of his own and other times, who have died in battle without the solace of knowing an adequate reason for their fate, beyond the fact that they had no choice in the matter, that it was 'the done thing', a convention to which a friendly company subscribed, and that it took nearly as much courage to reject it as to conform.

Nelson knew that all sane men feared death, feared wounds and pain, feared dishonour, and that it was by an outward *appearance* of courage that morale was sustained, discipline supported, self-conquest ensured—hence his sharpness to the lieutenant at Copenhagen. That was why, in battle itself, his exertions redoubled, and why he seemed to all around him his fullest self. It had been so at the Nile and in the Baltic: it was so now. We have been fortunate in examples of the quality in our own time, shown under circumstances which might have daunted even Nelson, though he would not have allowed the fact to appear.

At Trafalgar, though numerically the odds were somewhat against him, Nelson went into battle with the most complete assurance of victory in all his crowded life. Close knowledge of conditions in the opposing fleet could in fact only have reassured him still further, but if the enemy stood boldly up to his advance, it was inevitable that victory must be won at high cost.

The details of 21 October are established by abundant evidence. Villeneuve was directly between the British Fleet and Cape Trafalgar. which was about 21 miles east of the *Victory*. Soon after daylight, Nelson made four general signals. The first was to form order of sailing in two columns. The second and fourth gave the course. The third was to 'Prepare for battle'. He then summoned the captains of his four frigates, his friends Blackwood of the *Euryalus*, Dundas of the *Naiad*, Capel of the

Phœbe, who had been with him at the Nile, and Prowse of the *Sirius*—and it is not untypical of the change in the pace of warfare that, with a light wind, nearly six hours elapsed after the opposing fleets had come into visual contact, before battle was fairly joined, and that there was leisure in those hours to do much.

Nelson had three anxieties. The first was lest the enemy, when they discerned his numbers, should at once turn away and make for Cadiz. The second was the wind. It was uncertain, not more than sufficed to carry the ships over the Atlantic swell at a walking pace, which in the case of the indifferent sailers was more like a crawl. The third was the limit of daylight. It was autumn, and the fight could scarcely be general until noon, perhaps not then. That left all too few hours to complete the business he intended.

Nelson had expressed a general view of his responsibilities in a memorandum he had prepared during the chase to the West Indies.

> The business of an English Commander-in-Chief being first to bring the Enemy's fleet to battle on the most advantageous terms to himself (I mean that of laying his ships well on board the Enemy as expeditiously as possible), and secondly to continue them there without separating until the business is decided . . . if the two fleets are both willing to fight, but little manœuvring is necessary; the less the better: a day is soon lost in that business. . . .

It was in fact time for which he was striving—time for his pell-mell battle, and if the plan which he had circulated to his captains had to be sacrificed in some of its details in order to engage quickly, Nelson would not hesitate, whatever the risks to the leading ships. On the day, they 'scrambled into battle as soon as they could'.

The tactics of Trafalgar have led to countless arguments and much disagreement. What were Nelson's intentions? How far were they carried out? Where and why did he depart from his plan? Were his actions the best under the circumstances? Could they serve as a model for the future conduct of operations?

Some of these questions cannot now be answered completely, since Nelson did not live to write his own account of the battle, but to most of them there is a reasonable reply. His intention was victory, and it was achieved. The principal element in his plan, attack in column, was in fact carried out, and it was unquestionably the best in the circumstances since, if the enemy stood his ground, it ensured decision, while if he did not, conditions of chase—to which it could be adapted—would apply. But to elevate the tactics of Trafalgar to the status of a doctrine is carrying the matter too far, as all students of naval warfare have recognised. In any other hands than Nelson's, and against another opponent than Villeneuve, they could have led to disaster, to such an appalling risk did they expose the leading ships of each line. But the risk was calculated. Nelson had always worked to a low factor of safety. He knew his Fleet, and he knew his opponents. He had seized the essence—'laying his ships well on board the enemy as expeditiously as possible'—and that was what he did. There were extraordinary incidents in the process, tensions, comedy, pride, tragedy, triumph, and it is fortunate that so many were recorded.

The *Victory's* surgeon, William Beatty, wrote that 'soon after daylight, Lord Nelson came upon deck. He was dressed as usual in his Admiral's frockcoat, bearing on the left breast four stars of different Orders, which he always wore with his common apparel. He did not wear his sword in the Battle of Trafalgar. It had been taken from the place where it hung up in his cabin, and was laid ready on his table; but it is supposed he forgot to call for it. This was the only action in which he ever appeared without a sword. He displayed excellent spirits, and expressed his pleasure at the prospect of giving a fatal blow to the naval power of France and Spain; and spoke with confidence of obtaining a signal victory notwithstanding the inferiority of the British Fleet, declaring to Captain Hardy that "he would not be contented with capturing less than twenty sail-of-the-line". He afterwards pleasantly observed that "the 21st of October was the happiest day in the year among his family" but did not assign the reason for this. His lordship had previously entertained a strong presentiment that this would prove the auspicious day, and had several times said to Captain Hardy and Dr Scott (Chaplain of the Ship and Foreign Secretary to the Commander-in-Chief, whose intimate friendship he enjoyed) "the 21st of October will be our day!"'

The family occasion of which Nelson was thinking was an action which had taken place in West Indian waters in 1757, during the Seven Years War. His maternal uncle, Captain Suckling, under whom he had himself first gone to sea, made his name in command of the Dreadnought, when three British ships had attacked seven French vessels, and severely damaged them. Nelson also told his retinue that it pleased him to think that this was the day of the annual fair at Burnham Thorpe, his Norfolk birthplace.

When Blackwood arrived, he 'had the satisfaction to find the Admiral in good but very calm spirits. After receiving my congratulations at the approach of the moment he so often and so long had wished for, he replied: "I mean today to bleed the captains of the frigates, as I shall keep you on board until the very last minute." His mind seemed entirely directed to the strength and formation of the enemy's line, as well as to the effects which his novel mode of attack was likely to produce.'

Owing to conditions of light, Villeneuve had been about ten minutes later than Nelson in gaining a clear view of the fleet to which he was opposed. When he did so, it appeared to be in no recognisable formation. Then it divided, in accordance with Nelson's signal, steering for his centre and rear. Villeneuve now had to face the fact that if he held his immediate course he would be committed to the passage of the Straits, with Nelson in hard pursuit, and with the likelihood of further ships from Gibraltar disputing his intention. He took the action which Nelson had expected. Although his fleet was still in some disorder, Villeneuve reversed its course, heading it northwards, towards Cadiz. But already he was too late. The movement took too long; and Commodore Churruca, commanding the San Juan de Nepomuceno, now the rear ship of the Allied line, turned to his second-in-command with the words: 'The fleet is doomed. The French admiral does not understand his business. He has compromised us all.' He was not alone in his opinion. But placed as he was, and with Nelson set on battle, Villeneuve's problem had no satisfactory solution unless, by some miracle, the wind dropped, and night at length masked his retreat.

Nelson had every reason to be cheerful. His problems seemed over. He had gained the wish of his heart, the opportunity to defeat a principal fleet in the open sea.

At daylight [ran the famous last entry in his private diary], saw the Enemy's Combined Fleet from east to E.S.E.; bore away; made the signal for Order of Sailing and to Prepare for Battle. The Enemy with their heads to the southward. At seven the Enemy wearing in succession. May the Great God whom I worship, grant to my Country, and for the benefit of Europe in general, a great and glorious Victory; and may no misconduct in anyone tarnish it; and may humanity after Victory be the predominant feature in the British Fleet. For myself individually, I commit my life to Him who made me, and may His blessing light upon my endeavours for serving my Country faithfully. To Him I resign myself, and the just cause which is entrusted to me to defend. Amen, Amen, Amen.

Having composed his prayer, and added a codicil to his will which stated his view of Lady Hamilton's services to her country, a document which was witnessed by Blackwood and Hardy, Nelson had leisure to see and approve Hardy's arrangements for fighting the *Victory*. He visited every deck, spoke to the men at quarters, exchanged greetings with special friends, and made everyone cheerful and confident.

As the morning drew on, there were continual signals, first from Collingwood and later from Nelson, for ships to make more sail. The flagships were leading their respective lines, though this was not in accordance with the Memorandum, and it was a fact which added a touch of comedy to the proceedings. Blackwood at one time had urged Nelson to transfer his flag to a frigate, and when the idea was rejected by the admiral on the score of example, he was persuaded to agree that the *Téméraire* should precede the *Victory* into action. Yet Nelson would permit no taking in of sail, such as would have allowed the ships to change places, and when, at the last moment, Captain Harvey was on the point of overtaking, Nelson actually signalled him astern by flag, one account says by hailing in person.

Earlier in the day he had seen that Collingwood, in the *Royal Sovereign*, was beginning to outstrip the ships of his line by a considerable margin, and he grew so anxious for his old friend that he signalled to Duff of the *Mars*, which was fast, to draw ahead of his admiral. The order was without effect, for Collingwood, like Nelson, refused to take in sail. Nelson himself had packed his punch. There were three three-decked ships at the head of his line, the *Victory*, the *Téméraire* and the *Neptune*; Collingwood had no such powerful close support, for his other three-deckers the *Dreadnought* and the *Prince*, were nowhere near the van of his squadron.

At 11.40 Nelson telegraphed to Collingwood announcing: 'I intend to pass through the enemy's line to prevent them getting into Cadiz', an action in which he was to be foiled by the close formation of the Allies. This was followed by a general signal to: 'Make all sail with safety to the masts.' It was clear that some ships were intent on keeping the arranged 'Order of Battle'. Nelson's view was that even a moment's delay in grappling with an opponent might mean the loss of a prize. John Pasco, who was acting as signal lieutenant, was having a busy morning. He had already been concerned in one incident which affected his own future; he was soon to be involved in another, which has become legendary.

Pasco could have been doing duty as first lieutenant of the *Victory*, to which seniority entitled him, but in order to avoid a succession of executive officers, he had agreed to waive his rank while serving on Nelson's staff. The position was acceptable, at any rate as a temporary measure, in the course of a routine commission, but when a general action was in prospect it was a different matter, for the senior lieutenant would be sure to gain promotion if he survived, possibly to post-captain.

During the morning, Pasco had to make a report to Lord Nelson. 'On entering the cabin', so he afterwards told Sir Harris Nicolas, 'I discovered his Lordship on his knees, writing. He was then penning that beautiful prayer. I waited until he rose and communicated what I had to report, but could not, at such a moment, disturb his mind with any grievance of mine.' Pasco's delicacy cost him years of seniority in captain's rank, for he was only made a commander after the battle, Quilliam, the first lieutenant, receiving a double step, while poor Pasco had to wait for this. But he lived to become an admiral, and on the day of Trafalgar he ordered the hoist of Nelson's best-known message.

Blackwood records that as he was walking with Nelson on the poop the admiral said: 'I'll now amuse the Fleet with a signal', asking his friend if he did not think there was one yet wanting. Blackwood said he thought that everyone seemed clearly to understand what they were about, but Nelson kept to his opinion'.

His lordship came to me on the poop [Pasco afterwards related] and about a quarter to noon said: 'I wish to say to the Fleet, ENGLAND CONFIDES THAT EVERY MAN WILL DO HIS DUTY'; and he added: 'you must be quick, for I have one more to make, which is for Close Action.' I replied, 'If your Lordship will permit me to substitute *expects* for *confides*, the signal will soon be completed, because the word "expects" is in the vocabulary, and "confides" must be spelt.' His lordship replied, in haste, and with seeming satisfaction: 'That will do, Pasco, make it directly!' When it had been answered by a few ships in the Van, he ordered me to make the signal for Close Action, and to *keep it up*: accordingly, I hoisted No. 16 at the top-gallant mast-head, and there it remained until shot away.

There was, in fact, one intermediate signal made. This was to 'Prepare to anchor at close of day'. Nelson knew the danger of a lee shore, in this case the shoals of Trafalgar, especially to battle-damaged ships, and he believed that by nightfall there might be a gale of wind.

The effect of the famous hoist was various. According to one account, Nelson was delighted with his own inspiration. 'Now', he said, 'I can do no more. We must trust to the great Disposer of all events, and the justice of our cause! I thank God for this great opportunity of doing my duty!' But in the *Victory*, below decks, when the words were repeated by an officer of marines, some of the men—though they cheered—were nonplussed. Had they not always done their duty? Were they likely to falter now? As for Collingwood, his biographer reports that when the admiral saw it first, he said that he wished Nelson would make no more signals, for they all understood what they were to do! But in the Journal of Captain Redmill of the *Polyphemus* he noted that when the message was given to the ship's company it 'was answered with three cheers, and answered by the *Dreadnought* on our larboard beam', and when Napoleon heard that Nelson had flown it in battle, he ordered a similar message to be painted in a prominent place on all his own ships.

*Plan of Nelson's approach: the position of the two fleets at noon on 21
October 1805, showing the ships of the line and the Euryalus frigate.
(By kind permission of Rear-Admiral A. H. Taylor, C.B.)*

Soon after this incident the frigate captains took their leave. Blackwood was ordered to tell—

> all the captains of Line-of-Battle ships that Nelson depended on their exertions; and that if, by the mode of attack prescribed, they found it impracticable to get into Action immediately, they might adopt whatever they thought best, provided it led them quickly and closely alongside an Enemy. He then again desired me to go away; and as we were standing on the front of the poop, I took his hand, and said, 'I trust, my Lord, that on my return to the *Victory*, which will be as soon as possible, I shall find your Lordship well, and in possession of twenty Prizes.' On which he made this reply: 'God bless you, Blackwood, I shall never speak to you again.'

Within a few minutes, the *Royal Sovereign* came under concentrated fire. '*Here began the Din of War*. . . .' The words are from the journal of Lieutenant Barclay of the *Britannia*. The din did not cease until darkness, and until the day was decided by gunnery at short range, by boarding, or by a combination of the two.

In the *Royal Sovereign* Collingwood's hours had been less dramatic, at least until the time of encounter, than those of the Commander-in-Chief in the *Victory*, but equally characteristic. Mr Smith, the admiral's servant, entered the cabin about daybreak and found his master 'already up and dressing'. Collingwood asked Smith if he had seen the French Fleet. 'On my replying that I had not,' so Smith recorded, 'he told me to look out at them, adding that in a very short time we should see a great deal more. . . . I then observed a crowd of ships to leeward; but I could not help looking with still greater interest at the admiral, who during all this time was shaving himself with a composure which quite astonished me. . . .'

Collingwood dressed himself that morning with particular care, and soon afterwards, meeting Lieutenant Clavell, who was a favourite with him, advised him to pull off his boots. 'You had better put on silk stockings, as I have done,' he said, 'for if one should get shot in the leg, they would be so much more manageable for the surgeon.' He then proceeded to visit the decks, and addressing the officers said to them in his sober way: 'Now, gentlemen, let us do something today which the world may talk of hereafter.'

It was Collingwood's belief that if a ship could fire three well-directed broadsides in five minutes, no enemy could resist them, and in the *Dreadnought* he had been able to cut down the time to three minutes and a half. The *Royal Sovereign*, fresh from home, could not yet equal that speed, but her gunnery was already creditable, and was to show itself remarkable in battle. When, from his windward station, Nelson saw his friend beginning to come under close fire, he exclaimed: 'See how that noble fellow, Collingwood, takes his ship into action. How I envy him!'

Hercules Robinson, then a midshipman in the *Euryalus*, came to know Collingwood well, and was fond of telling how in action he walked the break of the poop 'with his little triangular gold-laced cocked hat, tights, silk stockings and buckles, musing over the progress of the fight, and munching an apple'. As Robinson said, an admiral's principal business took place before and after an engagement. During its course, the burden was on the individual captains.

Collingwood's instructions had been to pass through the enemy line at the twelfth ship from the rear, but seeing that the ship in question was a two-decker, and that near her was the great *Santa Ana*, which carried the flag of Admiral Álava, he chose her as his point of attack. The *Fougueux*, immediately astern, closed up, and when Collingwood saw the movement he ordered Rotheram, the captain of the *Royal Sovereign*, to steer straight at the Frenchman and carry away his bowsprit. To avoid this, the *Fougueux* backed her main topsail, and allowed Collingwood to pass through, at the same time beginning her own fire. Collingwood ordered a gun to be fired occasionally at her, in order to cover his own ship with smoke. Then, ranging along-side the Spaniard, he gave her a broadside and a half, killing and wounding about a hundred men, and in a matter of seconds the lower yards of the two ships were locked together. At one point, a top-gallant studding-sail, which had been shot away, was hanging over the gangway hammocks. Collingwood called out to Clavell to come and help him take it in, observing that they should want it some other day! The two officers rolled it carefully up, and placed it in a boat. By half-past two, after a fight which had lasted more than two hours, much of it at the closest quarters, the *Santa Ana* struck. By that time the *Royal Sovereign* was herself so damaged that she called on the *Euryalus*, whose captain had a way of being at the critical point, to take her in tow, and to make any necessary signals. Just before nightfall, when Collingwood had heard from Hardy's own lips of Nelson's fate, he transferred in person to the frigate, where he remained until the *Queen*, a three-decker not then present, became available for his flag.

Collingwood said of the *Santa Ana* that she was a 'Spanish perfection . . . She towered over the *Royal Sovereign* like a castle. No ship fired a shot at her but ourselves, and you have no conception how completely she was ruined.' Careful of his own property, as of that of the Admiralty, Collingwood had a serio-comic tale of destruction to tell a friend after the battle. 'I have had a great destruction of my furniture and stock,' he said, 'I have hardly a chair that has not a shot in it, and many have lost both legs and arms, without hope of pension. My wine broke in moving, and my pigs were slain in battle; and these are heavy losses where they cannot be replaced.'

The admiral perhaps claimed too much when he said that the *Royal Sovereign* alone engaged the *Santa Ana*, for the *Belleisle*, which followed Collingwood's lead as closely as she could, fired her first port broadside into Álava's ship, and her starboard into the *Fougueux*, which was now drifting to leeward. The *Belleisle* was on the point of raking another ship, the *Indomptable*, when the *Fougueux* loomed back out of the smoke, and struck her starboard gangway with her port bow, rolling her foreyard over the quarter-deck. The *Indomptable* then crossed the *Belleisle*'s bows, gave her a broadside, and drifted away. When she had gone, the *Belleisle* and *Fougueux* lay locked together for the greater part of an hour.

With the third ship it went hard: she was the *Mars*, and it was the *Fougueux* which did much of the damage. As she dropped to leeward after her encounter with the *Royal Sovereign*, she came into a position where she could rake the *Mars*. The captain of marines, Norman, who was on the poop, went to the quarter deck to report the situation to Captain Duff, who asked if any of their own guns would bear on the *Fougueux*. Norman said: 'I think not, but I cannot see for smoke.' 'Then', said Duff, 'we must point our guns at the ships on which they *can* bear. I shall go and look, but the men below may see better, as there is less smoke.' Duff went to the end of the quarter-deck to peer over the side, and then ordered a messenger to go below and tell the gunners to train more aft. 'He had scarcely turned round', wrote an eyewitness, 'when the *Fougueux* raked the *Mars*. A cannon shot killed Duff, and two seamen who were immediately behind him. The ball struck the captain on the chest, and carried off his head. His body fell on the gangway, where it was covered with a spare colour until after the action.' As Lieutenant Duff was also killed in the battle, poor young Norwich was the only member of his family left alive in the ship. A little later, Captain Cosmao of the *Pluton* gave the *Mars* another broadside, which completed the destruction of her masts and rigging. She drifted away, unmanageable. Grim sentences in her log tell her story more graphically than any formal account. 'At 1.15 Captain Duff was killed, and the poop and quarter-deck almost left destitute, the carnage was so great having every one of our braces and running rigging shot away which made the ship entirely ungovernable and was frequently raked by different ships of the enemy.' It was well that Captain Duff, as one of his last actions, had ordered his son below.

Successive ships followed the example of the *Royal Sovereign*, the *Belleisle* and the *Mars*, until the whole of the Allied rear was closely engaged, or had been driven to leeward. Seldom had there been a series of such grim encounters.

It was characteristic of sea fighting in the days of sail that gunfire itself hardly ever sank a ship, and that broadsides rarely damaged the wooden hulls of ships-of-the-line beyond repair. They struck their colours to an opponent more often because they were raked, that is, riddled from end to end by fire from astern or ahead, a process which dismounted guns and caused immense casualties along the decks, or because they were boarded and taken hand-to-hand, or becauses their masts and rigging were shot away, so that they became a prey to the natural hazards of the sea, unless their battle-weary and depleted crews could improvise jury-rigs, or anchor in security, or call upon a friendly tow. Battles under sail were clumsy, stubborn, protracted, and grim beyond belief.

Collingwood had given an example of how a flagship should be fought, and his line, in spite of the hammering suffered by the leading ships, succeeded in its allotted task. What of Nelson, whose business it was to prevent interruption of the work of his second-in-command? He had told his friend Lord Sidmouth: 'Rodney broke the line in one point. I will break it in two.'

Major-General Théodore Contamine, the senior military officer who sailed with Villeneuve, wrote an account some weeks after the action, for the benefit of the French Ministry of Marine. This is inaccurate in many details, but the general, as a soldier, had the advantage of being able to write objectively, while as a prisoner-of-war he had had opportunities of talking over the battle with his captors. His story of Nelson's approach differed in several respects from that of others.

49 'Battle of Trafalgar: Van Division'

Painted and engraved by Robert Dodd

50 'Battle of Trafalgar: Rear Division'

Painted and engraved by Robert Dodd

51 *Victory* grappled by *Redoutable*

52 *Redoutable* fighting
Victory and *Téméraire*

*From copies in the Musée
de la Marine, Paris, of
drawings made by an
officer of the 'Redout-
able' for Captain Lucas*

53 *Belleisle* after the
Action

*From a print published
12 August 1806*

54 *Naiad* taking
Belleisle in tow

*From a print published
12 August 1806*

Admiral Nelson [he wrote] had been begged by the officers of his Fleet to form his two columns with greater regularity; they were bearing down without formation on our line; but he, as became a genius, felt too keenly how essential it was to take prompt advantage of any favourable opportunity that presented itself.

Contamine maintained that, before the action became general, the wind was so light that it was almost impossible for the Combined Fleet to keep any steerage-way, when standing close-hauled to the wind:

... the enemy fleet, on the contrary, with a stern wind and carrying a press of sail, were able to profit by what little air was stirring and by the swell to bear down on us, to take up such positions as they chose, to direct their principal attacks against one point or another of our line, to disable some of our ships to commence with, to overwhelm them in detail, and to defeat them thus one after another.

Contamine continued:

So many advantages, which a little breeze would have unexpectedly dissipated, could not fail to be seized upon by Nelson, and could he tarry one minute in profiting by them, solely for the purpose of getting into more regular order ? The results unhappily justify only too well the decision he had taken to attack without delay.

The French view of Nelson was that he was impetuous. Villeneuve had before him an official appreciation of the admiral's character which gave Nelson little credit for brains, though some for trusting his officers, and much for bravery. 'The enemy will not trouble to form line parallel to ours and fight it out with the gun', Villeneuve himself had written, with memories of the Nile in mind. 'He will try to double our rear, cut through the line, and bring against the ships thus isolated, groups of his own to surround and capture them. Captains must rely on their courage and love of glory, rather than upon the signals of the admiral, who may already be engaged and wrapped in smoke. . . . The captain who is not in action is not at his post.' Conditions at the Nile and at Trafalgar were widely different, but Villeneuve was right in his idea that, whatever the circumstances, Nelson would never tolerate a battle on the old formal pattern. Almost any risk was preferable to that.

Knowledge of this fact, on Villeneuve's part, presented him with the unwelcome certainty that, if once a 'pell-mell' action was joined, no planned tactics, however skilled, could save his fleet. All would depend on individual capacity for fighting, and that was where Nelson, with his incomparable experience, believed that he had an overwhelming advantage.

Once committed to his attack, and having given his order to anchor after action or at nightfall, Nelson had nothing but details to attend to as he waited for the punishment which would be the inevitable result of his head-on approach to the enemy. He had already seen Collingwood face it, and for all he knew, Collingwood himself might already have been slain.

Nelson, tense by now, showed acute interest in detail, as he did so often under stress, never hesitating to interfere directly with the running of the ship in a way that might have exasperated a less phlegmatic flag-captain than Hardy. He rated a lieutenant for what he thought was taking in a studding-sail, though in point of fact it was being set afresh. Shortly before the opening shots were fired at the *Victory*, so one of the midshipmen recorded, Nelson ordered that the hammocks which were stowed along the side should be thoroughly soused with water, a wise measure against fire. During the process one of the seamen, too free with his bucket, splashed the uniform of an officer of marines who was stationed on the poop, and got cursed for his carelessness. Nelson overheard, and took the seaman's part, telling the marine officer that it was his own fault for getting in the way, and that he wished he had had the whole lot! Within a few minutes, at about 12.15, the *Victory* came under fire from the *Héros*, and the hammocks were soon proving their use against fragments of shot.

Shortly before Blackwood returned to his frigate Nelson asked him, as he had done several times before, what he would consider a victory satisfactory in the circumstances. He never, he said, doubted the outcome for an instant, despite the bold way the enemy were standing up to him, though he questioned the possibility of being able to save many prizes. Blackwood answered that 'considering the handsome way in which battle was offered by the enemy, and their apparent determination for a fair trial of strength, with the proximity of the land, I thought if fourteen ships were captured it would be a glorious result'. Nelson replied: 'I shall not, Blackwood, be satisfied with anything short of twenty.'

Soon the Union flags, and the white ensigns which had been flown in general actions since St Vincent's victory of 14 February 1797, were seen on every ship,[1] and at 12.24 the *Victory*, nearly 15 minutes after she had herself come under fire, opened with her starboard guns.

Throughout the near approach, every eye aboard the *Victory* had been looking for the ship wearing the flag of the Allied commander-in-chief—and apparently in vain. But at Trafalgar, everything seemed destined to befit a final battle conducted by Nelson, and he broke upon the French line—though not, as he had planned, through it—close to the *Bucentaure*. But before that event, much had happened.

Bands had struck up with stirring tunes, '*Rule, Britannia*', '*Britons Strike Home*', '*Heart of Oak*'. The gunners had stripped to the waist and tied handkerchiefs round their heads to deaden the noise of their pieces; others sharpened cutlasses; others even danced the hornpipe. Veterans, peering through the ports, recognised in the distance old acquaintances such as the *Santissima Trinidad*, dazzling in vermilion and white, and thought what fine prizes they would look at Spithead. Hardy had asked Nelson, probably at Dr Beatty's suggestion, whether he did not think that the four stars of chivalry on his admiral's coat did not make him too conspicuous, and Nelson had answered that no doubt it was true, but that it was no time to be changing it.

Ranging shots from the enemy at first fell short, then alongside, then over. Soon they began to hit, though, in the accepted style of the French, the aim was high. It

---

[1] Nelson, as a vice-admiral of the White, would have flown a white ensign in the *Victory* in the ordinary way, though Collingwood, as a vice-admiral of the Blue, would have flown a blue flag. The explanation of the practice, general though not universal, since 1797, of ships flying white ensigns in action was so that there should be no confusion with the flags of Spain or France, which could be mistaken at a distance for red and blue ensigns respectively. At Copenhagen, where no confusion could arise, the older tradition held good.

was masts and sails they wished to damage, since this affected an opponent's speed. One of the early casualties was John Scott, Nelson's Public Secretary, who was cut almost in two by a round-shot, as he spoke with Hardy on the quarter-deck. His body was thrown overboard, though not before Nelson had exclaimed: 'Is that poor Scott!' Whipple, the captain's clerk, was shortly afterwards killed by blast, and the marines on the poop began to suffer badly until, by Nelson's order, they were moved to positions less exposed. Soon the *Victory*'s sails were riddled, and her wheel smashed. Throughout the rest of the action the ship was steered from the gun-room, by tiller, an emergency which called for the services of many hands. 'This is too warm work, Hardy, to last long', said Nelson with a smile, and he congratulated his captain on the fact that, in all the battles he had been in, he had never seen more cool courage than was being shown by the company around him.

The *Victory*'s counter-stroke, though inevitably delayed, was fierce. About 20 minutes after she first opened fire, she passed across the stern of the *Bucentaure*. She fired her forecastle carronade into the cabin windows, and followed up with a double-shotted broadside. The smoke blew back in a choking cloud. Dust from broken woodwork covered the quarter-deck, and gun-crews listened with professional satisfaction to the crash of shot from end to end of the French flagship. The *Santa Ana* had not fared worse at Collingwood's hands, and the effect of the concentrated fire left the *Bucentaure* an easy prey to other ships.

Near Villeneuve's flagship was the French *Neptune*, which raked the *Victory*'s bows as she came round to starboard and ran on board the *Redoutable*, which had also kept station close to her admiral. Nelson had said to Hardy: 'It does not signify which we run on board of. Take your choice!' The *Redoutable*'s captain, seeing that the *Victory*'s lower guns were active, while her upper ones were almost silent from loss among the crews, shut most of her lower gun-ports, but kept her main-deck guns firing, and rained shot from her fighting-tops. Soon the two ships were firmly held together by an entanglement in their rigging, and both crews were anxious to board, but the French were prevented by the *Victory*'s starboard carronade, and by a broadside from the *Téméraire*, and the English by musketry and grenades, which made the upper deck almost untenable.

The *Victory* had already disabled the vessel she would have chosen, of all others, to encounter. She was now at grips with the best-trained ship in the entire Allied line, commanded by Captain Jean Lucas.

The battle had begun to resolve into its differing phases. Collingwood, with 15 ships, engaged the enemy rear. Nelson with 12, contained the van, of which the leading ships under Dumanoir stood at first so far to the northwards that they could take no part in the action. They were later turned, with much difficulty in the light air, and bore down with the intention of a counter-attack, a threat which was beaten off. The remainder of the day was given to the taking and manning of prizes, and to rendering serviceable such English ships as had been badly mauled. Never was a pell-mell battle better named, or better justified. No English ship hauled down her colours, but there was a time when, at the very centre of the struggle, there came acute crisis and tragedy. The credit of bringing this about belonged mainly to one ship, and it is seemly that her story should be distinguished from that of others.

The record of the French *Redoutable* at Trafalgar is one of the finest in the history of any navy. She fought two three-deckers, immobilised one of them, the *Victory*, and fired the shot which killed Nelson. For a 74-gun ship, the feat was brilliant almost beyond belief.

Before he made his way out of Cadiz, Villeneuve, listing the fleet, said of the *Redoutable* that she was 'a fine ship, fit for any employment'. The words were exact. Her narrative is best told in the report of her captain, Lucas, who survived the battle many years.

> Ever since the *Redoutable* was fitted out [so he wrote from England], no measures had been neglected to train the crew in every sort of drill. My ideas were always directed towards fighting by boarding. I so counted upon its success that everything had been prepared to undertake it with advantage. I had had canvas pouches to hold two grenades made for all captains of guns; the crossbelts of these pouches carried a tin tube containing a small match. In all our drills, I made them throw a great number of paste-board grenades, and I often landed the grenadiers in order to have them explode iron grenades. They had so acquired the habit of hurling them that on the day of battle our topmen were throwing two at a time.
>
> I had 100 carbines fitted with long bayonets on board. The men to whom these were served out were so well accustomed to their use that they climbed half-way up the shrouds to open musketry fire. All those armed with swords were given broadsword practice every day, and pistols became familiar weapons to them. The grapnels were thrown so skilfully that they would succeed in hooking a ship even though not exactly touching us. When the drum beat to quarters, each man went to his station fully armed, and with his weapons loaded; he placed them near his gun in nettings nailed between each beam. Finally the crew had themselves such confidence in this manner of fighting that they often urged me to board the first ship with which we should engage.

Even before the battle Lucas had had the chance to show his alertness. On 20 October, when the *Redoutable* was some distance in the wake of the *Bucentaure*, the flagship signalled: 'Man overboard.' 'I immediately hove-to', said Lucas, 'and lowered a boat, which saved the man who had fallen into the sea. I signalled the same at once, and a little later I resumed my station.'

Once in action, Lucas—

> laid the *Redoutable*'s bowsprit against the *Bucentaure*'s stern, fully resolved to sacrifice my ship in defence of the admiral's flag. I acquainted my officers and crew, who replied to my decision by shouts of '*Vive l'Empereur! Vive l'Amiral! Vive le Commandant!*' repeated a thousand times. Preceded by drums and fifes that I had on board, I paraded at the head of my executive round the deck; everywhere I found gallant lads burning with impatience to begin the fray, many of them saying: 'Captain, don't forget to board!'

Lucas could not prevent the *Victory* from raking the *Bucentaure*, but when she ran aboard the *Redoutable*, the two ships closed so that the Frenchman's poop was abeam of the *Victory*'s quarter-deck. 'In this position', said Lucas, 'the grapnels were flung. Those aft were cut loose, but those forward held. Our broadsides were fired muzzle to muzzle, and there resulted a horrible carnage.' Soon Lucas 'ordered the trumpet to sound. It was the recognised signal to summon boarding parties in our exercises. They came up in such perfect order, with the officers and midshipmen at the head of their divisions, that one would have said it was only a sham fight. In less than a minute the upper works were covered with armed men who hurled themselves on to the poop, on to the nettings, and into the shrouds.' For some moments the *Victory* was in danger, but the ships were rolling, and her height made it difficult for the eager French to cross. 'I gave orders to cut away the slings of the main yard and to lower it to serve as a bridge', said Lucas. 'Mr Yon, midshipman, and four seamen succeeded in getting on board the *Victory* by means of her anchor.' Captain Adair, of the *Victory*'s marines, then brought up a party from below, and although he himself was killed in leading the repulse, the alarm was soon over. A broadside from the *Téméraire* poured into the *Redoutable*, and she ceased to be a fighting ship, though her resistance was not quite at an end.

> It would be difficult to describe the horrible carnage caused by the murderous broadside [said Lucas]. More than 200 of our brave lads were killed or wounded. I was wounded at the same instant, but not so seriously as to prevent me from remaining at my post. . . . A little later a third ship came up and stationed herself astern of the *Redoutable* and fired into us at pistol range; in less than half an hour our ship was so riddled that she seemed to be no more than a mass of wreckage. In this state the *Téméraire* hailed us to strike, and not prolong a useless resistance. I ordered several soldiers who were near me to answer this summons with musket-shots, which was performed with the greatest zeal. At the very same minute the mainmast fell on board the *Redoutable*. All the stern was absolutely stove-in, the rudder-stock, the tiller, the two tiller-sweeps, the stern-post, the wing transoms, the transom knees were in general shot to pieces.
>
> All the guns were shattered or dismounted by the shots, or from ships having run us aboard [Lucas's description continued]. An 18-pounder gun on the main deck and a 36-pounder carronade on the forecastle having burst, killed and wounded many of our people. The two sides of the ship, all the lids and bars of the ports were utterly cut to pieces. Four of our six pumps were shattered, as well as our ladders in general, in such sort that communication between the decks and the upper works was extremely difficult. All our decks were covered with dead, buried beneath the debris and the splinters from the different parts of the ship. Out of the ship's company of 643 men we had 522 disabled, 300 being killed and 222 wounded, amongst whom were almost the entire executive. . . . He who has not seen the *Redoubtable* in this state can never have any conception of her destruction.
>
> I do not know of anything on board which was not cut up by shot. In the midst of this carnage the brave lads who had not yet succumbed, and whose who were wounded, with whom the orlop deck was thronged, still cried, '*Vive l'Empereur!* We're not taken yet. Is our Captain still alive?'

Lucas did not strike until he was certain that the leaks were such that his vessel would in any case soon founder. 'At the instant that I was assured of this I ordered the colours to be hauled down. They came down of themselves, with the fall of the mizzen-mast.' The *Redoutable*, *Victory* and *Téméraire* were by then still locked together; they had been joined by the *Fougueux*, which was quite out of control.

So ended the fiercest scene of the entire battle. Lucas's account of his casualties differed from the official return (490 killed; 81 wounded), but she had the highest in the Combined Fleet. Her men died in trying to prevent Nelson from carrying out his intention of passing through the enemy line, and cutting them off from Cadiz. One of them put an end to Nelson's life.

At about 1.15, which was nearly half an hour after the *Victory* had become embroiled with the Frenchman, Nelson and Hardy were still steadily pacing the quarter-deck. Already a shot, striking the fore-brace bits, had passed between them, and a splinter had bruised Hardy's foot, tearing off the buckle from his shoe. Just as the pair had arrived within a pace or two of their regular turning point at the cabin ladder-way, Nelson, who regardless of the usual custom was walking on the port side, suddenly faced about.

Hardy, as soon as he had taken one more step, turned, and saw his friend in the act of falling. He was on his knees, with his left hand just touching the deck. Then his arm gave way, and he fell on his left side, exactly at the place where Scott had been killed earlier in the battle. 'They have done for me at last, Hardy', said Nelson. 'My backbone is shot through.' The wound was from a musket-ball which had entered the left shoulder through the fore-part of the epaulette, and, penetrating, had lodged in the spine. The piece had been fired from *Redoutable*'s mizzen-top, the marksman being about 15 yards away. Serjeant Secker of the marines, together with some seamen, at once bore Nelson down to the cockpit.

Even as he was carried below, Nelson's thoughtfulness for detail did not desert him. First he covered over his face with a handkerchief, so that the men should not be discouraged at the sight of the Commander-in-Chief laid low. Then, on his way down, he noticed from beneath the covering that the tiller-ropes needed to be re-rove, and asked a midshipman to tell Hardy to see to it. In the *Victory*, most of the damage and almost all the casualties had been confined to the upper deck. Below, the gunners were still ready and able to take on all comers, and they were firing occasionally on the side not in contact with the *Redoutable*.

In order of going into action the British squadrons had formed as follows: Collingwood, leading in the *Royal Sovereign*, was supported by the *Belleisle*, *Mars*, *Tonnant*, *Bellerophon*, *Colossus*, *Achille*, *Revenge*, *Defiance*, *Polyphemus*, *Dreadnought*, *Swiftsure*, *Thunderer* and *Defence*. The *Prince* counted as among the ships destined to attack the rear of the enemy, but in fact her course appears to have lain somewhere between that of Collingwood and that of Nelson, and she came into action so late that by the time she did so, all order had long since crumbled.

Nelson, leading in the *Victory*, was supported by the *Téméraire*, *Neptune*, *Leviathan*, *Conqueror*, *Britannia*, *Ajax*, *Agamemnon*, *Orion*, *Minotaur* and *Spartiate*. His remaining ship, the little *Africa*, had lost touch with the main body of the fleet during the night of 20 October. She was on her own, well to the northward of Nelson, who signalled to her, after action had been joined, to 'Make all sail possible with safety to the masts'. Her part in the battle was in fact out of all proportion to her size.

The Combined Fleet were attacked as they ranged in the following order: *Neptuno* (Spanish), *Scipion* (French), *Intrépide* (French), *Formidable* (French), *Mont Blanc* (French), *Duguay-Trouin* (French), *Rayo* (Spanish), *San Francisco de Asis* (Spanish), *San Augustin* (Spanish), *Héros* (French), *Santissima Trinidad* (Spanish), *Bucentaure*

(French), *Redoutable* (French), *San Justo* (Spanish), *Neptune* (French), *San Leandro* (Spanish), *Santa Ana* (Spanish), *Indomptable* (French), *Fougueux* (French), *Monarca* (Spanish), *Pluton* (French), *Algésiras* (French), *Bahama* (Spanish), *Aigle* (French), *Swiftsure* (French), *Montañez* (Spanish), *Argonaute* (French), *San Ildefonso* (Spanish), *Argonauta* (Spanish), *Achille* (French), *Principe de Asturias* (Spanish), *Berwick* (French), and *San Juan de Nepomuceno* (Spanish).

It is not to be wondered at that the nomenclature among the ships has led to some confusion. For instance there was a French *Argonaute* and a Spanish *Argonauta*. The *Algéciras*, which might have been thought to be Spanish, was in fact French. There was a French *Swiftsure* and *Achille*, and British ships of the same name. There was a French *Neptune*, a Spanish *Neptuno*, and an English *Neptune*; and while the *Berwick* was French, the *Tonnant*, *Téméraire* and *Spartiate* were in Nelson's fleet.

According to her own account—and the time-keeping in the fleets was anything but synchronised—the *Africa*, detached as she was, came into action not long after the *Royal Sovereign*. 'Engaged the headmost Ship of the Enemies Van,' wrote Captain Henry Digby in his Journal, 'a Spanish two-Decker bearing the Flag of an Admiral' (she was actually the *Neptuno*, Commodore Valdez), 'and engaged the whole of the Enemies Van line as we passed them.' Just before she opened fire, the *Africa* 'hove overboard one hundred and three Bags bread two Casks Beef 3 Casks of Pork one Cask of Oatmeal One Cask Suet One Cask Sugar Ten butts Seven Puncheons twelve hogsheads Ten Lemon Juice Cases'—so Digby continued in his breathless way. Thus lightened, the *Africa* bore down to 'the Assistance of the *Neptune* engaging the *Santissima Trinidad*'. The *Africa* was now mixed up in a battle of giants, for Captain Fremantle's three-decker, third in Nelson's line, was worthy of her huge antagonist. 'At 1.58', so Digby noted with satisfaction, 'the whole of the Masts went by the Board. When she struck, sent Lieut. Smith with a party to take charge of her: at the same time Observed the Enemies Van hauling on the Starboard Tack.' Digby was wrong; the Spaniard had not yet struck, though it was true enough that Dumanoir was at last coming down to the help of his friends.

Unintentionally the *Africa* had played her part in distracting part of the Allied line, and as she suffered severely, there was some justice in her sending a party to the tall Spaniard. But Admiral Cisneros would have felt it beneath his dignity to surrender to a mere 64, and Lieutenant Smith returned to his ship, having been assured in polite Castilian that his visit was premature.

But the *Africa* still had a part to play, for she came into action at the final and most critical stage of the mêlée. 'It must be some time', so Nelson had written in his Memorandum, 'before they—the enemy van—could perform a manœuvre to bring their force compact to attack any part of the British Fleet.' As usual, he had gauged rightly, but the van would turn in time, and then the fire of such detached ships as the *Africa* would be invaluable.

It was only by using boats, and towing, that some of Dumanoir's ships could be got round at all, and it was nearly three o'clock before they were standing down to the scene of action. By that time the back of the Allies' resistance had been broken. Yet there was still a chance to redeem the day, for the British ships which had borne the brunt of the engagement were for the most part dismasted hulks, and Nelson himself was lying mortally wounded.

In the extreme rear there seemed the best opportunity for effective interference. Here the action was still hot, and Gravina, in the *Principe de Asturias*, was holding his own, though against a concentration which was increasing. He himself, like Nelson, had been gravely wounded, but Escano, his Chief of Staff, was keeping up the struggle with obstinate courage. The danger to the Spanish admiral was so acute that when Dumanoir led down to windward, ready to seize any chance that opened, only four ships followed him, three Frenchmen and the Spanish *Neptuno*. Nearly all the rest made for Gravina to leeward, but one, the *Intrépide*, went straight into the firing which was now dying round the *Bucentaure*. She was checked by the *Africa*, which wore round her stern, ran up her lee side, and quickly made her presence felt. Then fresh ships, the *Ajax* and *Orion* among them, completed the gallant Captain Infernet's discomfiture, and after more resistance, he struck.

By the time Dumanoir was well set in his course there were only the last two ships of Nelson's division, the *Spartiate* and *Minotaur*, not yet in close action, and it was these ships which the French admiral thought he might cut off. They saw the danger, but their concern was principally for the *Victory* and the *Téméraire*, as they lay almost helpless, cumbered with wreckage.

Captain Mansfield was leading, in the *Minotaur*, for the order of sailing had been preserved. But the *Minotaur* was slower than the *Spartiate*, and, seeing that there was not a moment to lose, Sir Francis Laforey, who commanded the faster vessel, asked leave to pass. The two ships held straight on across Dumanoir's bows, raking him at pistol shot, and then heaving-to between him and the group round the *Victory*. There they stood their ground, engaging Dumanoir's ships, and forcing them to keep their wind. It was an instance of initiative in the true spirit of Nelson's Memorandum. Dumanoir, finding how much fire-power was left in the centre of the battle, and finding, to his consternation, that the *Bucentaure* had struck, held on to see what could be done in the rear, where Gravina was in such peril.

Collingwood was ready for him. Seeing Dumanoir's threat, he made a general signal for ships to come to the wind in succession on the larboard tack. The result was that by the time Dumanoir was in a position to attack, he saw half a dozen ships hauling out, to form a new line to windward. To depress his spirits still more, he could now see Gravina's flagship bearing away out of action, flying the signal for the fleet to rally round her. Dumanoir, giving up all as lost, held on to the southward, for the Straits of Gibraltar.

By the time Collingwood had news that Nelson was dying, the day was won. Villeneuve and two of his flag-officers were prisoners in the British fleet, and of the 33 of the line which had left Cadiz, only 11 got back that night to safety. Four were with Dumanoir: 18 were still in the area of battle; 17 of these ships were largely or totally dismasted, 13 were actually in possession of prize crews, and one, the French *Achille*, was in flames.

Just as the burning and destruction of the great *L'Orient* at the Battle of the Nile had, with dreadful splendour, illuminated the night of Nelson's first achievement in independent command, so was the fire in the *Achille* symbolic of his victory at Trafalgar. The Frenchman had been engaged in turn by the *Revenge, Defiance, Swift-sure* and *Polyphemus*. Her captain and most of her officers had been killed or wounded, and at the last she was commanded by a young *enseigne de vaisseau*. Then, at about four o'clock, the mighty *Prince*, lumbering into action, bore down upon her, and fired two raking broadsides into her stern. These brought down her fore- and main-masts, and set her alight.

The *Achille* burnt for an hour and a half. As soon as they saw that the blaze was out of control, boats from the *Prince* rescued as many of her crew as they could, but nothing could save her. Soon her guns, those that were still shotted, were firing on their own, as the heat set off the charges. At sunset she blew up. The sea closed over her wreckage, and the battle was over.

5 The Fortunes of the Ships

As Collingwood's line was first in action, it is appropriate to consider the fortune of his ships before those to windward of them, which were led by Nelson.

By the time the *Royal Sovereign* had engaged the *Fougueux, Santa Ana, Indomptable* and others, and had been taken in tow by the *Euryalus*, it was well after two o'clock. The *Royal Sovereign* herself took little further part in the action, though she was at all times ready to drive off French or Spanish ships which ventured too close.

The next astern, *Belleisle*, broke away from her encounter with the *Fougueux* soon after one, when she was engaged in succession by the *Pluton, Aigle, San Justo, San Leandro* and others. Her next protracted duel was with the French *Neptune*. This lasted for three-quarters of an hour, when the Frenchman was driven off by the *Polyphemus*. Captain Hargood in the *Belleisle* had continued to fight splendidly, but it was half miraculous he could still fight at all, considering what the ship had endured as she went into action behind Collingwood. Nelson himself had watched her with admiration, and an officer of marines left an account of the tense moments before she opened fire.

> At a quarter before eleven [he wrote], seven or eight of the enemy's ships opened their fire upon the *Royal Sovereign* and *Belleisle*; and as we were steering directly for them we could only remain passive, and perseveringly approach the position we were to occupy in this great battle. This was a trying moment. Captain Hargood had taken his station on the forepart of the quarter-deck on the starboard side, occasionally standing on a carronade slide, whence he issued his orders for the men to lie down at their quarters, and with the utmost coolness directed the steering of the ship.
>
> The silence on board was almost awful, broken only by the firm voice of the captain, 'Steady!' or 'Starboard a little!' which was repeated by the master to the quartermaster at the helm, and occasionally by an officer calling to the now impatient men: 'Lie down there, you, sir!' As we got nearer and nearer to the enemy the silence was, however, broken frequently by the sadly stirring shrieks of the wounded, for of them, and killed, we had more than fifty before we fired a shot; and our colours were three times shot away and rehoisted during the time.

Seeing our men were fast falling, the first lieutenant ventured to ask Captain Hargood if he had not better show his broadside to the enemy and fire, if only to cover the ship with smoke. The gallant man's reply was somewhat stern, but emphatic: 'No. We are ordered to go through the line, and go through she shall, by God!'

The state of things had lasted about twenty minutes, and it required the tact of the more experienced officers to keep up the spirits of those around them by observing, 'We should soon now begin our work', when—like as on another occasion the welcome order was given, 'Up guards, and at 'em!' our energies were joyfully called into play by 'Stand to your guns'.

On the poop, where there were three marine officers, and some 30 men 'at small arms', the order to lie down was not given. One of the junior subalterns wrote:

The shot began to pass over us, and gave us intimation of what we should in a few minutes undergo. . . . A shriek soon followed—a cry of agony was produced by the next shot—and the loss of the head of a poor recruit was the effect of the succeeding, and, as we advanced, destruction rapidly increased. A severe contusion of the breast now prostrated our captain, but he soon resumed his station. Those only who had been in a similar situation to the one I am attempting to describe can have a correct idea of such a scene.

Some of the men were in fact now lying down, though not, apparently, by order.

I was half disposed to follow the example [continued the lieutenant], but turning round, my much esteemed and gallant senior fixed my attention; the serenity of his countenance and the composure with which he paced the deck, drove more than half my terrors away, and, joining him, I became somewhat infused with his spirit, which cheered me on to act the part that became me. My experience is an instance of how much depends on the example of those in command when exposed to the fire of the enemy, more particularly in the trying situation in which we were placed for nearly thirty minutes, from not having the power to retaliate.

Whether Hargood was right or not in refraining from firing a few guns to help conceal his ship with smoke, the accounts give a representative picture of the ordeal of the leading ships in both lines, and the discipline needed in order to maintain that regular advance which so impressed the enemy.

The *Belleisle*'s last act in the battle was befitting. She took possession of the *Argonauta*, one of the finest of all the Spanish two-deckers. This was one case among many where ships surrendered not to the opponent which had given them mortal wounds, but to an enemy who could take advantage of extreme conditions. In this case, the surrender was to a very battered and glorious ship.

In her duel with the *Neptune* the *Belleisle* had lost such masts and rigging as still remained standing, and she was in fact the only ship on the British side to be totally dismasted, being at one point as near destruction as any ship in either fleet. She was then almost unable to fire a gun, owing to wreckage, but an ensign was nailed to the stump of her mizzen, and she kept a Union flag flying at the top of a handspike. As they passed by, late in the battle, the men of the *Spartiate* gave her a cheer, as well they might. Earlier, the *Swiftsure* had come to her help. 'Though an immovable log,' wrote one of the *Swiftsure* lieutenants, 'she still kept up a smart fire upon the enemy whenever it was possible to bring a gun to bear. This was a scene that truly accorded with the feelings of an Englishman.'

'When we came up with her,' the account continued, 'the Ship's company was crowded upon the poop, Quarters and every other part of the ship to cheer us, which they did by giving loud Huzzas, which we were not dilatory in returning. Captain Hargood then requested our Captain to engage a ship to windward of him that was firing into the *Belleisle*, as it was impossible to return her fire.' The enemy in question was the *Achille*. The *Swiftsure* gave her the attention necessary. Later the *Belleisle* was taken in tow by the frigate *Naiad*, and again came within hail of the *Swiftsure*, when Captain Hargood thanked Captain Rutherford for his help.

There was a significant pause in the log of the *Mars*, soon after she had lost her captain. She asked for a tow from the *Euryalus*, Captain Blackwood replying that he would do it with pleasure, but that he was going to help the Second-in-Command, by Collingwood's order. The *Mars* then drifted towards the group of ships near the *Victory*, where she received an unexpected honour. The French Commander-in-Chief, together with officers of his retinue, came on board from the *Bucentaure*, and were received by Lieutenant William Hannah, who had succeeded to the command of the ship. The party were later transferred to the *Neptune*, since the *Mars* was in no state to accommodate them. Villeneuve in due course went to the *Euryalus*, and this gave Blackwood the chance of first-hand acquaintance with all the principal leaders in the battle. Nelson he knew well. For Collingwood he was now repeating signals. Soon he would discover the sort of man that Villeneuve was, and would grow to respect him.

Of the adventures of the *Tonnant*, Captain Tyler, there are various descriptions, among them one by Lieutenant Clements, who said that, 'we went down in no order, but every man to take his bird. They cut us up a good deal, until we got our broadside to bear on a Spanish ship in breaking the line, when we gave her such a thundering broadside that she did not return a gun for some minutes, and a very few afterwards.' She was the *Monarca*.

The *Tonnant* next engaged the French *Algéciras*, Magon's flagship. George Sartorius, a midshipman who rose later to become an Admiral of the Fleet, said of his ship:

> She was one of the very few, perhaps one of the four or five that had been constantly exercised at her guns. Had we not been well exercised, I think the Frenchman would have got the advantage of us. We had actually our fire-engine playing on her broadside to put out the fire caused by the flame of our guns.

One of the lieutenants wrote that the *Algéciras*—

> in the most gallant manner, locked her bowsprit in our starboard main shrouds and attempted to board us, with the greater part of her officers and ship's company. She had riflemen in her tops, who did great execution. Our poop was soon cleared, and our gallant captain shot through the left thigh and carried below. During this time we were not idle. We gave it her most gloriously with the starboard and main deckers, and turned the fore-castle gun, loaded with grape, on the gentlemen who wished to give us a fraternal hug. The marines kept up a warm destructive fire on the boarders. Only one man made good his footing on our quarter-deck, when he was pinned through the calf of his right leg by one of the crew with his half-pike, whilst another was going to cut him down, which I prevented, and desired him to be taken to the cockpit.

At length we had the satisfaction of seeing her three lower masts go by the board, as they had been shot through below the deck, and carrying with them all their sharpshooters, to look sharper in the next world; for as all our boats were shot through we could not save one of them. The crew were then ordered, with the second lieutenant, to board her. They cheered, and in a short time carried her. They found the gallant Admiral Magon killed at the foot of the poop ladder, and the captain dangerously wounded. Out of eight lieutenants, five were killed, with three hundred petty officers and seamen, and about one hundred wounded.

The exaggeration is here considerable. The actual casualty figures for the *Algéciras* were 77 killed and 142 wounded. The *Tonnant* had 26 killed and 50 wounded. 'During this time', added Lieutenant Clements, 'we were hard at it on a Spanish ship when at last down came her colours. I hailed him, and asked him if he had struck, when he said, "Yes".'

The *Algéciras* was soon taken possession of by another ship, but meanwhile the *Monarca* had rehoisted her colours, though she gained nothing from her change of mind, for she was soon engaged by the *Bellerophon*, the 'Billy Ruffian'—as her seamen called her. This was a ship which had already distinguished herself at the Glorious First of June and at the Nile. She got into action at the same time as the *Tonnant*, and was soon engaged on both sides. Her larboard broadside was fired at the *Monarca*, while her forward starboard guns were aimed at the *Aigle*. She was then attacked by the *Montañez*, by the French *Swiftsure* and by the *Bahama*. One of her officers reported that while she was thus beset, the '*Aigle* twice attempted to board us, and hove several grenades into our lower deck, which burst and wounded several of our people most dreadfully'.

She likewise set fire to our fore-chains. Our fire was so hot that we soon drove them from the lower deck, after which our people took the quoins out and elevated their guns, so as to tear their decks and sides to pieces. When she got clear of us she did not return a single shot while we raked her; her starboard side was entirely beaten in, and, as we afterwards learnt, four hundred men were *hors de combat*, so that she was an easy conquest for the *Defiance*, a fresh ship.

Once again, the casualties are a wild estimate, but it is known that the *Aigle* lost about two-thirds of her ship's company.

The *Bellerophon* herself suffered severely, having 27 killed, including her captain, and well over a hundred wounded. Much of this loss was caused by the *Aigle*'s grenades exploding loose powder near the guns. 'One of the grenades', said the first lieutenant, Cumby, 'in its explosion had blown off the scuttle of the gunner's store-room, setting fire to it and forcing open the door into the magazine passage. The door was so placed that the same blast that blew open the store-room door, *shut* the door of the magazine. Otherwise we must all in both ships inevitably have been blown up together.' The gunner, with a small party, got the fire under control, and Lieutenant Cumby took command after Captain Cooke's death. He wrote to his father that some of the men chalked on their guns 'Victory or Death'.

Although the *Monarca* struck to the *Bellerophon* at about two o'clock, she may well have regretted that the *Aigle* was not her prize instead, for according to the *Bellerophon* the *Aigle* was the best-manned ship in the Combined Fleet, and they thought themselves the same. Certainly the two ships in the British fleet which lost their captains, the *Mars* and the *Bellerophon*, had a record at Trafalgar to compare with any, but if the *Aigle* was in fact as well manned as Lucas's *Redoutable*, then she was good indeed, and deserved a victory.

The *Colossus* and English *Achille* came next. Some accounts speak of the *Achille* being 'close astern of the *Colossus*, and sailing well', others place them side by side in the column. Whatever may have been their earlier position, they came into action in line of bearing, to starboard of their leaders, and diverging from them. The *Achille* passed close astern of the *Montañez*, luffed up and drove her off, and then pressed on to help the *Belleisle*. On her way she attacked the *Argonaute*, and was herself fired at by the French *Achille*. These ships having left her, she engaged the *Berwick*, with whom she was at close quarters for half an hour. The result was success. 'Sent a Lieutenant and men on board the French Ship', said her log, 'and took possession of her. . . . Received French prisoners on board. Hove overboard sixty-seven butts to make room in the forehold for the prisoners.'

The *Colossus* engaged the French *Swiftsure* and the Spanish *Bahama*, both of which struck, the decisive incident in the capture of the French ship being a broadside from the *Orion*. She had left her own line, which was Nelson's, to come to the aid of the hardest-pressed ships in Collingwood's column. Both enemy ships were among the prizes which survived, but the *Colossus* herself suffered heavily, with 40 killed and 160 wounded.

The two next ships should have been the *Dreadnought* and the *Polyphemus*, but they were outsailed by the *Revenge*, a brand new 74 with a name whose battle honours stretched back to the reign of Elizabeth I. At about 12.30 she opened fire on the *San Ildefonso*, and soon afterwards on the French *Achille*, two of whose masts she brought down within a quarter of an hour. But her big battle was with Gravina. His three-decker, the *Principe de Asturias*, 'shot up on my lee quarter', said Captain Moorsom, while the *Revenge* was enduring a raking fire from elsewhere. 'My friend the Spanish admiral,' continued Moorsom, 'who had been trying hard to dismast me, and succeeded in carrying away all my topsail yards, at last bore up, on the approach of one of our three-decked ships.'

One of the *Revenge*'s seamen recalled that Gravina's ship 'ran her bowsprit over our poop, with a number of her crew on it, and in her fore rigging. Two or three hundred men were ready to follow; but they caught a Tartar, for their design was discovered, and our marines with their small-arms, and the carronades on the poop, loaded with canister-shot, swept them off so fast that they were glad to sheer off.' In spite of the severity of her encounter with her great antagonist, the *Revenge*, whose losses were heavy, was in good enough trim to form part of the line which prevented the threat from Dumanoir from becoming effective in the later stages of the battle.

The *Defiance* was able to engage about an hour and a quarter after the *Royal Sovereign*. By that time much of her running rigging had been shot away, as she made her approach. She too made at least a brief attack on Gravina, and then set about the *Aigle*, which was by then much the worse for wear, though still game. The *Defiance* 'ran alongside of her, and made fast. Boarded, and got possession of her quarter-deck and poop. Struck the French colours, and hoisted English. Her people still firing from the tops, forecastle and lower deck.' This was very much a case of disputed possession, so after 25 minutes the boarders were recalled, the ship was cast off, and broadside fire was opened once again. In another half-hour the French called for quarter. 'Ceased firing,' said the *Defiance*'s log: 'out boats, sent a Lieutenant with twenty men to take possession of her.' It had been a gallant resistance, for the *Aigle* had been engaged with at least six ships up and down the lee line. Her hull was battered in every direction, and she had nearly 300 killed and wounded.

Captain Durham had an extraordinary story to tell afterwards of the first attempt at boarding of the *Aigle*, differing from accounts in the log. A certain Mr Spratt, he said, 'an active young midshipman, took his cutlass between his teeth, called to the boarders to follow, leapt over board and swam to the *Aigle*, followed by a few men; he got in at the stern port, and was met by some of the crew, who resisted. He succeeded in cutting his way up and hauled down the Frenchman's colours, and in the act of doing so, was shot through the leg.'

He dragged himself to the side of the ship, and holding his bleeding limb over the railing, called out, 'Captain, poor Jack Spratt is done up at last!' Durham managed to warp alongside, and the midshipman was slung on board. Durham was himself by then wounded in the leg and side. Spratt, who was badly hit, refused to have his leg amputated, and the surgeon, feeling the operation was essential, asked the captain for a written order to authorise him to take the limb off. This was refused, though Durham promised to argue the matter with the midshipman. Spratt held out his other leg, which was a very good one, and said: 'Never; if I lose my leg, where shall I find a match for this?' Spratt was made a lieutenant after the action, and did not in fact lose his leg, but he was 17 weeks in hospital at Gibraltar, and was never able to go to sea again.

After the battle was over Hardy told Durham, by way of comforting him in his wounded state, that Nelson had said to him as they went in to action: 'What would poor Sir Robert Calder give to be with us now! Tell your friend Durham he was the most sensible man of the party to stick to his ship.'

The *Dreadnought*, so valuable in fire-power though so poor a sailer, fired her first broadside at Gravina, and later ran alongside Churruca's *San Juan de Nepomuceno*, which struck to her within ten minutes. Then she again attacked Gravina's flagship, which by that time was proceeding towards Cadiz; but she soon found herself outsailed, and broke off her pursuit to help to meet the threat from Dumanoir.

The remaining ships in Collingwood's line, the *Thunderer*, *Defence*, *Polyphemus*, *Swiftsure* and *Prince*, had, by comparison with their fellows, light trials and light casualties, the *Prince* having no killed or wounded whatsoever.

The *Thunderer* fired most of her shots at the *San Ildefonso*; the *Defence* was engaged with the French ship *Berwick* as well as the *San Ildefonso*, which struck to her towards the end of the day; the *Swiftsure* did her most useful work in aid of the *Belleisle*, while the *Polyphemus* engaged or pursued a number of ships, though none at very close quarters. As for the powerful *Prince*, handicapped like the *Dreadnought* by her slow speed, she crept up on the scene of violence longing to show her mettle, bent on engaging anything which had life in it.

The *Prince* had had bad luck from the beginning. When the enemy were first signalled, she had been supplying the *Britannia* with water and provisions, and she took some time to put herself in trim for the chase which Nelson ordered. Then on the early morning of the battle she split her fore-topsail, and had scarcely replaced it when the enemy were seen in line, away to leeward. She had a brief encounter with Gravina, raking his *Principe de Asturias* with two broadsides, and at about four o'clock she engaged the *Achille*, brought down her foremast and set her alight. Her boats saved most of the Frenchmen left alive in the ship, some 140 men. Her last act in the battle was to take formal possession of the *Santissima Trinidad*, the principal credit for whose capture belonged to the *Neptune*. Cisneros could yield to a fresh three-decker; the little *Africa* had been quite a different matter.

'How well I remember the *Achille* blowing up', wrote Hercules Robinson many years later. He had seen the event from the *Euryalus*, and recalled the frigate 'got hold of a dozen of her men, who were hoisted into the air out of the exploding ship, cursing their fate, tearing their hair, and wiping the gunpowder and salt water from their faces'. Such is human resilience that he was able to add: 'In the evening these same fellows, having got their supper and grog and dry clothes, danced for the amusement of our men, under the half deck.' Nor was the midshipmen's berth in the *Euryalus* without its compensations. Robinson helped in saving a black pig which swam over from the doomed ship: 'and what a glorious supper of pork chops appeared . . . instead of our usual refection of cheese, biscuits and salt junk.'

As with Collingwood's line, so with Nelson's. It was the leading ships which endured most, and in particular the *Victory* and *Téméraire*. Of the rest—apart from the *Africa*—only the *Britannia* had as many as ten killed, the other ships escaping lightly, thanks to the success of Nelson's plan. Had the van of the Combined Fleet turned earlier, it must have been a different story.

The *Victory*, first to engage, suffered most, but the *Téméraire* ran her close, and no admiral ever had better support than Nelson from Captain Eliab Harvey, a bold gambler, a man of outspoken temper, and a doughty fighter. 'When the *Victory* opened her fire,' said the ship's log, 'immediately put our helm aport to steer clear, and opened our fire on the *Santissima Trinidad* and two ships ahead of her.' Such spread of aim was exceptional. Then 'the action became general'. The fire of the *Téméraire* was decisive in removing all danger from the plucky *Redoubtable*, and soon after the Frenchman had ceased resistance, she was free to give the finishing touches to the damaged *Fougueux*, which had drifted over from Collingwood's side.

In his official despatch on the battle, begun in the *Euryalus* on 22 October, Collingwood included a story about the *Téméraire* which, though not supported by later evidence, showed the reputation which her prowess had given her. 'A circumstance occurred during the action which so strongly marks the invincible spirit of British seamen that I cannot resist the pleasure I have in making it known to Their Lordships', wrote Collingwood. 'The *Téméraire* was boarded by accident or design, by a French ship on one side, and a Spaniard on the other: the contest was vigorous; but in the end the Combined ensigns were torn from the poop, and the British hoisted in their places.' No doubt the scene immediately round the *Victory* was one of glorious confusion, and an observer had made up a picturesque story, which pleased the admiral. There is no likelihood that the *Téméraire* was in fact boarded at any time, though attempts were probably made to do so.

Captain Harvey, in a letter written to his wife after the battle, confirmed that Nelson had given him leave to lead the weather line 'and to break through the Enemy . . . about the 14th ship from the Van', but that afterwards he had annulled this permission by signal. In fact, when going into action the *Téméraire*'s stem almost touched the stern of the *Victory*, 'and', said Harvey, 'from this for 2 hours we were so nearly engaged that I can give you no other account of this part of the most glorious day's work'.

The ship had, in fact, at least one very near shave, for a 'stink pot', as the sailors called it, 'thrown from the *Redoutable* entered the powder screen on the quarter-deck, and caused a destructive explosion on the main-deck below. Had it not been for the presence of mind of the master-at-arms, John Toohig, who was quartered in the light-room, the fire would have communicated to the after magazine, and probably have occasioned the loss not only of the *Téméraire*, but of the ships near her.'

In the *Neptune*, which was close upon the heels of the *Victory* and *Téméraire*, the scene was recorded in Minutes kept by the signal officer, Lieutenant Andrew Green. These were sent home to his wife at Swanbourne by Captain Fremantle.

> The *Victory* open'd her fire and endeavoured to pass under Stern of the French Admiral in the *Bucentaure* [said Green]. The *Redoutable* closed so near, to support his Commander-in-Chief, that the *Victory* was obliged to lay that ship on board, when both ships paid off before the wind.
>
> The *Téméraire*, in following gallantly Lord Nelson's ship, fell on the opposite side of the *Redoutable*, from the same cause, and the *Intrépide* alongside the *Téméraire* [Green was wrong here, for it was the *Fougueux*]. The four ships lock'd in and on board each other, and their Sterns to us. We put the ship's helm a-Starboard and the *Neptune* passed between the *Victory* and *Bucentaure*, with which ship we were warmly engaged (the *Conqueror*'s Jib-boom touching our Taffrail). We passed on to the *Santissima Trinidad*, whose stern was entirely exposed to our fire without being able to return a single shot with effect. At 50 minutes past one observed her Main and Mizen Masts fall overboard, gave three cheers, she then paid off and brought us nearly on her lee Beam, in about a quarter of an hour more, her Foremast fell over her Stern, and shortly after an Officer threw a Union Jack over her Starboard Quarter, hailed the *Neptune* and said they had struck.

The *Neptune* did not take possession, and for the excellent reason implied in the next sentence in the lieutenant's Minutes.

> The Van of the Enemy now wore and were crossing us apparently with an intent to support their Admirals. The *Conqueror* at this time passed over to windward to engage them, Put our helm a-port and fired successfully with six sail-of-the-line that passed to windward, the remaining three going to leeward. Observed the *Leviathan* and another ship closely engaged with two of the Enemy's ships who had bore up and soon after struck.

The *Leviathan* in fact had engaged the French *Neptune*, and after her encounter with

55 The death of Nelson
Detail from the painting by A. Devis

PALMAM QUI MERUIT FERAT

TRAFALGAR

56 'The Trophied Bier'
From a print by J. Godby after W. M. Craig (1806)

57 H.M.S. *Victory* today: the stern

58 Reverse of a Trafalgar medal by Thomas Webb

Dumanoir's ships she bore down on the *San Augustin*. After a 20-minute fight, she carried her by boarding. Maistral in the *Neptune* went off before the wind to attack Collingwood's ships, and was in the final flight to Cadiz, where the ship arrived little damaged, living to fight another day.

As for the *Conqueror*, she at one time engaged both the *Bucentaure* and the *Santissima Trinidad*, but her most useful work was in the later stages of the battle, when she helped to foil Dumanoir. The *Britannia*,[1] *Ajax* and *Agamemnon* had no close encounters, but, together with the *Orion*, they took part in the mêlée, and it was to the *Orion* that the *Intrépide* struck. Captain Codrington, commanding the *Orion*, had first made his name under Howe at the Glorious First of June, when a young officer, and he lived to fly his flag at Navarino as commander-in-chief, a battle which may be said to have been the swan-song of the old sailing-ship of the line. Going into action he reserved his fire until he knew it would be effective, and he found some wry amusement in seeing Berry in the *Agamemnon* blazing away for all he was worth, apparently at friend and foe alike.

The action of the *Spartiate* and the *Minotaur* in foiling Dumanoir has already been described. They were a curious combination, for they had been on opposite sides seven years before, at the Nile, where the *Minotaur* had helped to capture her companion.

William Thorpe, who served in the *Minotaur*, left an interesting account of an address given by her captain, Mansfield, on the eve of going into battle. He turned all the hands up, and told them that they would shortly be in sight of the enemy, at which everyone began to cheer.

> There is every probability of engaging [he continued], and I trust that this day or to-morrow will prove the most glorious our country ever saw. I shall say nothing to you of courage. Our country never produced a coward. For my own part I pledge myself to the officers and ship's company never to quit the ship I get alongside of, till either she strikes or sinks, or I sink.
>
> I have only to recommend silence and a strict attention to the orders of your officers. Be careful to take good aim, for it is to no purpose to throw shot away. You will now repair to your respective stations, and I will bring the ship into action as soon as possible. *God Save the King*!

It was a scene that must have been repeated in other ships, as they made their stately way towards the Combined Fleet. Captain Mansfield in fact had his chance of running alongside a Spaniard. She was the *Neptuno*, and she duly struck her flag, being one of the last ships in the battle to do so.

Mr Midshipman Babcock, another Trafalgar survivor who lived to achieve his flag, was serving in the *Neptune*. He left one of the best accounts of the appearance of the enemy as the British fleet approached.

It was a beautiful sight when their line was completed, their broadsides turned towards us,

[1] The *Britannia*, nicknamed 'Old Ironsides', was the veteran of the British Fleet, having been launched in 1762, three years before the *Victory*, and a year earlier than the *Defiance*.

showing their iron teeth, and now and then trying the range of a shot to ascertain the distance, that they might, the moment we came within point blank (about six hundred yards), open their fire upon our van ships—no doubt with the hope of dismasting some of our leading vessels before they could close and break their lines.

Some of the enemy's ships were painted like ourselves, with double yellow sides, some with a broad single red or yellow streak, others all black, and the noble *Santissima Trinidad*, with four distinct lines of red, with a white ribbon between them, made her seem a superb man-of-war, which indeed she was. Her appearance was imposing, her head splendidly ornamented with a colossal group of figures, painted white, representing the Holy Trinity from which she took her name.

Álava's *Santa Ana* had an enormous effigy of the Virgin mother, clothed in red, for her figure-head. As a badge of nationality, every French ship bore on her stern a lozenge-shaped escutcheon, painted in three horizontal bands of blue, white and red, and both Cosmao of the *Pluton* and Valdez of the *Neptuno* had three colours flying. Spanish ships each had a large crucifix, and the Frenchmen 'Eagles', dedicated by and to Napoleon.

Accounts of the French and Spanish ships tell much the same story—of gallant resistance, made without any real hope of success; of dreadful carnage and material destruction; of comparatively ineffective gunnery; and of elaborate preparations to board (natural enough in a fleet which contained so many soldiers), which in no case came nearer realisation than the *Redoutable*'s brief moment when she might have made a lodgement in the *Victory*, or the *Algéciras*'s when she grappled with the *Tonnant*. It is a story of unrewarded courage, justifying Villeneuve's foreboding, and exemplifying the futility of his training when opposed to men of confident spirit, efficient both in gunnery and seamanship.

The matter is typified in an officer's description of the later stages of the *Bucentaure*'s death-throes.

The upper decks and gangways, heaped with dead and the wreckage from overhead, presented an appalling spectacle. Amid this scene of disaster Admiral Villeneuve, who from the first had displayed the calmest courage, continued tranquilly pacing up and down the quarter-deck. At length he saw his ship totally dismasted, and no hope of succour coming from any quarter. With bitter sorrow he exclaimed: 'The *Bucentaure* has played her part; mine is not yet over.' He gave orders for his boat to be got ready at once to take him with his flag on board one of the ships of the van squadron. He still cherished the hope that he might be able, with the fresh ships of the van, to make a supreme effort, and even yet snatch victory from the enemy.

But the unfortunate admiral's illusion did not last long. Word was soon brought him that his barge, which before the battle had been got ready against this very possibility, had several holes made in it by the enemy's shot, and, as a *finale*, had been crushed to pieces under a mass of fallen spars and rigging. Every single one of the ship's other boats had also been destroyed. On that they hailed across to the *Santissima Trinidad* for them to send a boat, but no reply was made and no boat was sent. Bitterly did Admiral Villeneuve realise his desperate position, and the hard fate that was in store for him. He saw himself imprisoned on board a ship that was unable to defend herself, while a great part of his fleet was in action and fighting hard. He cursed the destiny that had spared him in the midst of all the slaughter round about. Compelled by force of circumstances to think no more about his fleet, he had now only to think of the ship he was in. All he could do now was to see after the lives of the handful of brave men left fighting with him. Humanity forbade him to allow them to be shot down without means of defending themselves. Villeneuve looked away, and allowed the captain of the *Bucentaure* to lower the colours.

The Allied flagship actually surrendered to an officer of marines, Captain James Atcherley of the *Conqueror*. Israel Pellew, commanding the *Conqueror*, could not spare his first lieutenant, on whom the duty would normally have fallen, and ordered Atcherley to take his place. Atcherley went off with two seamen, and a corporal and two marines. When he gained the *Bucentaure*'s upper deck, and his red coat showed itself on the quarter-deck of the battered vessel, four French officers of rank stepped forward, all bowing and presenting swords. One was Villeneuve; one was Magendie, the captain of the ship; and one was Major-General Contamine, the senior soldier.

'To whom have I the honour of surrendering?' asked Villeneuve in English.

'To Captain Pellew of the *Conqueror*.'

'I am glad to have struck to the fortunate Sir Edward Pellew.'

'It is his brother, sir', said Atcherley.

'His brother! What, are there two of them!' exclaimed Villeneuve. '*Hélas!*'

'*Fortune de la guerre*', said Magendie, as he became a prisoner-of-war for the third time. All the Frenchmen knew of Sir Edward Pellew, who, when in command of a frigate, had driven the battleship *Droits de l'Homme* ashore in 1797. The younger brother was, it seemed, equally formidable.

Atcherley suggested that the swords of such senior officers should be handed to someone of higher rank than himself. He then went below to secure the magazines, passing through scenes of horror. 'The dead, thrown back as they fell, lay along the middle of the decks in heaps', he said, 'and the shot, passing through, had frightfully mangled the bodies. . . . An extraordinary proportion had lost their heads. A raking shot, which entered the lower deck, had glanced along the beams and through the thickest of the people, and a French officer declared that this shot alone had killed or disabled nearly forty men.'

The marine officer locked up the magazines and put the keys in his pocket, he posted his two marines as sentries at the doors of the admiral's and flag-captain's cabins and then, returning on deck, conducted Villeneuve, Magendie and Prigny down the side into his little boat, which went off in search of the *Conqueror*. Pellew, however, had ranged ahead to engage another opponent, and as Atcherly could not see her in the smoke, the Frenchmen were taken to the nearest British ship, which happened to be the *Mars*, the *Conqueror*'s sister-ship. And so it was that, for the second time, Villeneuve gave himself into the charge of a junior officer, Captain Duff having been killed about an hour before.

Nelson's Memorandum had enjoined that 'every effort must be made to capture their Commander-in-Chief'. His orders had now been obeyed, and for such direction as the Allied Fleet could receive for the rest of the battle, they would have to look to Admiral Gravina, who was hard-pressed himself, and away from the centre of the fighting. Villeneuve told Blackwood later that he thought 'such a victory and in circumstances so disadvantageous to the attack never was achieved before', and that he could 'scarcely credit it, and his despair and grief exceeds anything I ever saw. To resist such an attack, surrounded as Lord Nelson was, was vain', he said, and none of his subordinates would have disagreed with him, though their luck in the encounter varied greatly.

Admiral Álava's flagship, the *Santa Ana*, had better fortune than the *Bucentaure*, though only relatively, and chiefly because she had consistent support. According to the French captain Maistral of the *Neptune*, she did not at first put up a fight against the *Royal Sovereign* which in any way corresponded to her strength; Maistral's ship was ahead of the *Santa Ana* in the Allied line, and he turned to give her help, much as the *Redoutable* had done in the case of the *Bucentaure*, though less closely. As he approached, Maistral 'observed that several men were hiding themselves outside the ship on the opposite side to the enemy. It was therefore essential to assist this vessel in her defence, that she might not fall into the hands of the enemy from the very first shots.' Maistral was successful in preventing the *Santa Ana* from striking until 2.20 in the afternoon. Collingwood then sent Blackwood over, to convey Admiral Álava to the *Euryalus*, but he was told that Álava was on the point of death, and he returned only with the Spanish flag-captain.

That officer had already been to the *Royal Sovereign* to deliver his sword, and had asked one of the sailors the name of the ship to which he had struck. When told that it was the *Royal Sovereign* he replied in broken English, patting one of the guns: 'I think she should be called the Royal Devil!'

Blackwood had brought over a sword to Collingwood, which he had understood to be Álava's, but which was in fact that of Francisco Riquelme, the senior unwounded lieutenant. Álava was lying below unconscious, though his wound was not in fact as grave as had at first appeared. The *Santa Ana* was recaptured during the storm which followed the battle, with Álava still on board, and a courteous correspondence between him and Collingwood followed, Álava insisting that he had in fact never surrendered. As his nephew, who was serving with Gravina in the *Principe de Asturias*, survived to take service with the Spanish army against France in the Peninsular War, and was A.D.C. to Wellington at Waterloo, later becoming Spanish Ambassador in London, Collingwood's tacit acceptance of the Admiral's statement was in the long run indirectly rewarded, though he continued to believe that Álava's own conduct was wrong. Years later, writing from Minorca to Admiral Purvis about the Spanish ships which were then allied with his own, Collingwood said: 'Place no confidence in Álava nor in any person belonging to the ships; I have good reason for it: but carefully conceal any suspicions of their loyalty.' Collingwood did not forget.

Gravina's wound was much more serious, and in fact he died from its effects some weeks after the battle. He fought his ship with gallantry, and although it was he who, after the capture of Villeneuve, gave the signal for the Combined Fleet to rally and to make for Cadiz, this was a sensible course, considering how the day was going, and it was one which had the full concurrence of Cosmao of the *Pluton*, the ablest among the uncaptured French officers. Cosmao, like Nelson, saw that a storm was likely to blow up from the west, and that he might have a good opportunity to make a sortie later from Cadiz, and even to recapture some of the prizes lost to the British. Some writers have blamed his conduct as pusillanimous. Events showed that he was a wise man, and a realist. With a little better luck, his decision might have been well rewarded. As it happened, it only helped to make a decisive victory still more complete.

Gravina had with him, in addition to his own flagship, the French *Neptune*, the *Pluton* and the *San Leandro*. On his way to Cadiz he picked up the *San Justo*, *Argonaute*, *Montañez* and *Indomptable* from the centre, and the *Héros*, *Rayo* and *San Francisco* from the van, eleven ships in all. Four more, the *Formidable*, *Duguay-Trouin*, *Mont Blanc* and *Scipion* had withdrawn south-westward with Dumanoir. The rest remained in British hands, or were 'driving about, perfect wrecks, at the mercy of the waves', to quote the *Gibraltar Chronicle*.

'Partial firing continued until 4.30,' ran the battle entry in the *Victory*'s log, 'when a victory having been reported to the Right Honourable Lord Viscount Nelson, K.B. and Commander-in-Chief, he then died of his wound.'

The final scene in Nelson's life was recorded by Dr Beatty in an account which, by reason of its directness and authenticity, demands to be quoted exactly as he wrote it.

With the handkerchief still across his face, Nelson was carried to the orlop deck of the *Victory* by Serjeant Secker and his party.

> Several wounded officers and about forty men were likewise carried to the Surgeon for assistance just at this time [said Beatty] and some others had breathed their last during their conveyance below. Among the latter were Lieutenant William Alexander Ram and Mr Whipple, Captain's clerk. The Surgeon had just examined these two officers, and found that they were dead, when his attention was arrested by several of the wounded calling to him, 'Mr Beatty, Lord Nelson is here; Mr Beatty, the Admiral is wounded.'
>
> The Surgeon now, on looking round, saw the handkerchief fall from his Lordship's face; when the stars on his coat, which also had been covered by it, appeared. Mr Burke, the Purser, and the Surgeon, ran immediately to the assistance of his Lordship, and took him from the arms of the Seamen who had carried him below. In conveying him to one of the Midshipmen's berths, they stumbled, but recovered themselves without falling. Lord Nelson then inquired who were supporting him; and when the Surgeon informed him, his Lordship replied, 'Ah, Mr Beatty, you can do nothing for me. I have but a short time to live: my back is shot through.'
>
> The Surgeon said he 'hoped the wound was not so dangerous as his Lordship imagined, and that he might still survive long to enjoy his glorious victory.'
>
> The Reverend Doctor Scott, who had been absent in another part of the cockpit administering lemonade to the wounded, now came instantly to his Lordship: and in his anguish of grief wrung his hands, and said: 'Alas, Beatty, how prophetic you were!' alluding to the apprehensions expressed by the Surgeon for his Lordship's safety, previous to the battle.
>
> His Lordship was laid upon a bed, stripped of his clothes, and covered with a sheet. While this was effecting, he said to Dr Scott, 'Doctor, I told you so; Doctor, I am gone!' and after a short pause, he added in a low voice, 'I have to leave Lady Hamilton and my adopted daughter Horatia, as a legacy to my Country.'
>
> The Surgeon then examined the wound, assuring his Lordship that he would not put him to much pain in endeavouring to discover the course of the ball; which he soon found had penetrated deep into the chest, and had probably lodged in the spine.
>
> This being explained to his Lordship, he replied he 'was confident his back was shot through'.
>
> The back was then examined externally, but without any injury being perceived; on which his Lordship was requested by the Surgeon to make him acquainted with all his sensations.

He replied, that 'he felt a gush of blood every minute within his breast: that he had no feeling in the lower part of his body: and that his breathing was difficult, and attended with very severe pain about that part of the spine where he was confident that the ball had struck; for', said he, 'I felt it break my back.'

These symptoms, but more particularly the gush of blood which his Lordship complained of, together with the state of his pulse, indicated to the Surgeon the hopeless situation of the case; but till after the victory was ascertained and announced to his Lordship, the true nature of his wound was concealed by the Surgeon from all on board, except only Captain Hardy, Doctor Scott, Mr Burke, and Messrs Smith and Westerburgh, the Assistant-Surgeons.

The *Victory's* crew cheered whenever they observed an Enemy's Ship surrender. On one of these occasions, Lord Nelson anxiously inquired what was the cause of it; when Lieutenant Pasco, who lay wounded at some distance from his Lordship, raised himself up, and told him that another Ship had struck: which appeared to give him much satisfaction.

He now felt an ardent thirst; and frequently called for drink, and to be fanned with paper, making use of these words: 'Fan, fan', and 'Drink, drink.' This he continued to repeat, when he wished for drink or the refreshment of cool air, till a very few minutes before he expired. Lemonade, and wine and water, were given to him occasionally.

He evinced great solicitude for the event of the battle, and fears for the safety of his friend Captain Hardy. Doctor Scott and Mr Burke used every argument they could suggest to relieve his anxiety. Mr Burke told him 'the Enemy were decisively defeated, and that he hoped his Lordship would still live to be himself the bearer of the joyful tidings to his Country'.

He replied, 'It is nonsense, Mr Burke, to suppose I can live: my sufferings are great, but they will soon be over.'

Dr Scott entreated his Lordship not to despair of living, and said he 'trusted that Divine Providence would restore him once more to his dear Country and friends'.

'Ah, Doctor!' replied his Lordship, 'it is all over; it is all over.'

Many messages were sent to Captain Hardy by the Surgeon, requesting his attendance on his Lordship, who became impatient to see him, and often exclaimed: 'Will no one bring Hardy to me? He must be killed: he is surely destroyed.'

The Captain's Aide-de-camp, Mr Bulkeley, now came below, and stated that 'circumstances respecting the Fleet required Captain Hardy's presence on deck, but that he would avail himself of the first favourable moment to visit his Lordship'.

On hearing him deliver this message to the Surgeon, his Lordship inquired who had brought it.

Mr Burke answered: 'It is Mr Bulkeley, my Lord.'

'It is his voice', replied his Lordship; he then said to the young gentleman, 'Remember me to your father.'

An hour and ten minutes, however, elapsed, from the time of his Lordship's being wounded, before Captain Hardy's first subsequent interview with him; the particulars of which are nearly as follow. They shook hands affectionately, and Lord Nelson said: 'Well, Hardy, how goes the battle? How goes the day with us?'

'Very well, my Lord', replied Captain Hardy. 'We have got twelve or fourteen of the Enemy's Ships in our possession; but five of their van have tacked, and show an intention of bearing down upon the *Victory*. I have, therefore, called two or three of our fresh ships round us, and have no doubt of giving them a drubbing.'

'I hope', said his Lordship, 'none of *our* Ships have struck, Hardy?'

'No, my Lord', replied Captain Hardy; 'there is no fear of that.'

Lord Nelson then said: 'I am a dead man, Hardy. I am going fast; it will be all over with me soon. Come nearer to me. Pray let my dear Lady Hamilton have my hair, and all other things belonging to me.'

Mr Burke was about to withdraw at the commencement of this conversation; but his

Lordship, perceiving his intention, desired he would remain. Captain Hardy observed, that he 'hoped Mr Beatty could yet hold out some prospect of life'.

'Oh, no', answered his Lordship, 'it is impossible. My back is shot through. Beatty will tell you so.'

Captain Hardy then returned on deck, and at parting shook hands again with his revered friend and Commander.

His Lordship now requested the Surgeon, who had been previously absent a short time attending Mr Rivers (a midshipman who lost a leg), to return to the wounded and give his assistance to such of them as he could be useful to; 'for', said he, 'you can do nothing for me'.

The Surgeon assured him that the Assistant-Surgeons were doing everything that could be effected for those unfortunate men; but on his Lordship's several times repeating his injunctions to that purpose, he left him, surrounded by Dr Scott, Mr Burke, and two of his Lordship's domestics.

After the Surgeon had been absent a few minutes attending Lieutenant Peake and Reeves of the Marines, who were wounded, he was called by Doctor Scott to his Lordship, who said: 'Ah, Mr Beatty! I have sent for you to say, what I forgot to tell you before, that all power of motion and feeling below my breast are gone; and *you*', continued he, 'very well *know* I can live but a short time.'

The emphatic manner in which he pronounced these last words, left no doubt in the Surgeon's mind, that he adverted to the case of a man who had some months before received a mortal injury of the spine on board the *Victory*, and had laboured under similar privations of sense and muscular motion. The case had made a great impression on Lord Nelson; he was anxious to know the cause of such symptoms, which was accordingly explained to him; and he now appeared to apply the situation and fate of this man to himself.

The Surgeon answered: 'My Lord, you told me so before'; but he now examined the extremities, to ascertain the fact, when his Lordship said, 'Ah, Beatty! I am too certain of it; Scott and Burke have tried it already. *You know* I am gone.'

The Surgeon replied: 'My Lord, unhappily for our Country, nothing can be done for you'; and having made this declaration he was so much affected that he turned round and withdrew a few steps to conceal his emotions.

His Lordship said: 'I know it. I feel something rising in my breast', putting his hand on his left side, 'which tells me I am gone.'

Drink was recommended liberally, and Doctor Scott and Mr Burke fanned him with paper. He often exclaimed: 'God be praised, I have done my duty'; and upon the Surgeon's inquiring whether his pain was still very great, he declared, 'it continued so very severe, that he wished he was dead. Yet', said he in a lower voice, 'one would like to live a little longer, too'; and after a pause of a few minutes, he added in the same tone: 'What would become of poor Lady Hamilton, if she knew my situation?'

The Surgeon, finding it impossible to render his Lordship any further assistance, left him, to attend Lieutenant Bligh, Messrs Smith and Westphal, Midshipmen, and some Seamen, recently wounded.

Captain Hardy now came to the cockpit to see his Lordship a second time, which was after an interval of about fifty minutes from the conclusion of his first visit. Before he quitted the deck, he sent Lieutenant Hills to acquaint Admiral Collingwood with the lamentable circumstances of Lord Nelson's being wounded.

Lord Nelson and Captain Hardy shook hands again; and while the Captain retained his Lordship's hand, he congratulated him, even in the arms of death, on his brilliant victory, 'which', said he, 'was complete; though he did not know how many of the Enemy were captured, as it was impossible to perceive every Ship distinctly. He was certain, however, of fourteen or fifteen having surrendered.'

His lordship answered: 'That is well, but I bargained for twenty'; and then emphatically exclaimed: '*Anchor*, Hardy, *anchor*!'

To this the Captain replied: 'I suppose, my Lord, Admiral Collingwood will now take upon himself the direction of affairs.'

'Not while I live, I hope, Hardy!' cried the dying Chief, and at that moment endeavoured ineffectually to raise himself from the bed. 'No,' added he; 'do *you* anchor, Hardy.'

Captain Hardy then said, 'Shall *we* make the signal, Sir ?'

'Yes', answered his Lordship, 'for if I live, I'll anchor.'

The energetic manner in which he uttered these his last orders to Captain Hardy, accompanied with his efforts to raise himself, evinced his determination never to resign the Command while he retained the exercise of his transcendent faculties, and that he expected Captain Hardy still to carry into effect the suggestion of his exalted mind; a sense of his duty overcoming the pains of death.

He then told Captain Hardy he 'felt that in a few minutes he should be no more'; adding in a low tone: 'Don't throw me overboard, Hardy.'

The Captain answered: 'Oh no, certainly not.'

'Then', replied his Lordship, 'you know what to do; and', continued he, 'take care of my dear Lady Hamilton, Hardy. Take care of poor Lady Hamilton. Kiss me, Hardy.'

The Captain now knelt down and kissed his cheek, when his Lordship said: 'Now I am satisfied. Thank God, I have done my duty.'

Captain Hardy stood for a minute or two in silent contemplation. He knelt down again, and kissed his Lordship's forehead.

His Lordship said: 'Who is that ?'

The Captain answered: 'It is Hardy', to which his Lordship replied: 'God bless you, Hardy!'

After this affecting scene Captain Hardy withdrew, and returned to the quarter-deck, having spent about eight minutes in this his last interview with his dying friend.

Lord Nelson now desired Mr Chevalier, his Steward, to turn him upon his right side, which being effected, his Lordship said: 'I wish I had not left the deck, for I shall soon be gone.'

He afterwards became very low; his breathing was oppressed, and his voice faint. He said to Doctor Scott: 'Doctor, I have not been a *great* sinner', and after a short pause, '*Remember*, that I leave Lady Hamilton and my Daughter Horatia as a legacy to my Country: and', added he, 'never forget Horatia.'

His thirst now increased, and he called for 'drink, drink', 'fan, fan', and 'rub, rub', addressing himself in the last case to Doctor Scott, who had been rubbing his Lordship's breast with his hand, from which he found some relief. These words he spoke in a very rapid manner, which rendered his articulation difficult: but he every now and then, with evident increase of pain, made a greater effort with his vocal powers, and pronounced distinctly these last words: 'Thank God, I have done my duty'; and this great sentiment he continued to repeat so long as he was able to give it utterance.

His Lordship became speechless in about fifteen minutes after Captain Hardy left him. Doctor Scott and Mr Burke, who had all along sustained the bed under his shoulders (which raised him in nearly a semi-recumbent posture, the only one that was supportable to him), forebore to disturb him by speaking to him; and when he had remained speechless about five minutes, his Lordship's Steward went to the Surgeon, who had been a short time occupied with the wounded in another part of the cockpit, and stated his apprehensions that his Lordship was dying.

The Surgeon immediately repaired to him and found him on the verge of dissolution. He knelt down by his side and took up his hand, which was cold, and the pulse gone from the wrist. On the Surgeon's feeling his forehead, which was likewise cold, his Lordship opened his eyes, looked up, and shut them again.

The Surgeon again left him and returned to the wounded who required his assistance, but was not absent five minutes before the Steward announced to him that he 'believed his Lordship had expired'.

The Surgeon returned and found that the report was but too well founded; his Lordship had breathed his last, at thirty minutes past four o'clock, at which period Doctor Scott was in the act of rubbing his Lordship's breast, and Mr Burke supporting the bed under his shoulders.

From the time of his Lordship's being wounded till his death, a period of about two hours and forty-five minutes elapsed (or perhaps half an hour more): but a knowledge of the decisive victory which was gained he acquired of Captain Hardy within the first hour and a quarter of this period. A partial cannonade, however, was still maintained, in consequence of the Enemy's running Ships passing the British at different points; and the last distant guns which were fired at their Van Ships that were making off, were heard a minute or two before his Lordship expired.

6 The Storm

The darkness of the night after the battle hid scenes of confusion and distress. No Admiral's light burned in the *Victory*, and Collingwood could not for some time hope to get his ships into regular order, though discipline was unimpaired. It soon became clear that some vessels would have difficulty in keeping afloat. In a material sense, those which, battered as they were, had found refuge in Cadiz, were best off. Among the rest out at sea, victors and vanquished, the work of immediate repair, of tending the wounded, of disposing of the dead, and above all of incessant work at the pumps, to keep leaks within control, engaged the attention and energies of every able-bodied survivor. And it proved, soon enough, that Nelson had been right. The earlier swell from the westward had been the portent of a coming storm. The wind increased throughout the hours of darkness, and it continued, rising to gale force, for several days.

Most ships were short-handed, the British not only through casualties, but because men were detached to the prizes; the vanquished because the larger proportion of their people were demoralised, and incapable of sustained work. A few captains, remembering Nelson's signals to prepare to anchor, now obeyed it. Those who did so, profited. Of those who did not, some were incapable of carrying out the instruction owing to damage to anchors and cables, while others considered themselves better off with more sea-room. These made their way, or were towed, like the *Royal Sovereign*, farther from the shoals which were to leeward.

Conditions in the prizes were always difficult. In the case of ships which had been severely handled, they were sometimes shocking. Mr Midshipman Badcock, for instance, was sent from the *Neptune* to the *Santissima Trinidad*, which everyone in the British fleet, from Collingwood downward, longed to see their own. The first job to be done on board the great ship was the grisly one of heaving corpses overboard. There were over 200 killed, and the Spaniards were in no state to help. Badcock then had to see to the securing of prisoners, including many soldiers, and to get as many as possible away to British ships. Below, he found the beams covered with blood, the decks still slippery, and the after part of the vessel almost choked with wounded, many armless or legless, none of whom had been properly attended. Nor was there any prospect of giving them immediate relief.

The *Minotaur*'s experience was typical of those ships, relatively little damaged, which were best able to supply prize parties. Towards the close of day she sent a lieutenant of marines with 68 men to the Spanish *Neptuno*. They reached her at half-past five, sending the *Neptuno*'s first lieutenant back to their own ship, to deliver his dead captain's sword.

The prisoners, firearms and ammunition were duly secured, the magazines locked, after which the British discovered that the ship was very leaky, and that there was no shot-plug on board. Men were sent over to the *Minotaur* for the essential materials, and the party set about stopping the worst holes. Prisoners were set to work at the pumps, for the *Neptuno* had five feet of water in the hold, and this was increasing.

On the morning of the 22nd the party began clearing away wreckage, after which the *Minotaur* took the *Neptuno* in tow. But the wind rose, the hawser broke, and the Spaniard was once again left to the care of her prize party.

The *San Juan de Nepomuceno*, which had actually struck to the *Dreadnought*, was left to the *Tonnant* to secure. The *Tonnant*'s captain sent Lieutenant Clements to board her, but by that time, so the lieutenant recorded, 'there was no available boat but what was shot. However,' he continued, 'I was told I must try, so and I went away in the jollyboat with two men. I had not gone above a quarter of the way, when we swamped.' Clements could not swim, but the two men held him up, one of them being a negro. The trio were at length fished out of the water, and returned to comparative safety. Similar incidents occurred in other ships. Boats set out, were found to be damaged, and their people suffered. But eventually prize crews were in possession of most of the surrendered vessels, though one of them, the *Algéciras*, was retaken by her own men, and brought into Cadiz, adding another unit to the surviving force.

Again, it was the *Tonnant* that was concerned. She had sent a lieutenant and 50 men as prize crew, and they had under hatches in the hold 270 French officers and men. At dawn on 22 October the ship had drifted too far inshore to hope for help from the British fleet, and as the morning advanced, they came close to the rocks. Lieutenant Bennett and his men were too few to guard the prisoners as well as to rig jury-masts, which alone could save the ship. As the only chance for all on board, the lieutenant had the hatches taken off, and the Frenchmen were set free. They swarmed on deck and, headed by one of their officers, Lieutenant de la Bretonnière—whose action made his name in the French navy, and eventually brought him his flag—at once made it clear to Bennett that they resumed possession of the ship, and that if the British resisted, they would be thrown overboard. If, on the other hand, the prize crew helped to save the ship, they were promised their liberty. In the circumstances, Bennett agreed, and British and French, working together, succeeded in getting up three top-gallant masts, and so reached port.

Among the prisoners was a woman, Jeanette of the *Achille*. Her story was told by a lieutenant of the *Revenge*.

On the morning after the action I had charge of the deck [he said], the other officers and crew being at breakfast, when a boat-load of prisoners-of-war came alongside, all of whom, with one exception, were in the costume of Adam. The exception was apparently a youth, but clothed in an old jacket and trousers, with a dingy handkerchief tied round the head, and exhibiting a face begrimed with smoke and dirt, without shoes, stockings or shirt, and looking the picture of misery and despair.

The appearance of this person at once attracted my attention, and on asking some questions I was answered that the prisoner was a woman. It was sufficient to know this, and I lost no time in introducing her to my messmates, as a female requiring their compassionate attention. The poor creature was almost famishing with hunger, having tasted nothing for four and twenty hours, consequently she required no persuasion to partake of the breakfast table. I then gave her up my cabin, and made a collection of all the articles which could be procured to enable her to complete a more suitable wardrobe.

One of the lieutenants gave her a piece of sprigged muslin which he had obtained from a Spanish prize, and two new checked shirts were supplied by the purser; these, with a purser's blanket, and my ditty bag, which contained needles, thread, etc., being placed at her disposal she, in a short time, appeared in a very different, and much more becoming costume. Being a Dressmaker, she had made herself a sort of jacket, after the Flemish fashion, and the purser's shirts had been transformed into an outer-petticoat; she had a silk handkerchief tastily tied over her head, and another thrown over her shoulders; white stockings and a pair of the chaplain's shoes were on her feet, and altogether our guest, which we unanimously voted her, appeared a very interesting young woman.

Jeanette's quick recovery was astonishing, considering what she had been through. In action, she had been stationed in the passage to the fore magazine, to help in handing up the powder. When firing ceased, she went in search of her husband, but found that all the ladders to the upper decks had by that time been shot away. Then there came the alarm of fire, and poor Jeanette wandered to and fro among the dead and dying, while the flames raged above, and guns from the main deck began to fall through the burnt planks. Her only possible refuge was by now outside, and she scrambled out of the gun-room port 'and, by the help of the rudder-chains, reached the back of the rudder, where she remained some time, praying the ship might blow up, and put an end her misery'.

'At length,' so she told her captors, 'the lead which lined the rudder-trunk began to melt, and to fall upon her, and her only means of avoiding this was to leap overboard.' First she found a lump of cork, which kept her up for some time, and then a man, swimming near, gave her a piece of plank, which she placed under her arms, and this supported her until she was picked up. About four days later, she heard that her husband had also been rescued, and when she eventually landed at Gibraltar, it was with a small purse of dollars given her by the *Revenge*'s officers. This was one instance among many when Nelson's wish that 'humanity after victory' should be 'the predominant feature in the British Fleet', was fulfilled to the letter.

Another French woman from the *Achille* was picked up by the *Britannia*. She had been dressed in the costume of a harlequin, and was given a large cotton dressing-gown by the lieutenant of marines. It is also certain that there were one or two women on board the British ships, though no record of their adventures appears to have survived. It had been so at the Glorious First of June, when a woman in H.M.S. *Tremendous* had recently become a mother. Her son, Daniel Tremendous Mackenzie, duly received the Naval General Service medal, with the appropriate clasp, when it was issued in 1848, by which time he was an ageing man. Two women who were present at the Nile were refused this medal, but, with the illogicality which sometimes pervades such matters, it was allowed to Jane Townsend, who was on board *Defiance* at Trafalgar.

Among the curiosities of the time was the convention that frigates and other vessels which by reason of their size were not eligible to 'lie in the line of battle', were usually free from attack, in a large-scale action, by the big ships, though it was not one which was always strictly observed. At Trafalgar, the British frigates played a notable part throughout, not only in repeating signals, which was one of their normal duties, but in helping damaged ships. On the other hand the frigates of the Combined Fleet, the *Cornélie*, *Hermione*, *Hortense*, *Rhin* and *Thémis*, and the brigs *Argus* and *Furet*, did far less. They kept to leeward during the action, in which position they could see little but smoke and general confusion, and their signalling left much to be desired, though they helped in the later stages of the battle. For instance, it was the *Thémis* that towed Gravina's *Principe de Asturias* into Cadiz, while under Captain Cosmao's orders they were to be given their opportunity in the later sortie.

On 22 October there was a strong wind all day, with squalls. The weather was mainly from the south, which was of help in keeping prizes from driving ashore, but was foul for Gibraltar, where the British wished to take them. Next day the wind increased, and in the afternoon, conditions favouring his leaving Cadiz, Cosmao made his foray. His idea was both to rescue the prizes which he could see tossing about in the bay, and prove that, even if defeated, there was yet a high spirit among the French and Spanish survivors. He deserved better luck than befell him. He had three French and two Spanish ships-of-the-line, the *Pluton*, *Indomptable*, *Neptune*, *Rayo* and *San Francisco de Asis*, together with a number of frigates and brigs. Some of the battleships were seriously damaged, but Cosmao thought that they could hold off any counter-attack which Collingwood could launch before nightfall, while the frigates and brigs, which were undamaged and handy, could show their qualities in boarding and towing.

He had one success. The *Santa Ana*, with Álava on board, was retaken, the *Thunderer* first having time to withdraw her prize crew. He might well have had another, for in the Spanish *Neptuno* the ship's company, seeing what was happening, turned on the *Minotaur*'s party, and helped one of the French frigates to secure a tow. Even so, the *Neptuno* was soon in trouble, and she drove ashore off Rota, British and Spanish working hard until the last to save themselves and the ship. Otherwise, all was disaster. Collingwood soon called up a number of 74's to drive Cosmao back, and the Frenchman actually lost no less than three of his main force. The *Indomptable* blundered across to Rota, and was wrecked near the *Neptuno*, with the loss of all hands. The *San Francisco de Asis* parted her cables after anchoring, and drove ashore near one of the Cadiz forts, while the three-decked *Rayo*, unable to regain harbour, rolled her masts out off San Luca, and had to surrender at discretion to the *Donegal*, Captain Sir Pulteney Malcolm. This officer, fresh from Gibraltar, not only had the mortification of missing Trafalgar, but even his unexpected prize was lost to him later, by weather.

Cosmao's ineffective gallantry was not popular in Cadiz. The citizens had seen two more of their own nation's ships perish off their shore, and even the rescue of Álava was imperfect compensation. But what Cosmao could not accomplish in denying the victors the fruits of their skill, the elements took in their stride. The *Redoutable* sank while in tow of the *Swiftsure*, five of whose men, with 13 from the *Téméraire*, went down with her; four others were wrecked, the *Berwick*, *Aigle*, *Bucentaure* and *Fougueux*, the *Bucentaure* taking part of her own crew, and the *Fougueux* all her own men, as well as 30 from the *Téméraire*. And on 24 October, as the weather still proved furious, Collingwood gave the order to 'Quit and withdraw men from prizes after having destroyed or disabled them.'

This was a sad moment for the fleet, even though, as Collingwood said, 'I can only say that in my life I never saw such exertions as were made to save those Ships; and would rather fight another Battle, than pass such a week as followed it.' Officers and men were robbed of the visible signs of their triumph; still more important to them (since that triumph needed no trophies to establish its extent), they saw their prize money vanish beneath the waves.

First there was the task of removing not merely the prize crews, but the remaining prisoners, and particularly the wounded. Then the demolition and fire parties set to work. Saddest perhaps was the case of the *Santissima Trinidad*. Badcock noted that she was built of cedar, and thought that the order to abandon her was premature. But it was with the greatest difficulty that she had been kept afloat so long, and already tired men worked themselves to exhaustion in moving her sick. Even when she finally disappeared, she was thought to have carried at least some living men with her, though her cat was one of the earlier rescues.

In the end, the four ships which were brought to Gibraltar, the French *Swiftsure*, the Spanish *Bahama*, *San Ildefonso* and the *San Juan de Nepomuceno*, were a damaged and undistinguished lot, though in fact the number of prizes was to be increased in an unexpected way, in an action which took its place as a pendant to the main battle.

At Cadiz, when parties landed from the British fleet (mainly survivors from prize crews which had been wrecked), nothing could have exceeded the kindness of the Spaniards, from the Governor to the meekest nursing sister. They had little to offer, but everything they had was given unstintingly, and with unfailing courtesy. Every account speaks of the kindly spirit which continued between the Spanish and the British.

Hercules Robinson was sent in later with his captain, Blackwood, to arrange an exchange of prisoners, Blackwood 'rather short, but of extraordinary strength and finely made, well set up, a fresh complexion and small hands and feet'. The Spaniards were impressed with his bearing and his fine uniform, 'a gold-laced cocked hat, gold-laced coat and epaulettes, white pantaloons and Hessian boots, a light crooked sabre, and a great shirt frill'. Robinson, as Blackwood's aide-de-camp, found himself enjoying pineapple and old sherry at the house of the Governor, the Marquis of Solano.

Codrington of the *Orion* recorded one case in which the master of a boarding party landing at Cadiz in a boat, was received by a carriage 'backed into the water for him to step into; all sorts of cordials and confectionery were placed in the carriage for him, and clean linen, bed, etc., prepared for him at a lodging on shore; added to which the women and priests provided him with delicacies of all sorts as the carriage passed along the streets'. In short, he says, 'and with very great truth, that had he been wrecked in any part of England he would never have received one-half the attention which he did from these poor Spaniards, whose friends we had just destroyed in such numbers; but, I must add, the survivors amongst whom we had been at the greatest pains and risks in saving from the jaws of death.'

Formerly allies, British and Spanish would end the long war on the same side, and their enmity was never deep throughout the years when Spain was politically linked with France. The Spaniards were monarchists and religious—so, in their differing ways, were the British. With the French it was different. They were prickly allies, and, so the Spaniards thought, ungenerous foes. Most of them had at one time publicly professed atheism, and although they now boasted an Emperor, and made a great show of the allegiance to the new dynasty, it was as a soldier that Napoleon had made his name, and his action in throwing away both his own fleet and that of his allies did not endear him to the victims.

When Rosily at last arrived from Madrid on his master's business, he found cold comfort, and a destroyed command. He must privately have blessed the day that Villeneuve decided to put to sea without him. His mission now devolved into holding enquiries and writing reports, an activity which was familiar to him. He could blame the absent Villeneuve to his heart's content, secure in the knowledge that he himself would be spared that unhappy man's successive dilemmas.

Collingwood, in his clear and graceful way, summed up the whole matter in a letter to Admiral Sir Peter Parker, written from the *Queen*, off Cadiz, within 11 days of the battle. It had been Parker who, many years before, had 'made' both him and Nelson, giving them command of frigates in the West Indies during the War of American Independence. Collingwood and Nelson had in their turn been in a position to help younger members of Parker's family, which they did with faithful gratitude.

> You will have seen from the public accounts that we have fought a great Battle [said Collingwood], and had it not been for the fall of our noble friend, who was indeed the glory of England and the admiration of all who ever saw him in Battle, your pleasure would have been perfect—that two of your own pupils, raised under your eye, and cherished by your kindness, should render such Service to their Country as I hope this Battle, in its effect, will be.
>
> . . . It was a severe Action, no dodging or manœuvring. They formed their line with nicety, and awaited our attack with great composure, nor did they fire a gun until we were close to them, we began first.

Not all accounts agree with Collingwood's on this point, but those are his words.

> . . . our Ships were fought with a degree of gallantry that would have warmed your heart. Everybody exerted themselves, and a glorious day was made of it.
>
> People who cannot comprehend how complicated an affair a Battle at sea is, and who judge of an Officer's conduct by the number of sufferers in his Ship, often do him a wrong. Though there will appear great differences in the loss of men, all did admirably well; and the conclusion was grand beyond description; eighteen hulks of the Enemy lying among the

British Fleet without a stick standing, and the French *Achille* burning. But we were close to the rocks of Trafalgar, and when I made the signal for anchoring, many Ships had their cables shot, and got an anchor ready. Providence did for us what no human effort could have done, the wind shifted a few points and we drifted off the land.

The storm being violent, and many of our Ships in most perilous situations, I found it necessary to order the captures, all without masts, some without rudders, and many half full of water, to be destroyed, except such as were in better plight; for my object was their ruin and not what might be made of them.

Collingwood's words, particularly the last sentence, might have been written by his dead friend. Though so differing in temperament, they were at one in their purpose. 'What might be made of them' proved in fact little enough, to most of the fleet. When the Prize Money and Grant were at last distributed, there were five classes of share. The highest amounted to a total of £3,362 7s. 6d.; which was no despicable award; then there was a great drop to £225 11s.; the third and fourth classes were £148 12s. and £27 respectively; while the share of the ordinary seaman was the princely sum of £6 10s. In the case of those wounded, the Committee of Lloyd's added sums ranging from £100 to severely wounded lieutenants, to £10 to slightly wounded seamen, which gave an unfair advantage to those ships which had made the most of their casualties.

Prize was one thing, credit another. However severe his outward aspect (and Collingwood never received from his captains half the affection which Nelson could summon at once, and keep throughout their lives), Collingwood was like Nelson in the generosity of his praise of dead and living alike. Captain Durham of the *Defiance* had an excellent example of the trait when he went to call on Collingwood in the *Euryalus* after the action. As so often, Collingwood was writing in his cabin. Blackwood was with him. Durham mentioned several ships of which he had knowledge, and praised the noble conduct of some of the frigates. But 'the captain of the *Euryalus* hinted that there had been a want of exertion on the part of some particular ship.'

'Collingwood started up and said: "Sir, this has been a glorious victory for England and for Europe—don't let there be a reflection against a cabin boy."' 'This', added Durham, 'quite silenced the captain of the *Euryalus.*'

Durham then left the cabin, and going on deck saw a French officer leaning on the capstan. He entered into conversation with him, and found it was Villeneuve.

The admiral said to Durham: 'Sir, were you in Sir Robert Calder's action?' Durham said that he was, and that he had commanded the ship which had discovered the Combined Fleet. Villeneuve sighed and said: 'I wish Sir Robert and I had fought it out that day. He would not be in his present situation, nor I in mine.'

Robinson of the *Euryalus* was still more particular about Villeneuve, whom he described as 'a tallish thin man, a very tranquil, placid, English-looking Frenchman; he wore a long tailed uniform coat, high and flat collar, corduroy pantaloons of a greenish colour, with stripes two inches wide, half boots with sharp toes, and a watch chain with long gold links'. Magendie on the other hand was 'a short, fat, jocund sailor, who found a cure for all ills in the Frenchman's philosophy, "*Fortune de la guerre*"'.

Villeneuve's retinue were accommodated some days after the battle in the comparative comfort of the *Neptune*. Captain Fremantle wrote to his wife on 28 October to say that he was that instant towing the *Victory*, and that Collingwood 'has just made the signal for me to go with her to Gibraltar', though he later changed his mind, and Fremantle was ordered elsewhere.

> Admiral Villeneuve was with me on board over two days [he continued]. I found him a very pleasant and Gentlemanlike man, the poor man was very low . . . but I still have the pleasure of feeding and accommodating his Captain and his 2 Aid du Camps and his Adjutant General, who are true Frenchmen, but with whom I am much amused. . . . I have found also an excellent French cook and a true Spanish pug-dog. . . . These Frenchmen make me laugh at the gasconade as well as at their accounts of Bonaparte, the Palais Royal, Paris etc. . . . The French Captain drinks your health regularly every day at dinner. The poor man is married and laments his lot; one of the younger ones is desperately in love with a lady in Cadiz and Frenchmanlike carries her picture in his pocket. . . .

Fremantle's pug, which quickly grew attached to him, and long served to alleviate the boredom of future service on blockade, had been another of the animals snatched from the *Santissima Trinidad*.

Another Frenchman happily accommodated was Infernet of the *Intrépide*, who had fought so gallantly and became the guest of Codrington in the *Orion*. Codrington found him 'much like us in his open manner, a good sailor and . . . he has more delicacy in his conduct, although perhaps boisterous in his manner, than any Frenchman I have before met with'. Codrington asked his wife to supply Infernet's wants when he reached England on parole, while Captain Hallowell of the *Tigre*, a particular friend of Nelson's, 'although not in the action, insisted on sending him a trunk with two dozen shirts, stockings, a bed, and some cloth to make a coat, and a draft for £100, as an acknowledgment of the civility he met with from Ganteaume and his officers when a prisoner'. Infernet remarked to Codrington, of the censure on Sir Robett Calder: 'It is very well for you gentlemen that you can feel justified in finding fault with an admiral who, when in command of *fifteen* sail-of-the-line fights a battle with *twenty*, because he only makes two of them prizes!'

7 Afterwards

It is a commonplace in the history of warfare that victory is rarely exploited to the hilt. The victors are too exhausted by battle, too weakened by losses, too satisfied with the fact that they have won. In Nelson's time it had been as true of sea actions as of land, though there had been some notable exceptions.

Nelson himself had sometimes talked of a 'Lord Howe victory', despite his reverence for that seaman; his feeling that the Glorious First of June had been a strategic failure, and only a half-developed tactical success, was shared by many officers who studied their profession closely; while his admired friend Lord Hood had made his anger all too apparent when Rodney had failed to turn the battle of the Saints into one of annihilation.

Collingwood, tried as he was by the events of 21 October and the storm which followed, never for one moment lost his grip of the strategic as well as the tactical situation, never relaxed, never tolerated negligence in his captains, either in principle or in detail. So far as the wider campaign was concerned, there were still loose ends, which must be attended to. He thought at first that Dumanoir had entered Cadiz with Gravina and Cosmao, and kept inshore watch on that port until it was certain that the Frenchman was elsewhere, when the strength of blockaders was decreased. Again, Allemand was still at large, and it was even possible that he might appear from the west, though the chances of such a bold course were not great. Above all, there was Craig and his Italian expedition to be supported and kept informed, and Pitt's whole policy to be implemented.

One of Collingwood's earliest Trafalgar despatches was to Elliot at Naples, and it is certain that, had Nelson lived, he would have written in much the same terms and with quite the same speed. 'As it is of great importance', he wrote, 'to the affairs of Italy and Europe in general that the events which have lately taken place on this coast should be known as soon as possible at the Court at which you reside, I lose no time in informing you, Sir, that on the 19th instant the Combined Fleet sailed from Cadiz, their destination certainly for Italy.' Collingwood then described the battle, 'the most decisive and complete victory that ever was gained over a powerful enemy', and the escape of Dumanoir to the south. 'I will venture to say,' he added, 'had the battle been fought in the Ocean far from land and unembarrassed by the rocks and shoals of Gibraltar, there probably would not one of the enemy's ships have escaped.' He concluded: 'As soon as I can make the necessary arrangements, I propose coming into the Mediterranean, and if the Spanish squadron of Cartagena is in motion and at sea, to use my utmost endeavours to destroy them also and send to the Italian coast such a force as will check any operations the enemy may have in contemplation there.'

Elliott and the Court of Naples could now be assured that there could be no possibility of serious interference at sea in the immediate future. Collingwood's own detachments would continue to watch what he called the 'Spanish beauties' at Cartagena, for although no threat seemed likely to come from that place, the fleet was well provided, and British seamen, with appraising eye, could never withhold admiration for Spanish shipbuilding, which had established a pattern of excellence such as was the envy of most shipyards.

Collingwood, in fact, took over all Nelson's burdens. While he lived, he was never to be relieved of them, and five weary years were to pass before he joined his friend in the crypt of St Paul's.

It was Sir Richard Strachan, henceforward to be known to contemporaries, from a sentence in his despatch, as 'the delighted Sir Dicky', who added four more to the depleted prizes of Trafalgar. Earlier in the campaign he had rendered notable service in warning Orde of Villeneuve's escape from the Mediterranean. He was to add a sparkling pendant to the events of the battle.

Dumanoir, after leaving the stricken scene, had made for Gibraltar, but had not entered the Straits. On 22 October the southerly gale had struck his damaged squadron, and he had found it impossible to stand up to it. Then, towards evening, he saw sails which be believed to be Rear-Admiral Louis and his ships, and he decided to reach to the westwards, in the hope of falling in with Allemand. For two days he searched for him, doing the best he could to repair his sails and stop his leaks, and then, on the 25th, he decided to go northward. On the 29th, as Louis was on the point of joining Collingwood, Dumanoir doubled Cape St Vincent. Neutrals were questioned, but not a word of Allemand could be had. Dumanoir therefore stood on for Rochefort, unaware that Strachan was ahead of him .

Strachan had remained in constant touch with the cruiser-line off Vigo until the day of Nelson's battle. Then, hearing that the ships which Villeneuve had left in Vigo were ready for sea, he moved away to let them out. On 24 October he took station off Finisterre, convinced that, with Nelson before Cadiz, the enemy must go north. He was thus well placed to intercept Dumanoir, of whose presence at large he was, of course, quite unaware.

As for Dumanoir, his ships were making so much water that he was forced to keep near the coast. He passed Finisterre early on 2 November, inshore of Strachan, without being sighted—but his luck then failed him. Captain Thomas Baker of the *Phoenix*—a skilled and successful frigate officer who had already had a lion's share of fighting and excitement, was once again at the right place at the right moment. He had been rewarded for good service by the opportunity of a lucrative detached cruise, but had heard news of Allemand through a Danish skipper. The information was false, but it suggested that Allemand was somewhere in the Bay of Biscay, making for his home port of Rochefort. Baker flung the certainty of prize money to the winds, and made straight for Ferrol, where he expected to meet Strachan. Not finding him there, he headed for the Finisterre rendezvous, and at daylight on 2 November discovered himself inshore of what he believed to be Allemand's squadron, but what in fact was Dumanoir's.

The French admiral detached the *Duguay-Trouin* to chase the *Phoenix*, but Baker, instead of trying to escape, held on for Strachan's rendezvous. The *Duguay-Trouin* failed to cut him off, and he was soon in sight of Sir Richard.

Baker was fired on before he could make his identity clear to Strachan in the *Caesar*. When he had done so, he reported that he had just been chased by Allemand, and that the French were close by, to leeward. 'I was delighted', wrote Strachan, in words which echoed round the fleet, 'and told him to tell the captains astern that I meant to engage at once.'

The *Phoenix* sailed away to rally the squadron, while Strachan held on after the chase. He sighted the French in the moonlight, standing away in line abreast, but when the moon set, they were free to alter course, safe from observation. Dumanoir altered to south-east, towards Cape Ortegal. Strachan was not deceived. He waited for two of his 74's to join him, the *Hero* and the *Courageux*, together with one more frigate, Lord William Fitzroy's *Aeolus*, and headed in the same direction. He had reasoned that Dumanoir would probably try to slip into Ferrol, and he was right.

By daybreak on 3 November, with another frigate, the *Santa Margarita*, added to his force, Strachan had Dumanoir once more in sight. The British were soon to be joined by the *Phoenix* and the *Révolutionnaire*, a heavy frigate taken from the French, and as the *Phoenix* was bringing up the *Namur*, the last of Strachan's big ships, Strachan was in the happy position of having four ships-of-the-line, to oppose an equal number of the enemy, besides which he had the help of four frigates. For once, the frigates could play an essential part in an action between big ships, and they could, indeed, tip the scale decisively.

All day the chase continued, and as Strachan's position prevented any possibility of Dumanoir making Ferrol, his direction was across the Bay towards Rochefort, with the British slowly gaining. The night was fine, and Strachan was able to keep Dumanoir in sight throughout. By the morning of 4 November the *Caesar*, Strachan's flagship, and the *Scipion*, Dumanoir's rearmost vessel, were barely six miles apart.

The British frigates were well ahead of the ships-of-the-line, and were just within gunshot. As early as six o'clock the *Santa Margarita* and *Phoenix* had got near enough to give the *Scipion* their broadsides, though Dumanoir was still hoping to be able to avoid an action. He had had to jettison a number of guns to keep his flagship seaworthy, and was in no condition to fight an inferior force, much less the one which was now hard on his heels. But by eleven o'clock he had no choice. The *Scipion* was unable to drive off the frigates, and was beginning to suffer badly, so Dumanoir hauled to the wind in line of battle. Action became as inevitable as it had been when Villeneuve took the same course at Trafalgar, and expectations on both sides were much the same.

When Strachan saw the movement of the enemy, he had only three of his heavy ships with him. He hailed his captains to tell them that he intended to attack the enemy centre and rear. He himself led into action with the *Caesar*, which was the most powerful vessel he had with him—once again, an echo of Trafalgar was apparent.

The usual practice in such a situation was for the leading ship to engage the enemy's windward vessel, and for the second astern to pass on, under cover of her fire, and to make for the next ahead, the process being repeated down the line. Strachan did not do this, probably because Dumanoir was second in the French line, and Strachan wished to bring the flagships together. Like Nelson, he wished to seek out the enemy commander.

In the action which followed, the frigates, instead of taking up the more orthodox position to windward of their own force, placed themselves to leeward of the *Scipion* and continued to engage her. They hoped to take a full part in what could scarcely fail to be a successful encounter.

Strachan secured a concentration on the rear, but left the van ship, the *Duguay-Trouin*, disengaged. Dumanoir promptly signalled for his squadron to tack in succession, his intention being to cover his rear, which was in acute danger, and perhaps to cut off the *Namur*, which was now seen approaching. It was a bold move. It had to be done under a destructive fire from the *Caesar* and the *Hero*, and it brought the French within pistol shot of the British line.

Strachan had difficulty in turning, and for more than half an hour action ceased. Seeing that the French might weather him and get away, Strachan ordered the *Namur* to bear up and engage the French van—alone. Of his other three ships, the *Hero* got round first, and Strachan ordered her to lead. Action was renewed with a fresh attack on the French rear, the frigates keeping their position astern and to leeward. Presently the *Namur* was able to place herself in line, behind the *Hero*, and—the *Duguay-Trouin* being by this time out of action—Strachan's four battleships could concentrate on the other three. 'The French squadron fought to admiration', said Strachan in his despatch, 'and did not surrender until their ships were unmanageable.' But by four o'clock all was over, and by nightfall the four French ships were in Strachan's possession.

It was not until Dumanoir came on board the *Caesar* that Strachan knew whom he had been fighting. 'Judge of my surprise', he wrote, 'when I found the ships we had taken were not the Rochefort squadron, but four from Cadiz.' Allemand's movements were still a mystery, but Strachan had the satisfaction not only of taking four useful vessels, one of which, the unlucky *Duguay-Trouin*, survived until after World War II as H.M.S. *Implacable*, a notable example of French shipbuilding, but he heard at least the general outcome of Trafalgar. Collingwood's official despatch in fact reached England just about the time that Strachan's Biscay action was ending. Soon after the news of his success reached London, Strachan found himself promoted Rear-Admiral of the Blue, though this was in the ordinary course of seniority. For his services against Dumanoir he was given the star of the Bath, and a pension of £1,000 a year. He had every reason to be delighted, but although he showed himself a skilful tactician, the result could never have been in doubt.

Strachan had a way with words, not unlike Nelson's. He was also generous in praise of his people. 'I have returned thanks to the Captains of the Ships-of-the-Line and the Frigates', he wrote, 'and they speak in high terms of approbation of their respective Officers and Ships' Companies. If anything could add to the good opinion I have already formed of the Officers and Crew of the *Caesar*, it is their gallant conduct in this day's battle. The enemy suffered much, but our ships not more than is expected on these occasions.'

The British casualties were 24 killed and over 100 wounded. Strachan commented: 'I daresay Their Lordships will be surprised we have lost so few men. I can only account for it from the enemy firing high, and we closing suddenly.' The French lost heavily in men, particularly in the *Scipion*, which suffered 111 killed and wounded, a sign of the efficient work of the frigates.

The makers of popular songs and ballads, full as they were of the death of Nelson, did not overlook Strachan, and to the fine old tune of *Heart of Oak* (composed originally in honour of Hawke) they put some new words.

> *Though with tears we lament our great Nelson's demise,*
> *Let the nations rejoice that more Nelsons arise;*
> *'Twas Collingwood finished what the hero begun*
> *And brave was the conquest accomplished by Strachan.*

The rhyme at least has the merit of showing how the man in the street pronounced Strachan's difficult name.

With the disposal of Dumanoir, the immediate naval campaign was over, for the few remaining ships in Cadiz, though they continued to be watched, proved no further use in the war, and the surviving French vessels were handed over when Spain changed sides, three years later. Only Allemand remained at large.

Just before Trafalgar, this intrepid admiral had decided to run for the Canaries, in the hope of injuring British trade. Within a fortnight he was close to Teneriffe, and on the day that Strachan met Dumanoir he was being made welcome by the Spanish garrison. He stayed some days, landed his sick, re-victualled, sold his prizes, and then gave out that he intended to cruise in the neighbourhood of Madeira, after which he would proceed to the coast of Portugal, where he hoped to disorganise the British lines of communication.

After three days he captured a British merchantman, outward bound, and learnt from her captain that before leaving Portsmouth he had heard a rumour that a great battle had been fought, and that Nelson had been killed. Allemand reasoned that if this were indeed so, the coast of Portugal might be less well guarded than it had been for some time, and his arrangements held.

In mid-December he took three small prizes. He learnt from them that there was a powerful squadron on the look-out for him, and that Nelson and Strachan between them had annihilated the Combined Fleet. 'The indiscretion of those who brought me the news struck consternation aboard, and aroused keen anxiety to get into port', wrote Allemand. This was not surprising, and his own luck held till the last. Thick weather helped him to elude the network of watchers, and he ran into the safety of Rochefort on Christmas Eve, 1805. His foray, which had caused so much disturbance to the Admiralty in London, and so much loss among the British trade, proved how right Decrès had been when he had urged Napoleon not to plan in terms of large-scale naval movements, but to engage in war against commerce, conducted by small and efficient detachments. Allemand had shown the way.

It was the *Pickle* schooner, one of the smallest ships at Trafalgar, commanded by a lieutenant of French descent, which brought official news of the battle to London. The *Pickle* was fast, she had done well in rescue work after the action, and Lapenotière, who was in charge of her, was a favourite with Collingwood. Blackwood had hoped for the chance to be sent, but the *Euryalus* was too useful to be spared for the time, and her captain had to be content with carrying home the principal French and Spanish prisoners, a later honour sufficient in itself.

The *Pickle* had sight of land on 4 November, and Lapenotière was able to land at Falmouth early next day. He posted at once to London, made extraordinarily good time, considering the season of the year and the state of the roads, and arrived at the Admiralty at one o'clock in the morning of 6 November.

On her way north, the schooner had fallen in with the frigate *Nautilus*, and had given her captain the news. The *Nautilus* had put into Lisbon, and had been sent home by the British Consul with urgent despatches. Sykes, her captain, made an exceptional passage to Plymouth, and managed to reach Whitehall at the same moment as Lapenotière, who was promoted to the rank of commander.

This time Marsden, the Secretary of the Admiralty, made no mistake, though no immediate re-disposition of forces was involved. Barham was in bed and asleep, but he roused him personally, and gave him the news at once, as architect of the great campaign. Secretary and First Lord then summoned all the clerks who could be found, and spent the rest of the night making copies for the King, for Pitt, and for the *London Gazette*. Private messages were sent to Nelson's brother, to Lady Hamilton at Merton, and to Lady Nelson, who received a note in Barham's own hand.

Collingwood's despatch was printed in *The Times* in its issue dated Thursday, 7 November, by which time the main outline of events had been circulated by word of mouth in the countryside through which Lapenotière and Sykes had ridden, and in the metropolis itself. It was a time when London crowds were capable of much more violence and disorder than is ever seen today, but for once the nation was sobered in its triumph by a sense of irreparable loss. Lord Malmesbury declared that 'not one individual who felt joy at this victory, so well-timed and complete, but first had an instinctive feeling of sorrow. I never saw so little public joy. The illumination seemed dim, and as if it were half clouded by the desire of expressing the mixture of contending feelings; every common person in the streets speaking first of their sorrow for Nelson, and then of the victory.'

Barham, old as he was, had done his work, and could face retirement with equanimity. He was in fact soon out of office, returning to an obscurity which long concealed his immense services to the country, and which even today are recognised mainly by historians, since his role was unspectacular and administrative. Though this was so, he was none the less the brain behind every movement of the fleets, and to the conduct of the naval war he brought the experience of a lifetime, and a devotion to his profession which was not exceeded even by Nelson and Collingwood, who were his instruments.

As for Pitt, at the very centre of affairs, he had known Nelson personally for many years, he had seen him at length during his last visit to London, and he felt his loss in the way that all men did who had ever fallen beneath his spell. Malmesbury happened to dine with him the day after he received the news. Pitt was then himself on the verge of his last illness, but active as always. 'I shall never forget', said Malmesbury, 'the eloquent manner in which he described his conflicting feelings when roused in the night to read Collingwood's dispatches. Pitt observed that he had been called up at various hours in his eventful life by the arrival of news of various hues, but that, whether good or bad, he could always lay his head on his pillow and sink into sound sleep again. On this occasion, however, the great event announced brought with it so much to weep over, as well as to rejoice at, that he could not calm his thoughts, but at length got up, though it was three in the morning.'

The effect on George III, when he read the despatch at Windsor, was perhaps even more remarkable. He was silent for the space of about five minutes, which must have caused consternation among his entourage. Then he summoned the Queen and the Princesses, had the news read to them, and ordered that a Thanksgiving Service should be held in St George's Chapel.

8 Apotheosis

Everything conspired to make Trafalgar different from and more conclusive than any earlier battle under sail. In one sense it was the naval counterpart of Waterloo; in another, it was even more the end of an era, since, while the British soldier continued to engage in set-piece encounters throughout much of the nineteenth century, the next full-scale fleet action in which the Royal Navy would be involved—that off Jutland, in 1916—was fought under circumstances which bore only the faintest resemblance to earlier naval warfare.

If it should have need to fight them, the navy of an island power must always win its battles first, otherwise its soldiers cannot be transported in safety to the countries where they will meet the enemy. The principle is timeless; and Trafalgar helped to make Waterloo possible. It was won almost ten years earlier than the land battle, and the two events may seem to have no other connection, except as illustrating the art of the admiral and that of the general, exercised in full flower by the two men who represented, for Englishmen, all that was highest in leadership against Napoleon.

Because Trafalgar was won so early in the renewed war with France, it seemed at the time to have effected little. The country had grown used to having its way afloat. A sea victory was nothing new, however grand, tragic or triumphant its details. Soon after the news came that Nelson was dead, it became known that Pitt was dying, and it seemed that his Third Coalition against France, the combination of Great Britain, Russia, Austria and Sweden, might be no more effective than earlier combinations. The capitulation of Ulm was followed, in less than two months, by the Battle of Austerlitz, by the end of the ancient Holy Roman Empire, by the alliance of Prussia with Napoleon, and by the eclipse of Austria as a military power. Pitt lived to hear the dismal news, and died broken-hearted.

Trafalgar in fact seemed doubly disappointing, first by reason of Nelson's loss, and again because there appeared to be so little to show for it. Even at the time when the press was full of the battle, it was also loud with a possible threat to Hanover, a matter which affected George III very closely, since he was Hereditary Elector.

The first and most obvious legend to establish was that Nelson had died to save his country from invasion. Although the facts were against it, they were not realised by the public at large, and such a cause did appear great enough for the sacrifice even of such a paragon. It was allowed to pass for truth almost until our own day. It was comfort in loss, and such matters are not strictly susceptible to reason. It was at least true that Nelson had removed the last *possibility* of a threat to this country. There was now no fleet capable of making an attempt, even if Napoleon had been rash enough to revive his project.

There were various ways in which the edge of public disappointment could be blunted, and by which an aura of magic, such as still surrounds the battle, could be fostered. Trafalgar afforded, with its inevitability, its tension and its climax, the finest opportunity which had been given to artists since the death of Wolfe on the Heights of Abraham, in 1759, the 'Year of Victories', nearly half a century before, when the country was at a peak of greatness. It could be made the occasion of a splendid funeral, and it could show a new instance of how generously compatriots could endow the family of a national hero. Each of these possibilities was exploited to the full. Each helped to divert thoughts from a Continent where Napoleon seemed unassailable.

According to Benjamin West, the historical painter, Nelson himself had foreseen the possibility of legend. His retinue were familiar enough with his discourse on the likelihood of his losing another limb, and they all knew that, if he were killed, he would prefer to be buried in St Paul's rather than in the Abbey. He believed that the Abbey, having been built on a marsh, would one day disappear, while he thought that St Paul's, on its eminence, would last longer. West had a tale of his own to tell.

Shortly before his last campaign, Nelson and West had found themselves sitting next to one another at a public dinner. Nelson had none of the man of action's supposed indifference to artists, and he lamented to West that his own artistic education had been so limited. However, he added, there was one picture he admired beyond most others; it was West's *Death of Wolfe*. This was familiar to him through engravings. His friend Sir William Hamilton, an excellent judge, and in his younger days a close friend of Wolfe's, always commended it. Nelson asked West why he had done no more pictures of the same kind. 'Because', said West, 'there are no more subjects.' 'Damn it!' exclaimed Nelson: 'I did not think of that!' A short pause followed, and Nelson then asked West to drink a glass of champagne with him, the wine he favoured. 'My Lord,' ventured the painter, 'I fear that your own intrepidity may yet furnish me with another such scene, and if it should, I shall certainly avail myself of it.' 'Will you?' said Nelson, pouring out bumpers. '*Will* you, Mr West? Then I hope I shall die in the next battle.'

The story may sound rather too good to be true, but West did in fact lose no chance when the time came, and Trafalgar gave him his 'new subject'. He even painted an Apotheosis, showing Nelson's heroic spirit being borne heavenwards by angels, Victory crowning him, and a beneficent Deity no doubt ready to welcome him to a peculiarly British version of heaven. This, if it were to please Nelson, would need to have resembled the famous naval dining club founded in 1765, of which he had been so appreciative a member.

Trafalgar had every concomitant upon which legend could be built. Those with a taste for history could point to the fact that it was fought in the very waters where, eight years earlier, Nelson had shown an extraordinary example of valour, when with Fremantle, he had engaged the commander of the Spanish gunboats hand to hand. The incident had been prophetic, and Fremantle had been with him again, closely in support, at Trafalgar. The battle had been fought not far distant from the scene of his exploits at Cape St Vincent, where he had won the star of chivalry of which he was so proud. Moreover, Trafalgar was close to the gateway into the Mediterranean, where Nelson had made so brilliant a name in the opening phases of the war. It all fitted.

Away off Spain in the *Victory*, one of Dr Beatty's first tasks as soon as circumstances allowed, was to preserve Nelson's remains, for what everyone knew would be a state funeral. There was no lead out of which to make a coffin, so, said Beatty, 'a cask called a leaguer, which is of the largest size on ship-board, was chosen for the reception of the body; which, after the hair had been cut off, was stripped of the clothes except the shirt, and put into it, and the cask was then filled with brandy.'

'In the evening', the account continued, 'after this melancholy task was accomplished, the gale came up with violence, and continued that night and the succeeding day without any abatement. During this boisterous weather, Lord Nelson's body remained under the charge of a sentinel on the middle deck. The cask was placed on its end, having a closed aperture at its top and another below; the object of which was, that as frequent renewal of the spirit was thought necessary, the old could thus be drawn off below and a fresh quantity introduced above, without moving the cask, or occasioning the least agitation of the body.

Nelson was not the man to be placed in a cask of spirits without at least a touch of drama. 'On the 24th', said Beatty, 'there was a disengagement of air from the body to such a degree, that the sentinel became alarmed on seeing the head of the cask raised.' For sheer understatement, this sentence must be hard to equal. The sentry was terrified, and the rumour was soon flying round the decks that the admiral was rising from the dead, angered, no doubt, that his ships were not anchoring. 'The spirit was drawn off at once', said Beatty, 'and the cask filled again, before the arrival of the *Victory* at Gibraltar on 28 October, where spirit of wine was procured; and the cask, showing a deficit produced by the body's absorbing a considerable quantity of the brandy, was then filled up with it.'

After landing her badly wounded, and with the barest essentials of repair to ensure reasonable safety for a long voyage, the *Victory* re-passed the Straits mouth early on 4 November, joined Collingwood's squadron off Cadiz next day, and after a passage protracted by bad weather, anchored at Spithead, where, less than four months earlier, Rose and Canning had bade Nelson farewell. By that time Blackwood had reached Portsmouth with the *Euryalus* and his eminent prisoners. He and Hardy at once arranged for a message to be sent to Lady Hamilton concerning Nelson's last codicil.

Late in December the *Victory* proceeded to the Nore, where on the 23rd the Commissioner's yacht received the body, now enclosed in a splendidly decorated coffin. With bells tolling, minute-guns firing, and colours at half-mast, the yacht made her way to Greenwich, for the Lying-in-State in Wren's Painted Hall. 30,000 people are believed to have filed past, Dr Scott keeping ceaseless, self-appointed vigil.

On 8 January 1806, in a violent south-west gale, the coffin was brought by river to the Admiralty in a long procession, attended by nine admirals, 500 Greenwich pensioners, and the Lord Mayor and Corporation of London in State barges. At Whitehall Stairs the body was received by Norroy King of Arms, with nine heralds and pursuivants.

Next day the funeral, the most elaborate within memory, made its slow way to St Paul's. The Chief Mourner was Nelson's old friend and patron, Sir Peter Parker, and he was followed by 30 flag-officers and 100 captains. The Royalty present included another old friend, the Duke of Clarence, later King William IV, with whom Nelson had served in the West Indies.

As so often, the most moving tributes were those not rehearsed. Dr Scott wrote afterwards to Lady Hamilton: 'One trait I must tell you; the very beggars left their stands, neglected the passing crowd, and seemed to pay tribute to his memory by a look. Many did I see, tattered and on crutches, shaking their heads with plain signs of sorrow. This must be truly unbought affection of the heart.'

As the coffin was being lowered into the crypt, a party of sailors from the *Victory* each seized a piece of the white ensign, the largest of the ship's three flags which had been flown in battle, and kept it as their memorial. 'That was *Nelson*', said Mrs Codrington, wife of the captain of the *Orion*, 'the rest was so much the Herald's Office.' But even the Heralds themselves were moved on this singular occasion, for Sir Isaac Heard, Garter King of Arms, after reciting Nelson's many titles of honour, as if conscious that the roll of words included no adequate description of the dead, added in breach of all precedent—'the Hero who in the moment of Victory fell, covered with Immortal glory. . . .'

Epilogue

Napoleon on Board the Bellerophon

('Mark the end'—Nelson)

By the year 1816, Nelson had lain in the crypt of St Paul's for more than a decade. He had been buried in a coffin made from wood from the mainmast of *L'Orient*, Brueys's flagship at the Nile. The memento had been given him by Hallowell of the *Swiftsure*, and Nelson had valued the gesture, macabre as it might have seemed. During the summer of 1815 the painter John James Chalon had made studies for a picture which captured popular imagination when it appeared in 1816 with the title 'Napoleon on Board the Bellerophon'. It showed the emperor, with members of his party, off Plymouth on 15 August 1815, two months after his defeat at Waterloo. The reasons for this general and sustained favour may have become rather less clear with the passage of time.

Napoleon, the giant who for so long held Europe in thrall, was at last the prisoner of the Royal Navy, and was close to those island shores upon which he was destined never to set foot, and on which he had hitherto looked but distantly, when he had encamped his army about Boulogne in the earlier years of the century, preparing an invasion which was never begun.

That it should have been the *Bellerophon* to which Napoleon had made his way from a French brig, as the ship lay off the coast of France near the estuary of the Gironde, was so appropriate that it would have escaped the attention of no sea officer, and indeed of no Englishman with a sense of history. For of all ships in the Navy, the 'Billy Ruffian', as her men called her, with 30 years activity already behind her, was perhaps best suited to receive the foremost enemy. She had fired her broadsides at the Glorious First of June, where she had worn the flag of Admiral Pasley, always in the forefront of the fighting; she had played an heroic part in the assault on *L'Orient* at the Nile, and only narrowly escaped destruction: at Trafalgar, where her captain had been killed, she had been in the thick of the mêlée. Within a month or so she had been patched up, and she was afloat, generally operationally, for half a century. The first ship of her name to appear in the British Fleet, her fame was such that the Navy has never since lacked a *Bellerophon*, and if tradition is any guide, it never will do.

Napoleon, ever alert and ever curious, was appreciative. He praised the ship, admired the neatness and method of her company, and charmed her captain, Maitland. 'In all my plans', he said, 'I have always been thwarted by the British Fleet.' It was not quite true, but it was a shrewd thing to say, and it was certainly the case that both then and later, when he was on his way to exile at St Helena in the newer ship *Northumberland*, he never ceased to examine the reasons for his enemy's success at sea.

On the long voyage towards the South Atlantic he discussed naval tactics with the

British officers, and he had a life of Nelson read to him, possibly that by Southey, which had recently appeared. The great admiral was one of the few he recognised as being of his own stature, though in another department of war. In the days of his power he had kept a bust of Nelson in his apartments, and had been seen to study it as if he would wrest some truth from its very features. Nelson symbolised all that was vital and enduring in a great Service, and, like Napoleon, he had risen to his challenges. Experience, together with careful reading of history, was Nelson's principal guide, and as the years went by it became increasingly true that as he rose in rank, so did his exertions.

Although Nelson read such manuals on the science or practice of war as came his way, sea officers of his era were left, extraordinary as it may seem, without theoretical instruction on the higher lines of their profession. Nor was this remedied after the long struggle with France, when there was time to digest its lessons, Indeed, the profit which could have been derived from Nelson's career, such as the value of delegation and disciplined freedom for subordinates, the soundness of that empirical attitude to tactical and strategical problems which had been the basis of his achievements, was forgotten or misapplied by later Boards of Admiralty. It was a sad waste.

Had Napoleon cared to pursue enquiries about his adversary further, he would have remarked that while almost all the more illustrious of Nelson's contemporaries and immediate predecessors, Howe, St Vincent and Barham among them, had experience in Admiralty administration and hence in the formulation of policy, as well as of the exercise of command afloat, the nearest that Nelson ever came to regulating matters of far-reaching consequence from a position ashore was when, after the Nile, he assumed responsibility for advice on the military as well as the naval affairs of the Kingdom of Naples. Napoleon could have smiled as he remembered the ineptitude of certain decisions and attempts in the Italian theatre of war, and would have seen proof that Nelson's more obvious gifts lay in tactics, where his outstanding leadership could find scope, and not in strategy.

Yet there is this to be noted: St Vincent, a shrewd judge, saw in Nelson a future head of the Navy, particularly after his services in the Baltic, where he took an almost visible step forward in the range of his understanding. In the event, he died at a level of rank in which only fortunately placed men have been able to show themselves world-scale influences, But even in strategy, Nelson was always *aware* of the broader issues. His mistakes at Naples arose from feeble instruments. His wrong surmises in the earlier stages of the campaign of Trafalgar were not without a reasoned basis, and when Barham called for the *Victory*'s log and journal, when Nelson returned home in the summer of 1805, he was not dissatisfied with what he read. Striking instances of Nelson's sense of the wider scene were his actions in sending word to India immediately after the Nile, and his crystal-clear picture of the state and balance in the Baltic world of 1801, even though this was a sphere with which he had hitherto been unfamiliar.

Tactically, Nelson's intentions were always to annihilate the enemy by the swiftest and most direct methods, sometimes in total disregard of familiar systems. As a very young man serving ashore, he was impatient at time-honoured military ways of reducing strong-points, and was for ever seeking means for gaining more immediate results. At sea, his method was to probe for a weakness or to detect a false move almost before it was made, and at once to exploit it. There are no better instances in history than the battles of St Vincent and the Nile.

At Trafalgar, his ideas have been described in some detail, and the opening words of the memorandum which he issued to his captains, and which was drafted probably before the long chase began, would have won Napoleon's instant approval. 'The business of an English Commander-in-Chief', wrote Nelson, 'is first to bring the Enemy's fleet to battle on the most advantageous terms to himself (I mean that of laying his ships well on board the Enemy as expeditiously as possible), and secondly to continue them there without separating until the business is decided. . . .' That was the aim he always pursued: consistent; simple in idea though more subtle in execution; above all, supremely confident.

Nelson was not given the necessary time, since he died so young, to synthesise all he had learnt, or to lay down broad principles as a guide to future admirals, so that he added little to the body of naval doctrine, and such lessons as could be drawn from his career were often faultily applied. He would certainly have held, with Napoleon, that the moral factor is of paramount importance, and, partly as a result of his know-ledge of the calibre of the officers and men beside whom he fought, he was at all times prepared to act with the lowest possible margin of safety, sometimes from necessity, at others because he was sure of the soundness of his own judgment.

If Nelson was remembered by Napoleon as the exemplar of the fighting seaman, it was not because he was incapable of becoming something more, or because a body of sound doctrine could not be culled from his letters and memoranda: but he would have frowned upon the giving of undue weight to deductions made from fragmentary expression. He would have preferred—and it has been his fate—to be looked upon as an instance of dedication to a single end, the defeat of his country's foes by means of such material as had been given him. Nelson rarely theorised (in this respect unlike Napoleon) and the best service which can be rendered to his memory is to examine his deeds. He stands on his column because of what he was and what he did, not because he discovered some infallible recipe for victory.

As the *Northumberland* dipped over the horizon with her dejected passenger, it was natural enough that Nelson should have preoccupied one who had caused much suffering, as well as adding abundant glory to the history of France, and that, of Nelson's battles, it should have been the Nile that he dwelt upon the longest. For the Nile had been Napoleon's first major reverse, and had given fresh hope to a shaken Europe. He knew and cared nothing about Nelson's failures—the long-forgotten affairs of Turks Island and Teneriffe, even the repulse at Boulogne, which had been almost under the Emperor's eye. These rebuffs had been against shore positions, or against vessels strongly protected within harbour. Afloat, Nelson had been invincible, and Trafalgar had merely confirmed what the Emperor knew already, that it was from the sea, from the limitless land spaces of Russia, and from the enduring wells of nationalism whence strength had been drawn which had at last put a term to his power

Appendix 1

Nelson's Ships and Captains

THE NILE, 1 August 1798	COPENHAGEN, 2 April 1801
Vanguard, 74 guns, *flag*	*Elephant*, 74 guns, *flag*
Captain Edward Berry	Captain Thomas Foley
Orion, 74 guns	*Edgar*, 74 guns
Captain Sir James Saumarez	Captain George Murray
Culloden, 74 guns (*grounded*)	*Glatton*, 56 guns
Captain Thomas Troubridge	Captain William Bligh
Bellerophon, 74 guns	*Isis*, 50 guns
Captain Henry Darby	Captain J. Walker
Minotaur, 74 guns	*Polyphemus*, 64 guns
Captain Thomas Louis	Captain J. Lawford
Defence, 74 guns	*Bellona*, 74 guns (*grounded*)
Captain J. G. G. Peyton	Captain Sir Thomas Thompson
Alexander, 74 guns	*Russell*, 74 guns (*grounded*)
Captain Alexander Ball	Captain W. Cuming
Zealous, 74 guns	*Ganges*, 74 guns
Captain Samuel Hood	Captain Thomas Fremantle
Audacious, 74 guns	*Monarch*, 74 guns
Captain Davidge Gould	Captain J. R. Mosse (*killed*)
Goliath, 74 guns	*Defiance*, 74 guns
Captain Thomas Foley	Rear-Admiral Thomas Graves
Theseus, 74 guns	Captain R. Ratalick
Captain Ralph Miller	*Agamemnon*, 64 guns (*grounded*)
Majestic, 74 guns	Captain F. D. Fancourt
Captain George Westcott (*killed*)	*Amazon*, 38 guns
Leander, 50 guns	Captain Edward Riou (*killed*)
Captain Thomas Thompson	*Desirée*, 36 guns
Swiftsure, 74 guns	Captain H. Inman
Captain Benjamin Hallowell	*Blanche*, 36 guns
Mutine, 18-gun brig	Captain G. E. Hamond
Captain Thomas Hardy	*Alcmene*, 32 guns
	Captain Samuel Sutton
	Arrow, 30 guns
	Captain W. Bolton
	Dart, 30 guns
	Captain J. F. Devonshire

NOTE: Ranks etc., are as at the time of the actions concerned. At Copenhagen two sloops, seven bomb-vessels and two fire-ships were also at Nelson's disposal.

TRAFALGAR, 21 October, 1805

WEATHER COLUMN

Victory, 100 guns, *flag*
Captain Thomas Hardy

Téméraire, 98 guns
Captain Eliab Harvey

Neptune, 98 guns
Captain Thomas Fremantle

Conqueror, 74 guns
Captain Israel Pellew

Leviathan, 74 guns
Captain Henry Bayntun

Ajax, 74 guns
Lieutenant John Pilfold (*acting*)

Orion, 74 guns
Captain Edward Codrington

Agamemnon, 64 guns
Captain Sir Edward Berry

Minotaur, 74 guns
Captain Charles Mansfield

Spartiate, 74 guns
Captain Sir Francis Laforey Bt.

Britannia, 100 guns
Rear-Admiral the Earl of Northesk
Captain Charles Bullen

Africa, 64 guns
Captain Henry Digby

Frigates:

Euryalus: Captain Hon. Henry Blackwood
Naiad: Captain Thomas Dundas
Phoebe: Captain Hon. Thomas Capel
Sirius: Captain William Prowse
Pickle: Lieutenant John Lapenotière (schooner)
Entreprenante: Lieutenant R. B. Young (cutter)

LEE COLUMN

Royal Sovereign, 100 guns
Vice-Admiral Cuthbert Collingwood
Captain Edward Rotheram

Mars, 74 guns
Captain George Duff (*killed*)

Belleisle, 74 guns
Captain William Hargood

Tonnant, 80 guns
Captain Charles Tyler

Bellerophon, 74 guns
Captain John Cooke (*killed*)

Colossus, 74 guns
Captain James Morris

Achille, 74 guns
Captain Richard King

Polyphemus, 64 guns
Captain Robert Redmill

Revenge, 74 guns
Captain Robert Moorsom

Swiftsure, 74 guns
Captain William Rutherford

Defence, 74 guns
Captain George Hope

Thunderer, 74 guns
Lieutenant John Stockham (*acting*)

Defiance, 74 guns
Captain Philip Durham

Prince, 98 guns
Captain Richard Grindall

Dreadnought, 98 guns
Captain John Conn

NOTE: Hardy was the only captain present at all three actions. He was a volunteer in the *Elephant* at Copenhagen. Berry was at the Nile and Trafalgar, Foley and Thompson at the Nile and Copenhagen, and Fremantle at Copenhagen and Trafalgar.

The *Orion*, *Bellerophon*, *Defence* and *Swiftsure* were at the Nile and Trafalgar, but the Nile *Swiftsure* was on the enemy's side in 1805, for she had been captured in 1801. Rutherford's *Swiftsure* was a brand new ship. After her recapture during the battle, the Nile *Swiftsure* was renamed *Irresistible*. The *Polyphemus*, *Defiance* and *Agamemnon* were at Copenhagen and Trafalgar.

Appendix 2

A Note on Sources

The principal manuscript material relating to Nelson, wide and ramified in subject and provenance, was assessed by Miss K. F. Lindsay MacDougall in the *Mariner's Mirror* (1955: pp. 227–32) for the benefit of the Society for Nautical Research. Next to this primary material, the long series of volumes published by the Navy Records Society, including as it does correspondence and papers of such men as Barham, St Vincent, Keith and Collingwood, makes them essential for any detailed and proportioned view of Nelson's Navy and the age to which he belonged.

Of the large, unequal library of books about Nelson which has continued to increase at a steady rate for over a century and a half, the principal items are listed and annotated in *Lord Nelson: a Guide to Reading*, compiled by the present writer in 1955; it includes a brief note on the iconography. Since that time there has been at least one book of major importance, *Nelson's Letters to his Wife and Other Documents 1785–1831*, edited by G. P. B. Naish (1958). This is an invaluable supplement to what will always be the mainstay of the Nelsonian, the seven volumes of *Dispatches and Letters* edited by Sir Harris Nicolas (1844–46). Some new details will be found in *A Portrait of Lord Nelson* (1958), and as regards individual actions, there is a glimpse of the aspiring hero in *A Memoir of James Trevenen*, edited by Professor Christopher Lloyd (1959). The same writer's *St. Vincent and Camperdown* (1963) in the British Battles Series, is a re-assessment of the events of 1797. Mr Dudley Pope's *England Expects* (1960) is based on a fresh look at the evidence regarding Trafalgar. It is also appropriate to recall Captain S. W. Roskill's reference to Nelson's qualities in *The Art of Leadership* (1964).

O. W.

Index

The numerals in **bold type** denote the *figure numbers* of illustrations